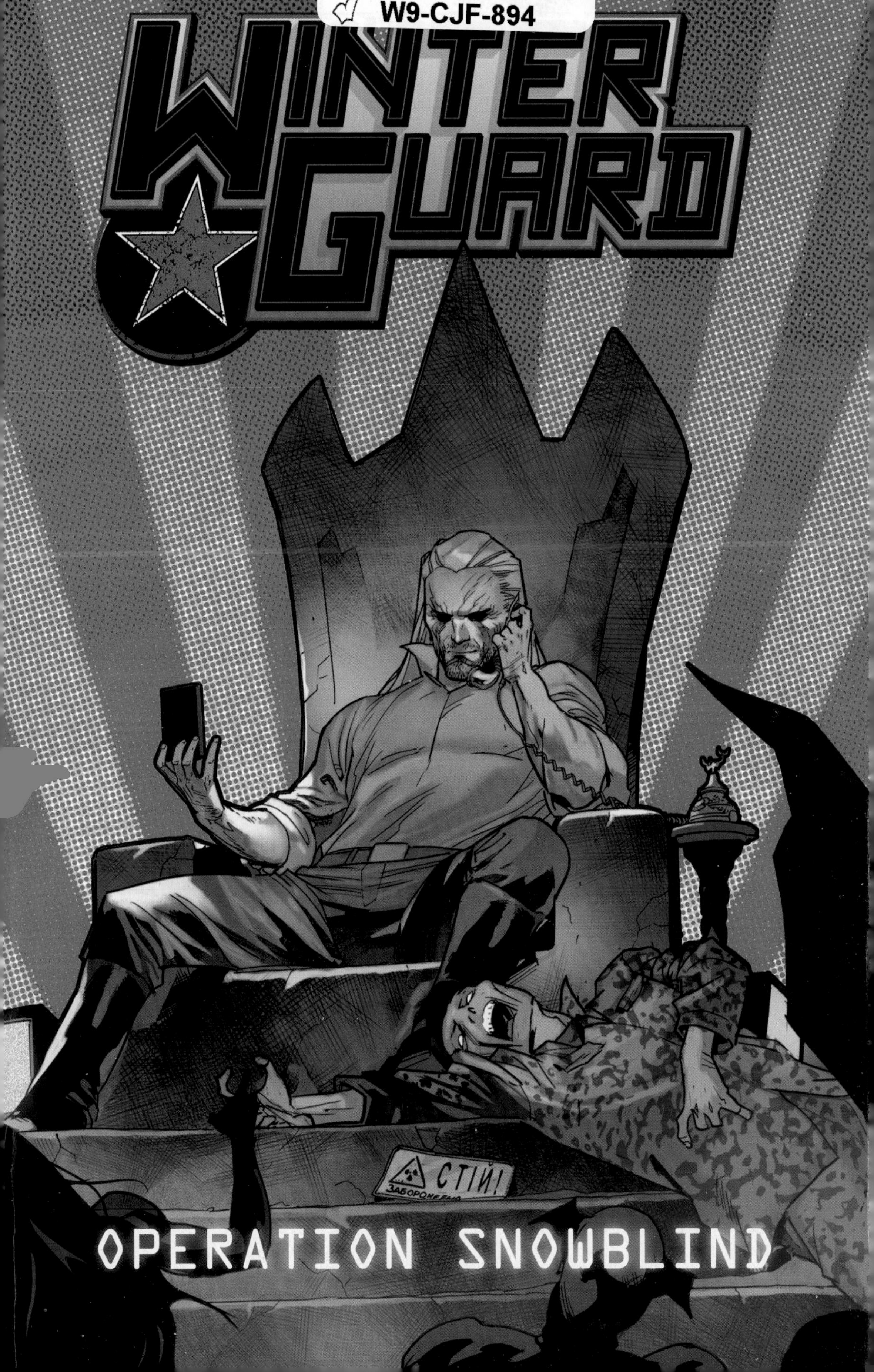
WINTER GUARD
СТІЙ!
OPERATION SNOWBLIND

Collection Editor **JENNIFER GRÜNWALD**
Assistant Editor **DANIEL KIRCHHOFFER**
Assistant Managing Editor **MAIA LOY**
Assistant Managing Editor **LISA MONTALBANO**
VP Production & Special Projects **JEFF YOUNGQUIST**
SVP Print, Sales & Marketing **DAVID GABRIEL**
Book Designer **SARAH SPADACCINI**
Editor in Chief **C.B. CEBULSKI**

WINTER GUARD: OPERATION SNOWBLIND. Contains material originally published in magazine form as WINTER GUARD (2021) #1-4 and WIDOWMAKERS: RED GUARDIAN AND YELENA BELOVA (2020) #1. First printing 2021. ISBN 978-1-302-92875-9. Published by MARVEL WORLDWIDE, INC., a subsidiary of MARVEL ENTERTAINMENT, LLC. OFFICE OF PUBLICATION: 1290 Avenue of the Americas, New York, NY 10104. © 2021 MARVEL No similarity between any of the names, characters, persons, and/or institutions in this book with those of any living or dead person or institution is intended, and any such similarity which may exist is purely coincidental. **Printed in Canada.** KEVIN FEIGE, Chief Creative Officer; DAN BUCKLEY, President, Marvel Entertainment; JOE QUESADA, EVP & Creative Director; DAVID BOGART, Associate Publisher & SVP of Talent Affairs; TOM BREVOORT, VP, Executive Editor; NICK LOWE, Executive Editor, VP of Content, Digital Publishing; DAVID GABRIEL, VP of Print & Digital Publishing; JEFF YOUNGQUIST, VP of Production & Special Projects; ALEX MORALES, Director of Publishing Operations; DAN EDINGTON, Managing Editor; RICKEY PURDIN, Director of Talent Relations; JENNIFER GRÜNWALD, Senior Editor, Special Projects; SUSAN CRESPI, Production Manager; STAN LEE, Chairman Emeritus. For information regarding advertising in Marvel Comics or on Marvel.com, please contact Vit DeBellis, Custom Solutions & Integrated Advertising Manager, at vdebellis@marvel.com. For Marvel subscription inquiries, please call 888-511-5480. Manufactured between 11/12/2021 and 12/14/2021 by SOLISCO PRINTERS, SCOTT QC, CANADA.

OPERATION SNOWBLIND

RYAN CADY
WRITER

JAN BAZALDUA
ARTIST

DJIBRIL
MORISSETTE-PHAN
PRELUDE ARTIST

FEDERICO BLEE WITH
FERNANDO SIFUENTES
OF PROTOBUNKER (#3-4)
COLOR ARTISTS

VC's ARIANA MAHER
LETTERER

TONI INFANTE
COVER ART

KAT GREGOROWICZ &
KAITLYN LINDTVEDT
ASSISTANT EDITORS

SARAH BRUNSTAD
WITH ALANNA SMITH
EDITORS

Widowmakers: Red Guardian & Yelena Belova

DEVIN GRAYSON
WRITER

MICHELE BANDINI
ARTIST

ELISABETTA D'AMICO
INKING ASSISTS

ERICK ARCINIEGA
COLOR ARTIST

VC's CORY PETIT
LETTERER

MIKE McKONE &
CHRIS O'HALLORAN
COVER ART

SARAH BRUNSTAD
EDITOR

SPECIAL THANKS TO WINTER KOIFMAN

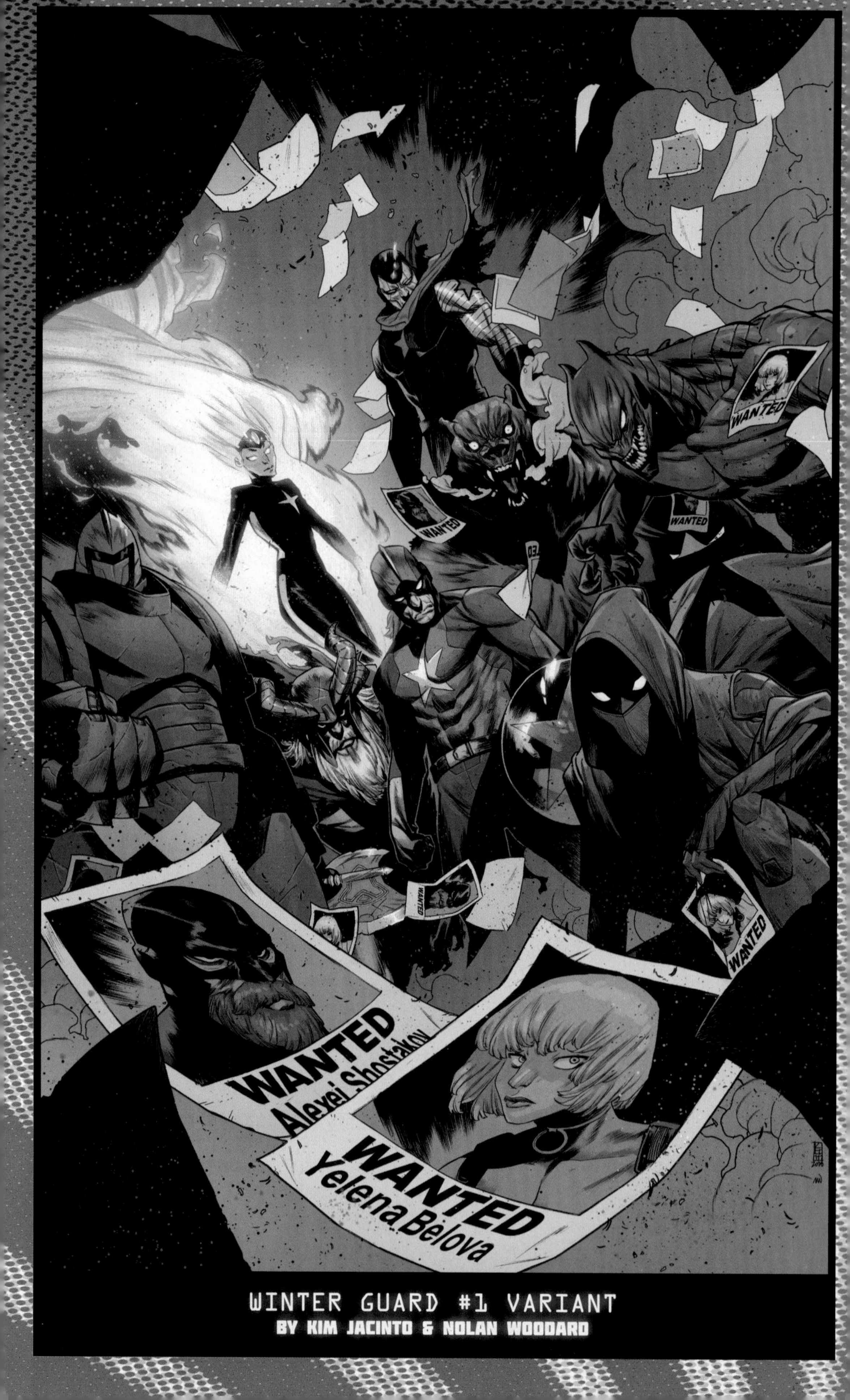
WANTED
Alexei Shostakov
WANTED
Yelena Belova

WINTER GUARD #1 VARIANT

BY KIM JACINTO & NOLAN WOODARD

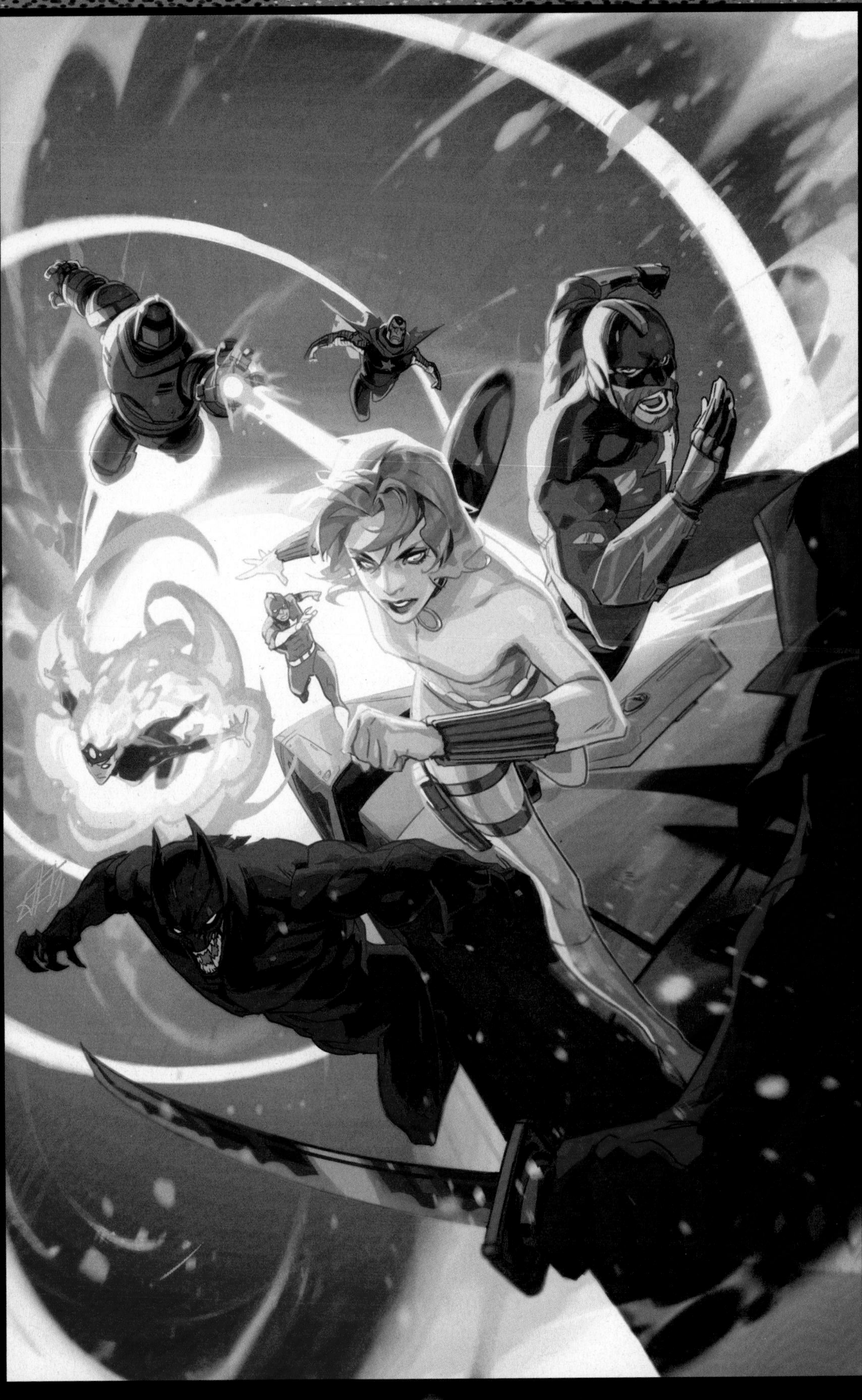

1

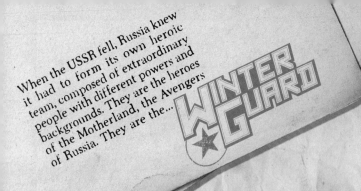

When the USSR fell, Russia knew it had to form its own heroic team, composed of extraordinary people with different powers and backgrounds. They are the heroes of the Motherland, the Avengers of Russia. They are the...

TOP SECRET

PERSONS OF INTEREST

RED GUARDIAN   YELENA BELOVA

MISSION BRIEF:

Jennifer Walters, alias She-Hulk [affiliation: AVENGERS] was taken into custody by the Winter Guard for crimes against Russia and was held and processed in ▮▮▮▮▮▮▮. Any agents who disclose the details of her arrest, whether voluntarily or under duress, will face the highest consequences under Russian law.

AGENTS

CRIMSON DYNAMO   RED WIDOW   VOSTOK   PERUN

CHERNOBOG   VANGUARD   DARKSTAR   URSA MAJOR

Withdrawn

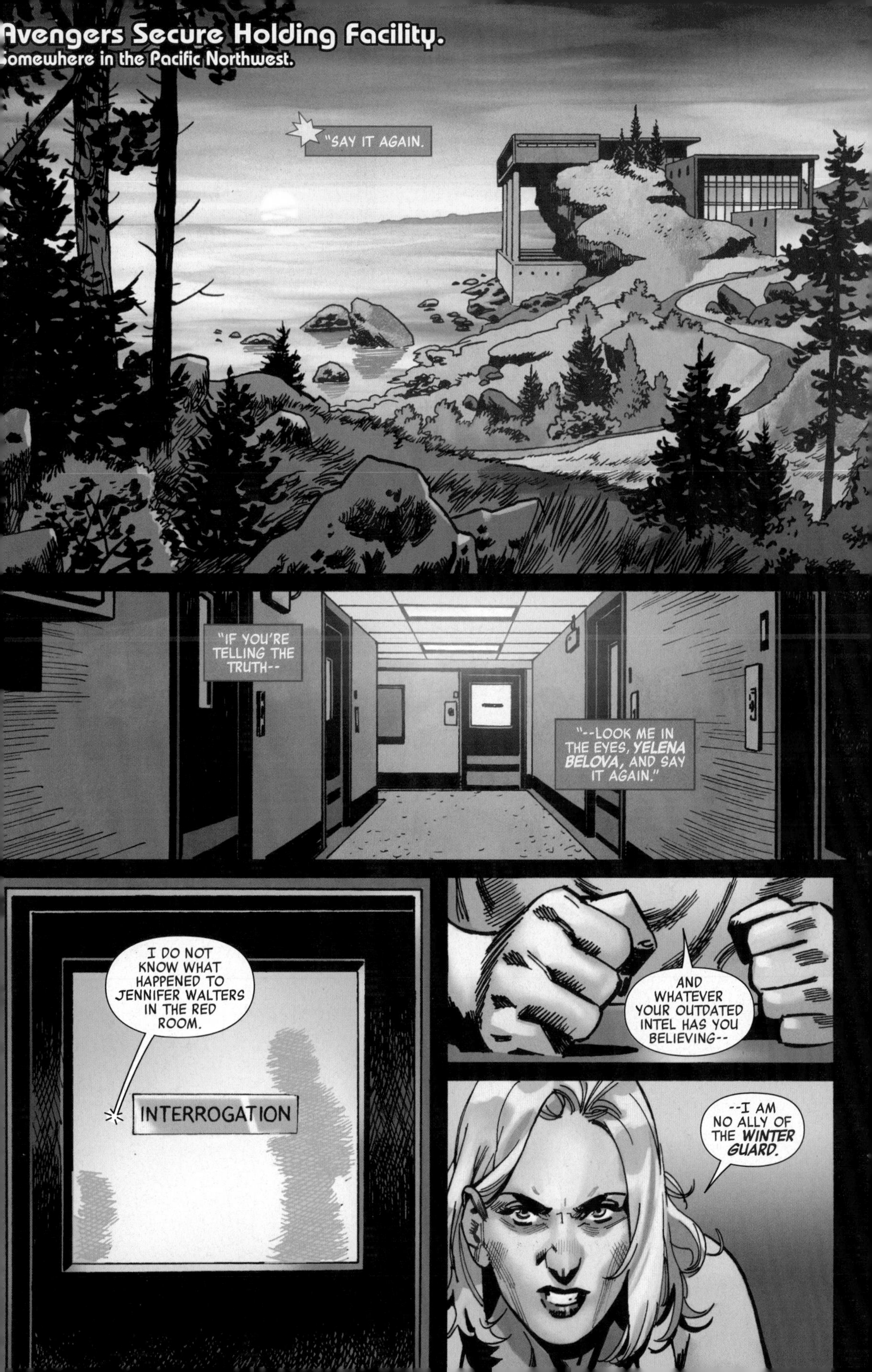
Avengers Secure Holding Facility.
Somewhere in the Pacific Northwest.
"SAY IT AGAIN.
"IF YOU'RE TELLING THE TRUTH--
"--LOOK ME IN THE EYES, YELENA BELOVA, AND SAY IT AGAIN."
I DO NOT KNOW WHAT HAPPENED TO JENNIFER WALTERS IN THE RED ROOM.
INTERROGATION
AND WHATEVER YOUR OUTDATED INTEL HAS YOU BELIEVING--
--I AM NO ALLY OF THE WINTER GUARD.

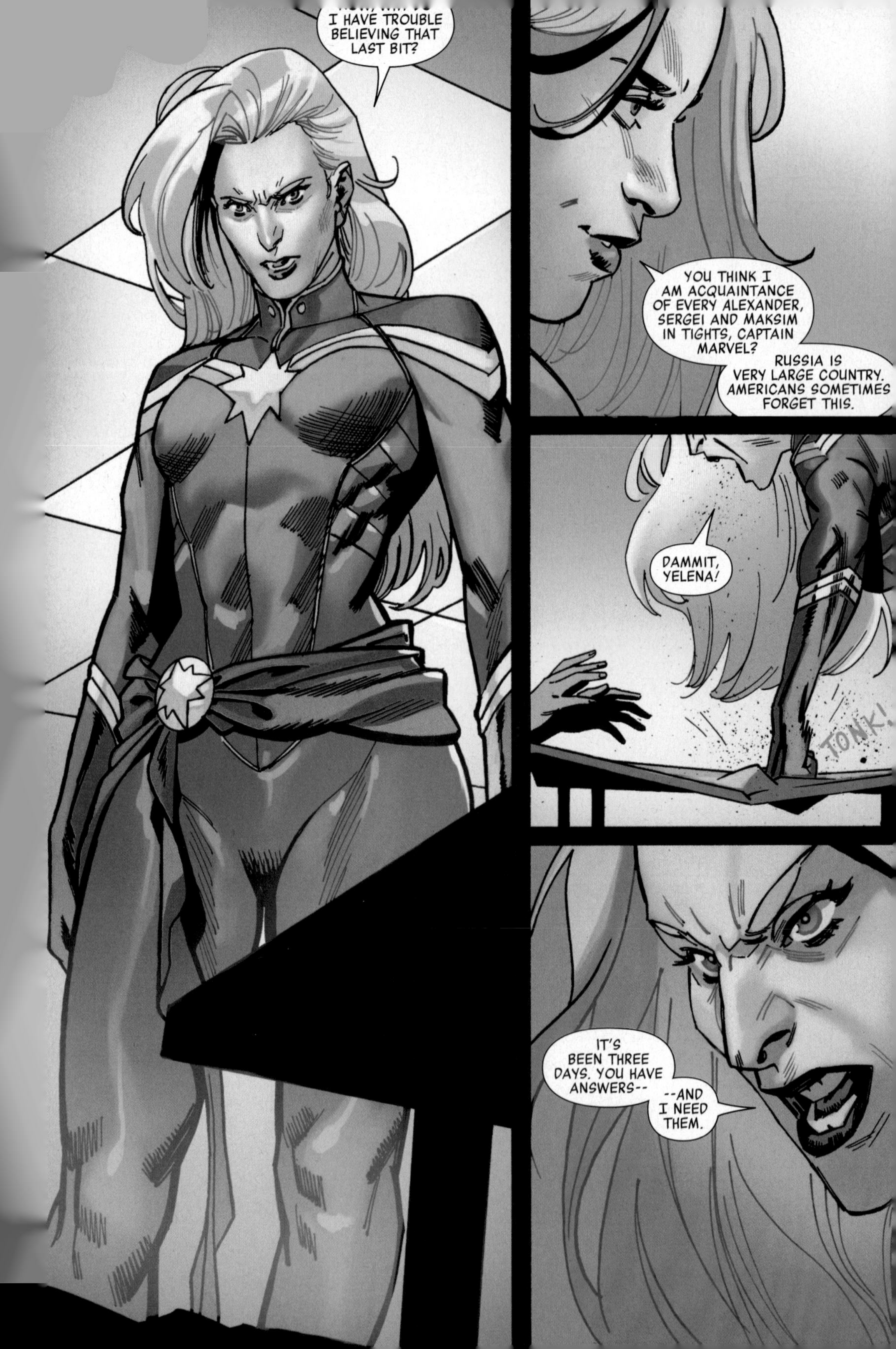
I HAVE TROUBLE BELIEVING THAT LAST BIT?
YOU THINK I AM ACQUAINTANCE OF EVERY ALEXANDER, SERGEI AND MAKSIM IN TIGHTS, CAPTAIN MARVEL?
RUSSIA IS VERY LARGE COUNTRY. AMERICANS SOMETIMES FORGET THIS.
DAMMIT, YELENA!
TONK!
IT'S BEEN THREE DAYS. YOU HAVE ANSWERS--
--AND I NEED THEM.

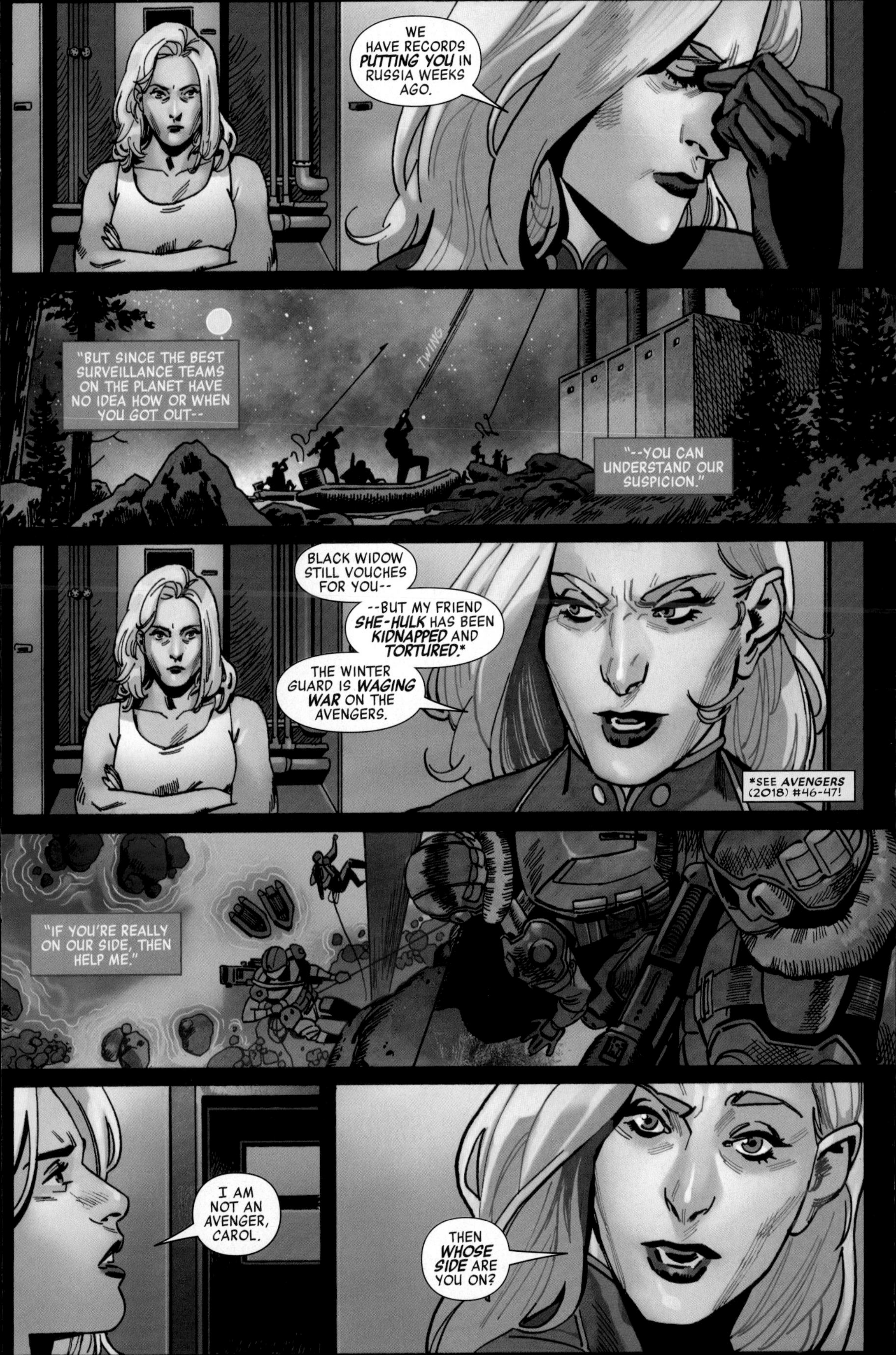
WE HAVE RECORDS PUTTING YOU IN RUSSIA WEEKS AGO.
"BUT SINCE THE BEST SURVEILLANCE TEAMS ON THE PLANET HAVE NO IDEA HOW OR WHEN YOU GOT OUT--
TWING
"--YOU CAN UNDERSTAND OUR SUSPICION."
BLACK WIDOW STILL VOUCHES FOR YOU--
--BUT MY FRIEND SHE-HULK HAS BEEN KIDNAPPED AND TORTURED.*
THE WINTER GUARD IS WAGING WAR ON THE AVENGERS.
*SEE AVENGERS (2018) #46-47!
"IF YOU'RE REALLY ON OUR SIDE, THEN HELP ME."
I AM NOT AN AVENGER, CAROL.
THEN WHOSE SIDE ARE YOU ON?

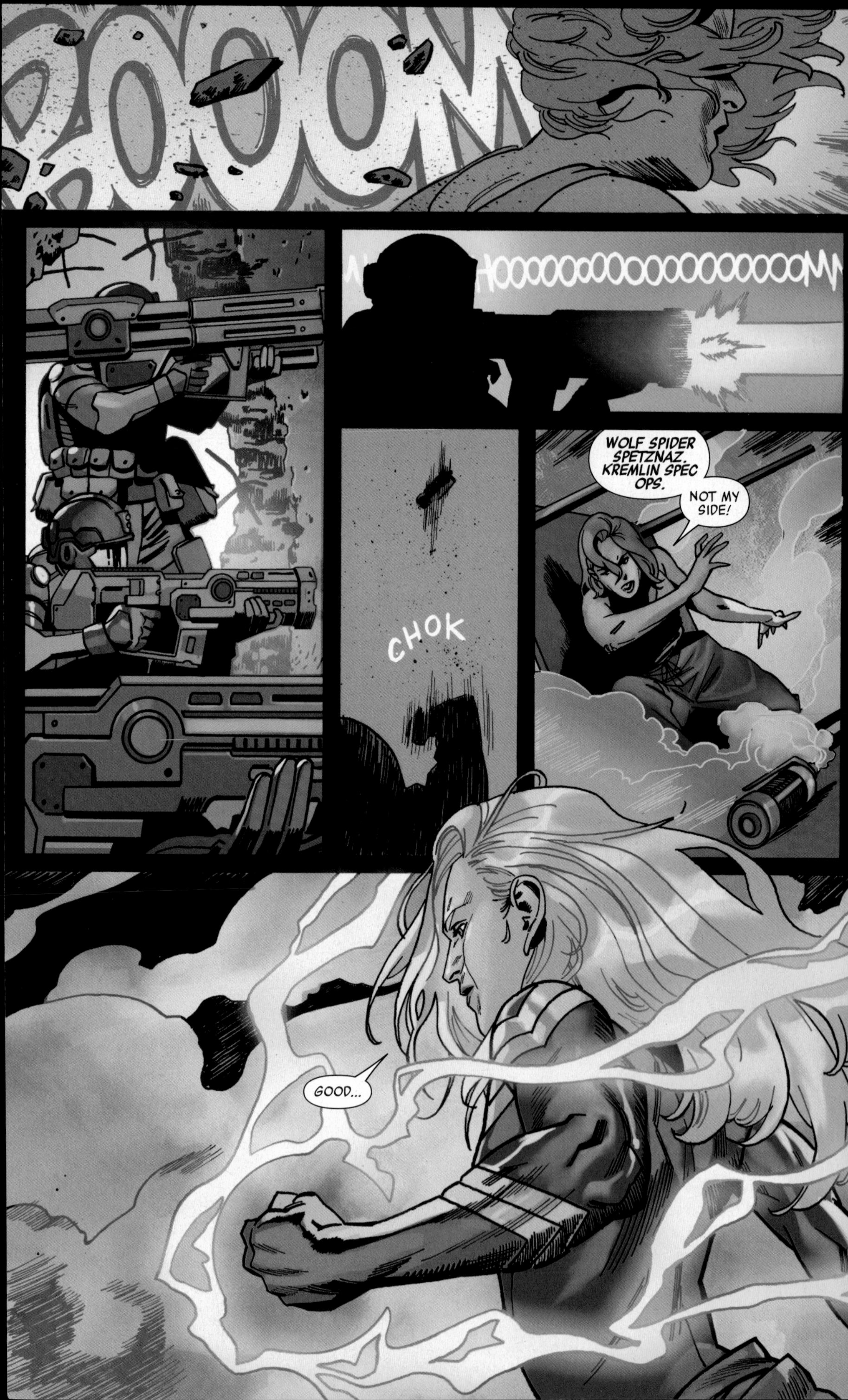
BOOOOOM
WHOOOOOOOOOOOOOOOOOOOOOM
CHOK
WOLF SPIDER SPETZNAZ. KREMLIN SPEC OPS.
NOT MY SIDE!
GOOD...

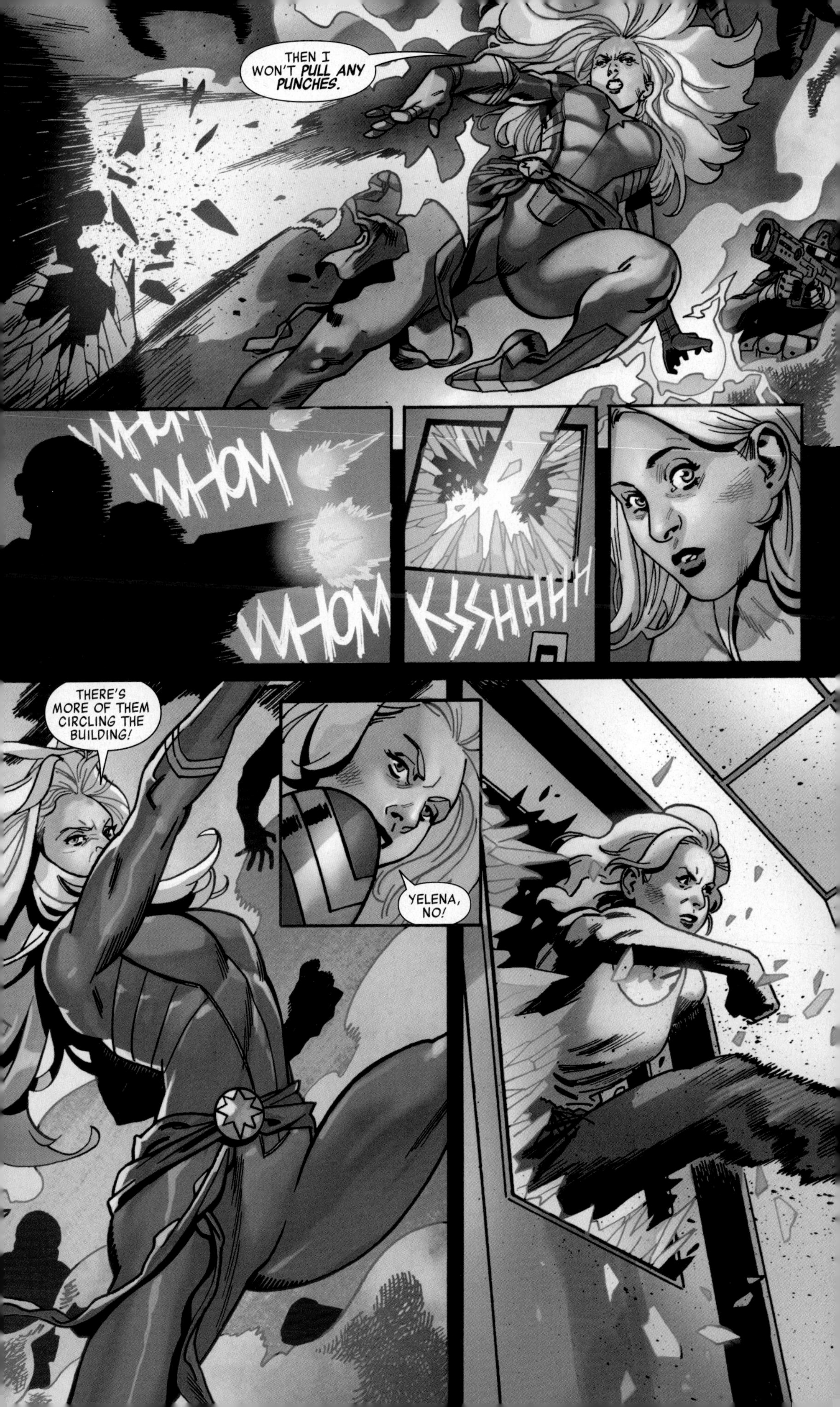

THEN I WON'T PULL ANY PUNCHES.
WHOM WHOM
WHOM
KSSHHHH
THERE'S MORE OF THEM CIRCLING THE BUILDING!
YELENA, NO!

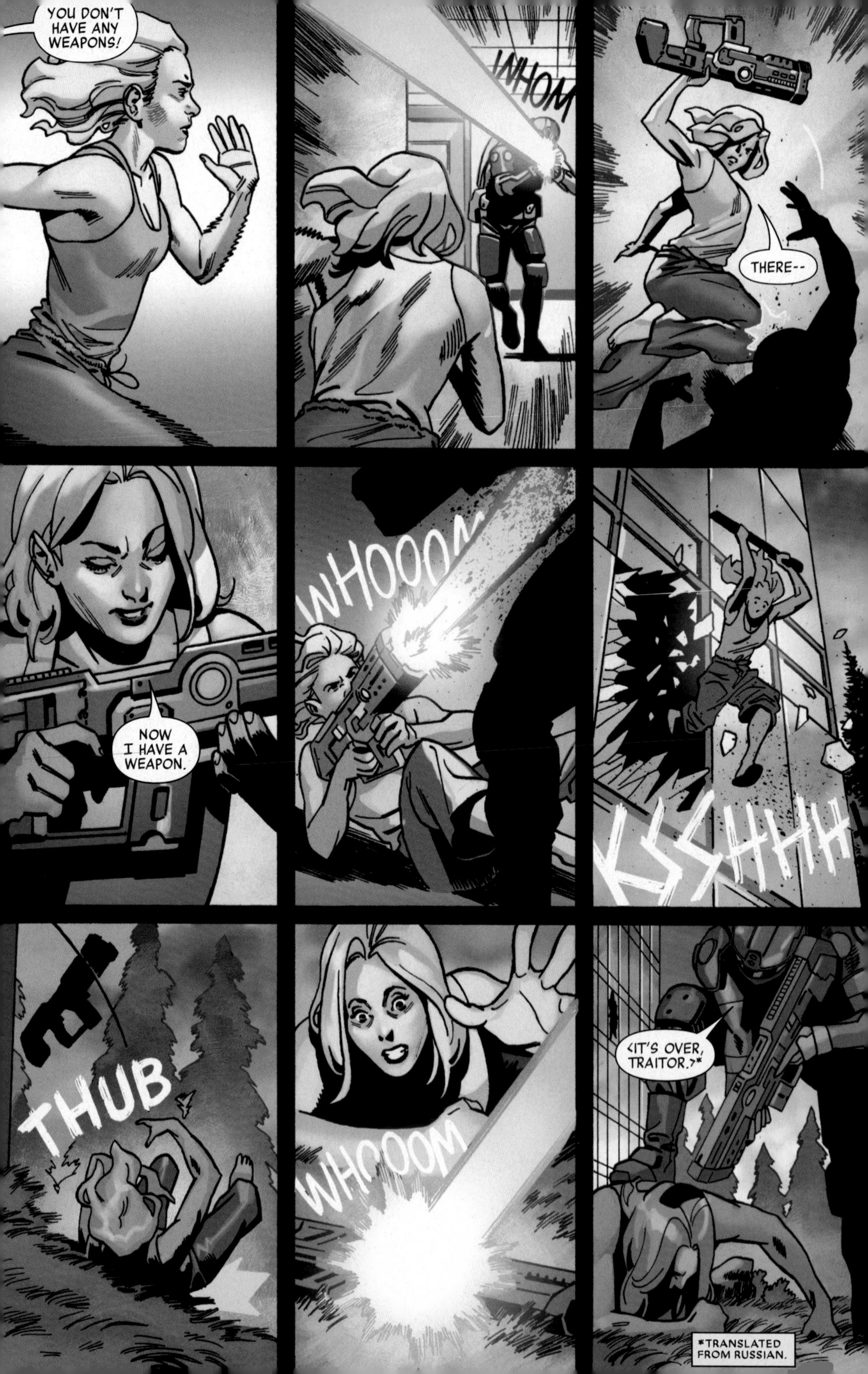
YOU DON'T HAVE ANY WEAPONS!
WHOM
THERE--
NOW I HAVE A WEAPON.
WHOOOM
KSSHHH
THUB
WHOOOM
<IT'S OVER, TRAITOR.>*
*TRANSLATED FROM RUSSIAN.

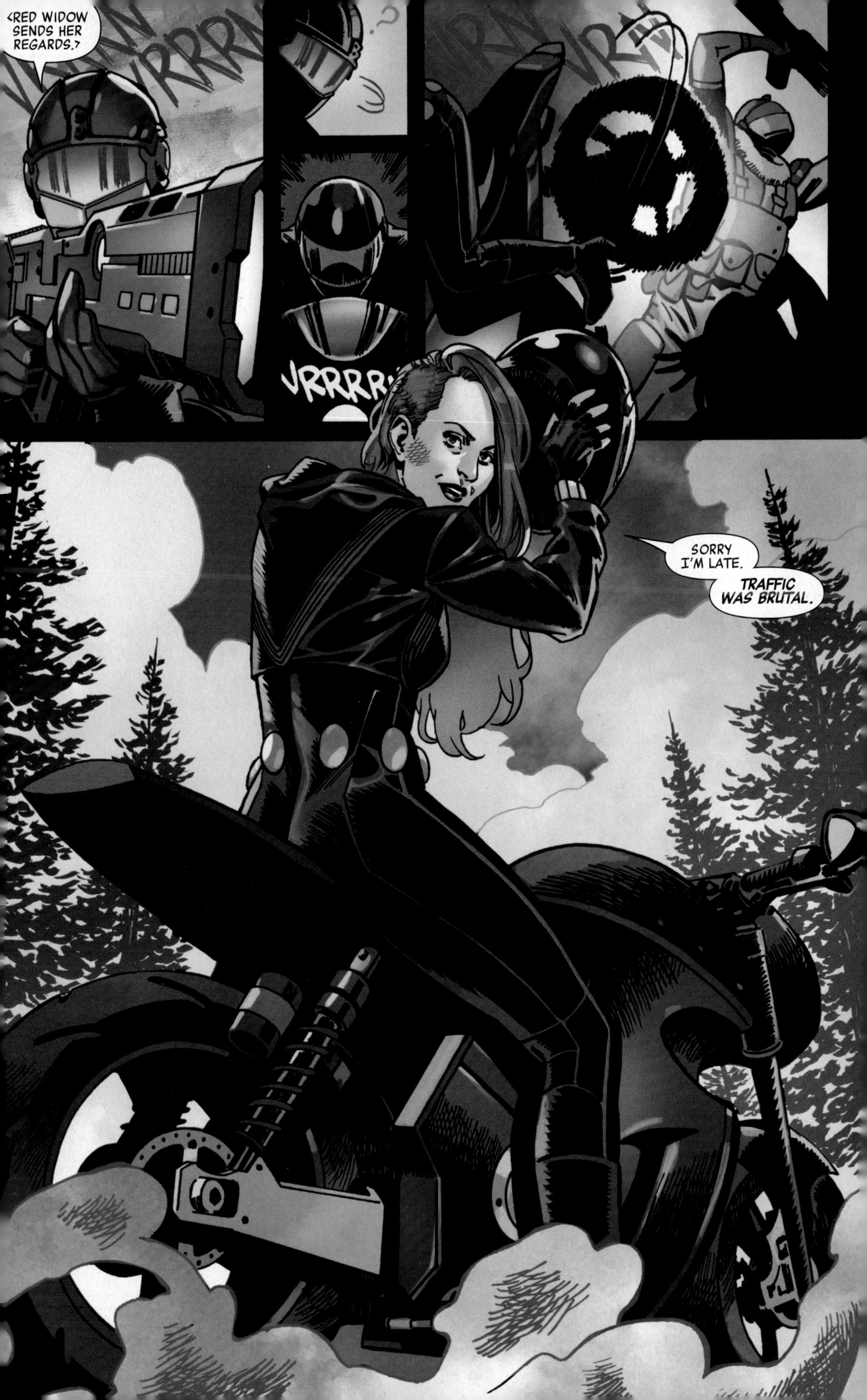
<RED WIDOW SENDS HER REGARDS.>
VRRRR
SORRY I'M LATE.
TRAFFIC WAS BRUTAL.

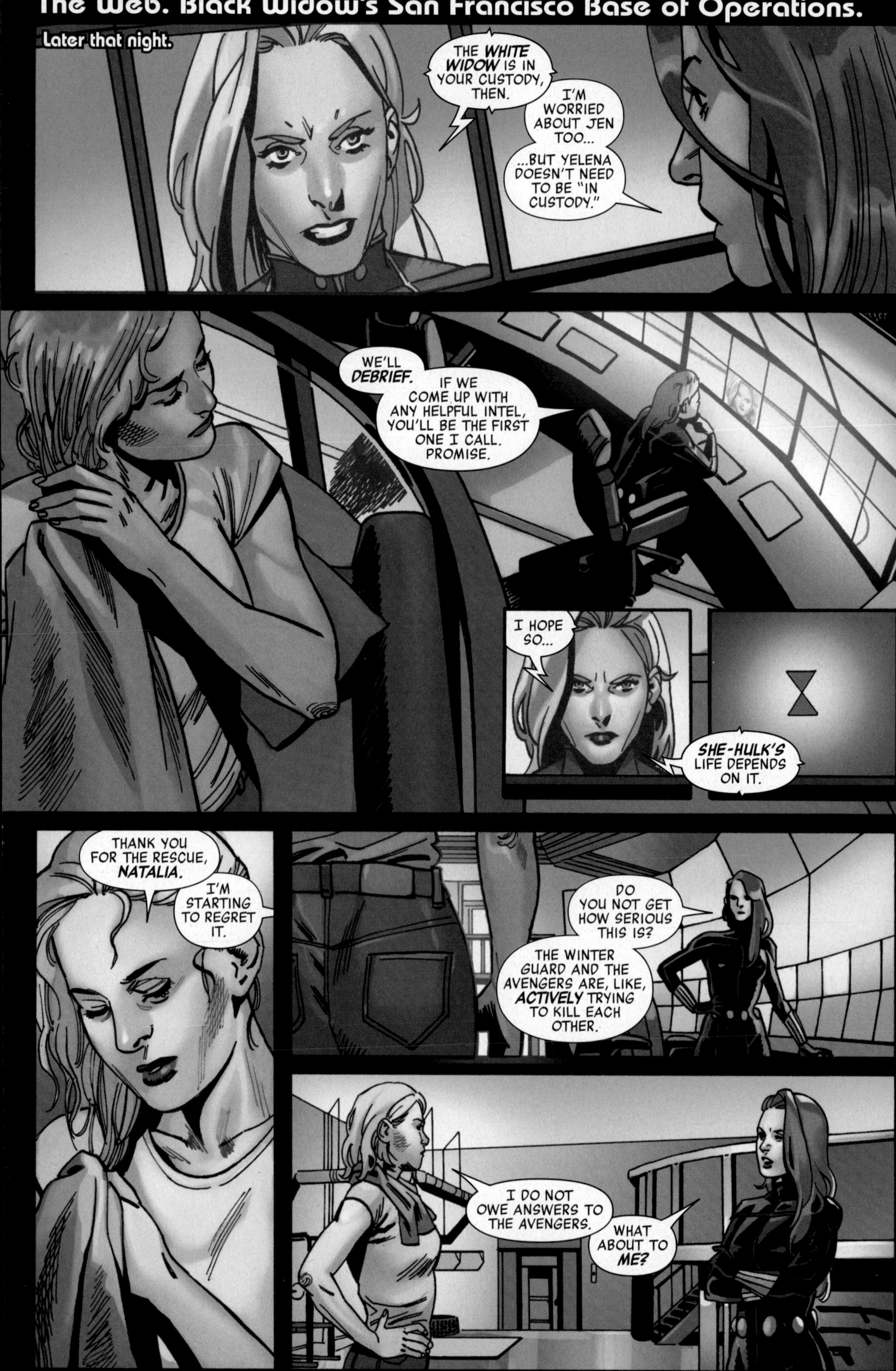
The Web. Black Widow's San Francisco Base of Operations.
Later that night.
THE WHITE WIDOW IS IN YOUR CUSTODY, THEN.
I'M WORRIED ABOUT JEN TOO...
...BUT YELENA DOESN'T NEED TO BE "IN CUSTODY."
WE'LL DEBRIEF.
IF WE COME UP WITH ANY HELPFUL INTEL, YOU'LL BE THE FIRST ONE I CALL. PROMISE.
I HOPE SO...
SHE-HULK'S LIFE DEPENDS ON IT.
THANK YOU FOR THE RESCUE, NATALIA.
I'M STARTING TO REGRET IT.
DO YOU NOT GET HOW SERIOUS THIS IS?
THE WINTER GUARD AND THE AVENGERS ARE, LIKE, ACTIVELY TRYING TO KILL EACH OTHER.
I DO NOT OWE ANSWERS TO THE AVENGERS.
WHAT ABOUT TO ME?

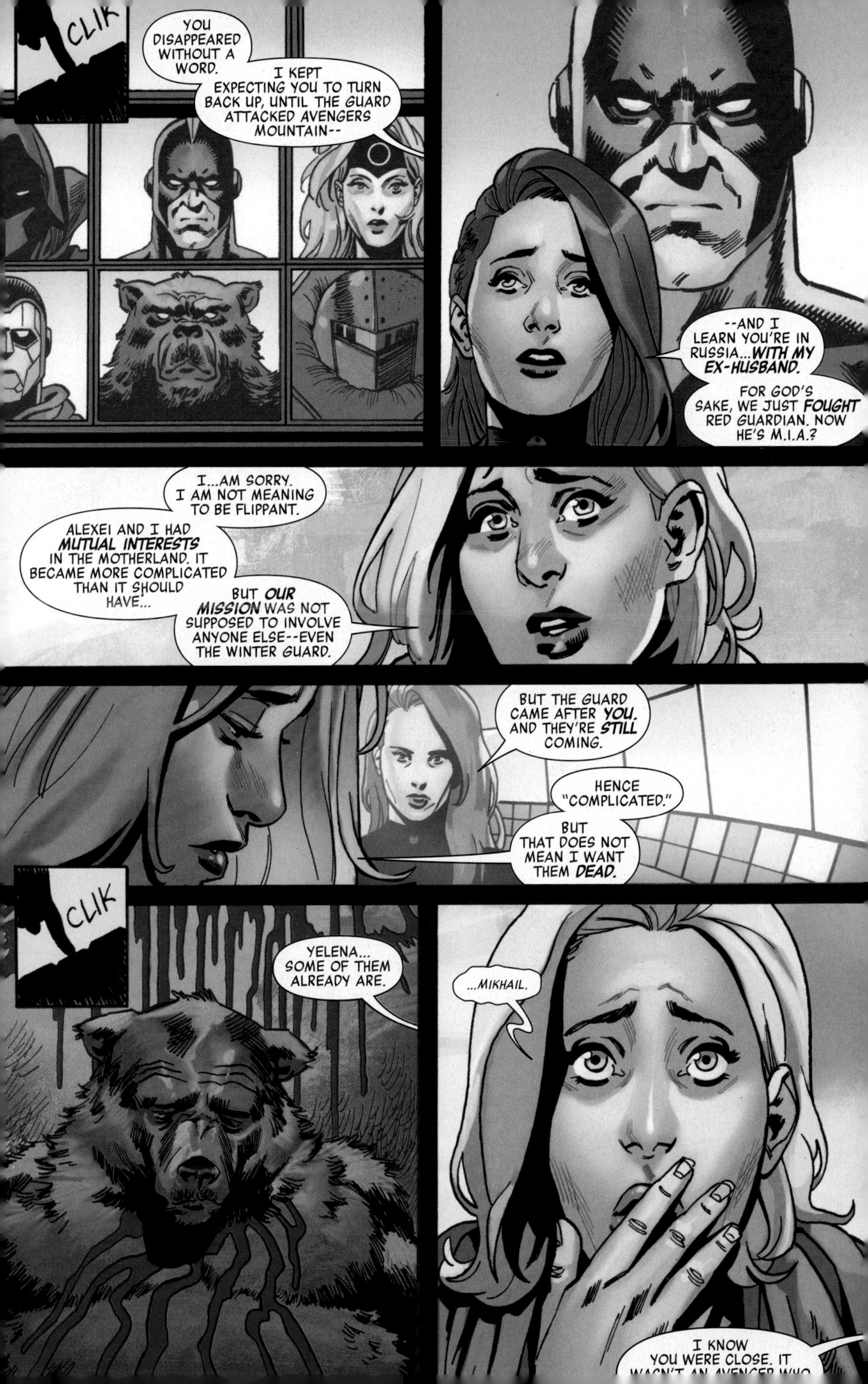
CLIK
YOU DISAPPEARED WITHOUT A WORD.
I KEPT EXPECTING YOU TO TURN BACK UP, UNTIL THE GUARD ATTACKED AVENGERS MOUNTAIN--
--AND I LEARN YOU'RE IN RUSSIA...WITH MY EX-HUSBAND.
FOR GOD'S SAKE, WE JUST FOUGHT RED GUARDIAN. NOW HE'S M.I.A.?
I...AM SORRY. I AM NOT MEANING TO BE FLIPPANT.
ALEXEI AND I HAD MUTUAL INTERESTS IN THE MOTHERLAND. IT BECAME MORE COMPLICATED THAN IT SHOULD HAVE...
BUT OUR MISSION WAS NOT SUPPOSED TO INVOLVE ANYONE ELSE--EVEN THE WINTER GUARD.
BUT THE GUARD CAME AFTER YOU. AND THEY'RE STILL COMING.
HENCE "COMPLICATED."
BUT THAT DOES NOT MEAN I WANT THEM DEAD.
CLIK
YELENA... SOME OF THEM ALREADY ARE.
...MIKHAIL.
I KNOW YOU WERE CLOSE. IT

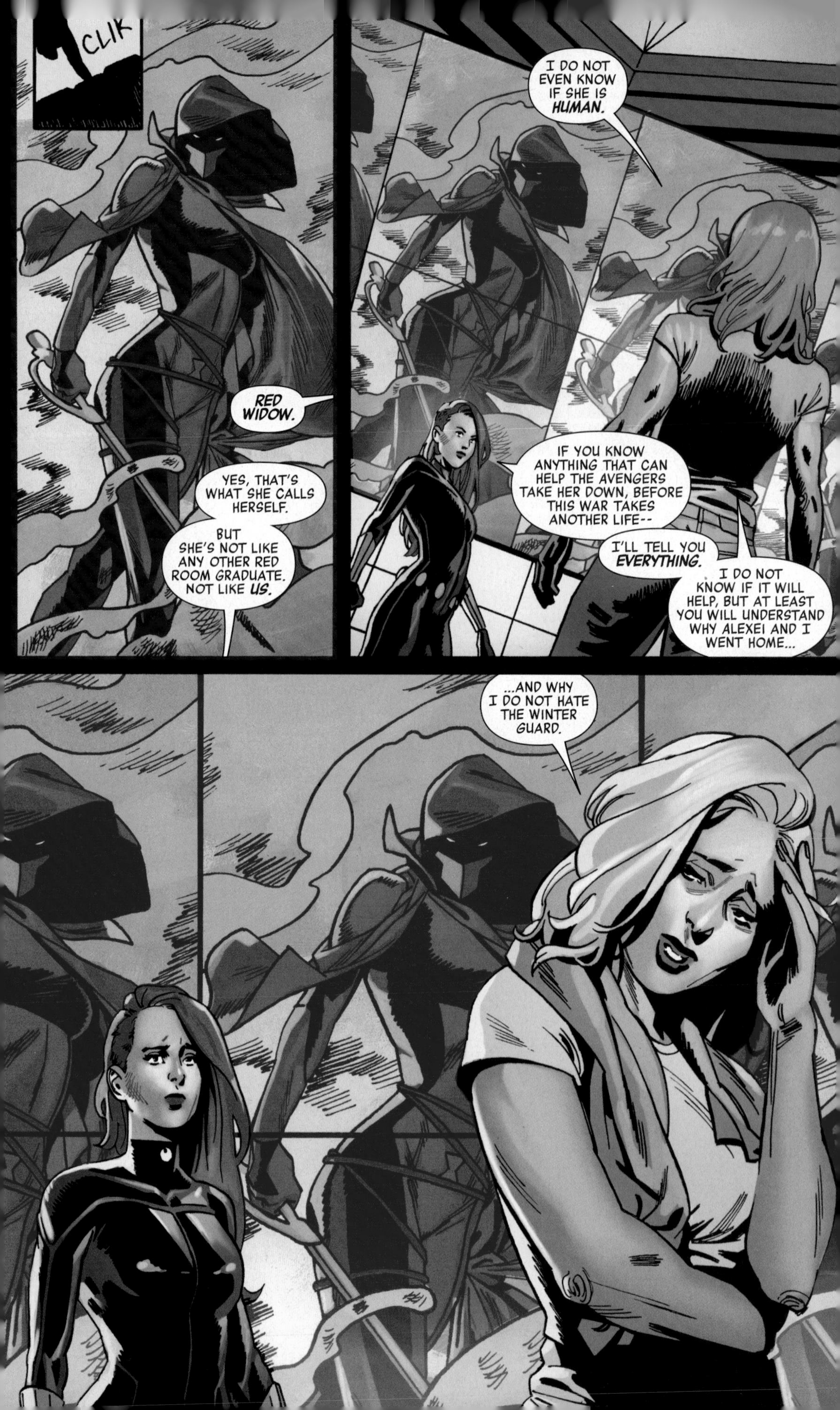
CLIK
RED WIDOW.
YES, THAT'S WHAT SHE CALLS HERSELF.
BUT SHE'S NOT LIKE ANY OTHER RED ROOM GRADUATE. NOT LIKE *US.*
I DO NOT EVEN KNOW IF SHE IS *HUMAN.*
IF YOU KNOW ANYTHING THAT CAN HELP THE AVENGERS TAKE HER DOWN, BEFORE THIS WAR TAKES ANOTHER LIFE--
I'LL TELL YOU *EVERYTHING.*
I DO NOT KNOW IF IT WILL HELP, BUT AT LEAST YOU WILL UNDERSTAND WHY ALEXEI AND I WENT HOME...
...AND WHY I DO NOT HATE THE WINTER GUARD.

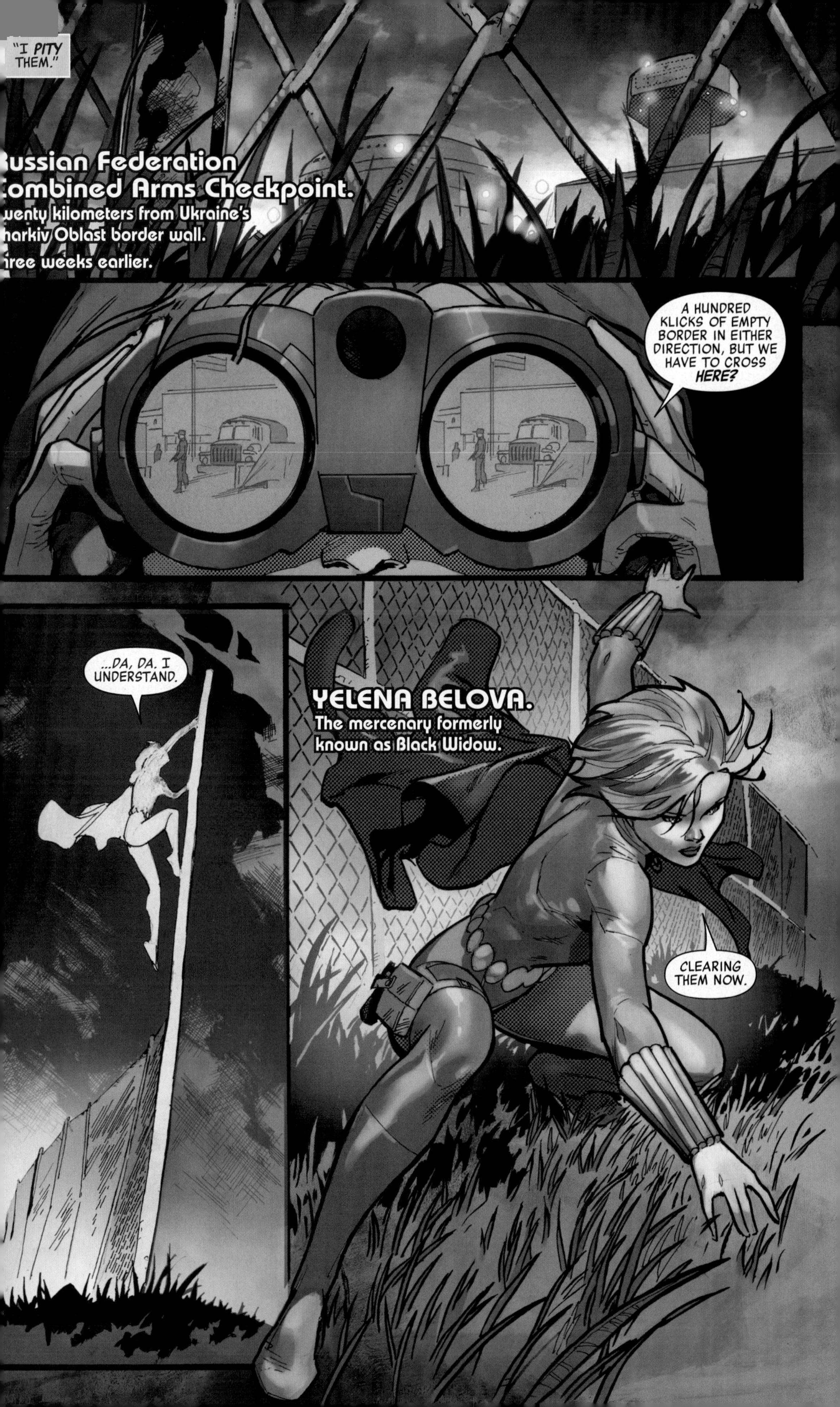
"I PITY THEM."
ussian Federation
ombined Arms Checkpoint.
wenty kilometers from Ukraine's
harkiv Oblast border wall.
hree weeks earlier.
A HUNDRED KLICKS OF EMPTY BORDER IN EITHER DIRECTION, BUT WE HAVE TO CROSS HERE?
...DA, DA. I UNDERSTAND.
YELENA BELOVA.
The mercenary formerly known as Black Widow.
CLEARING THEM NOW.

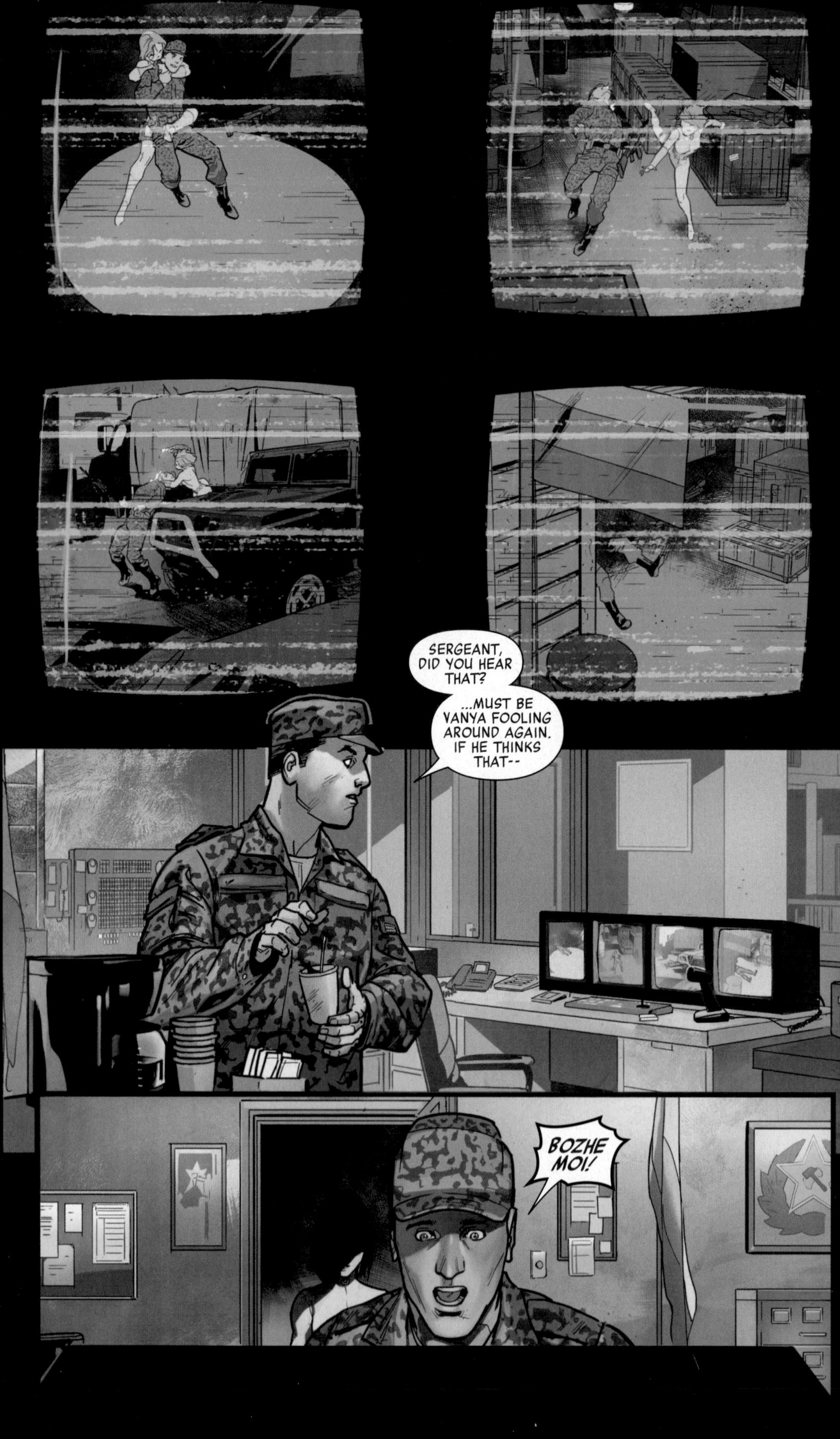
SERGEANT, DID YOU HEAR THAT?
...MUST BE VANYA FOOLING AROUND AGAIN. IF HE THINKS THAT--
BOZHE MOI!

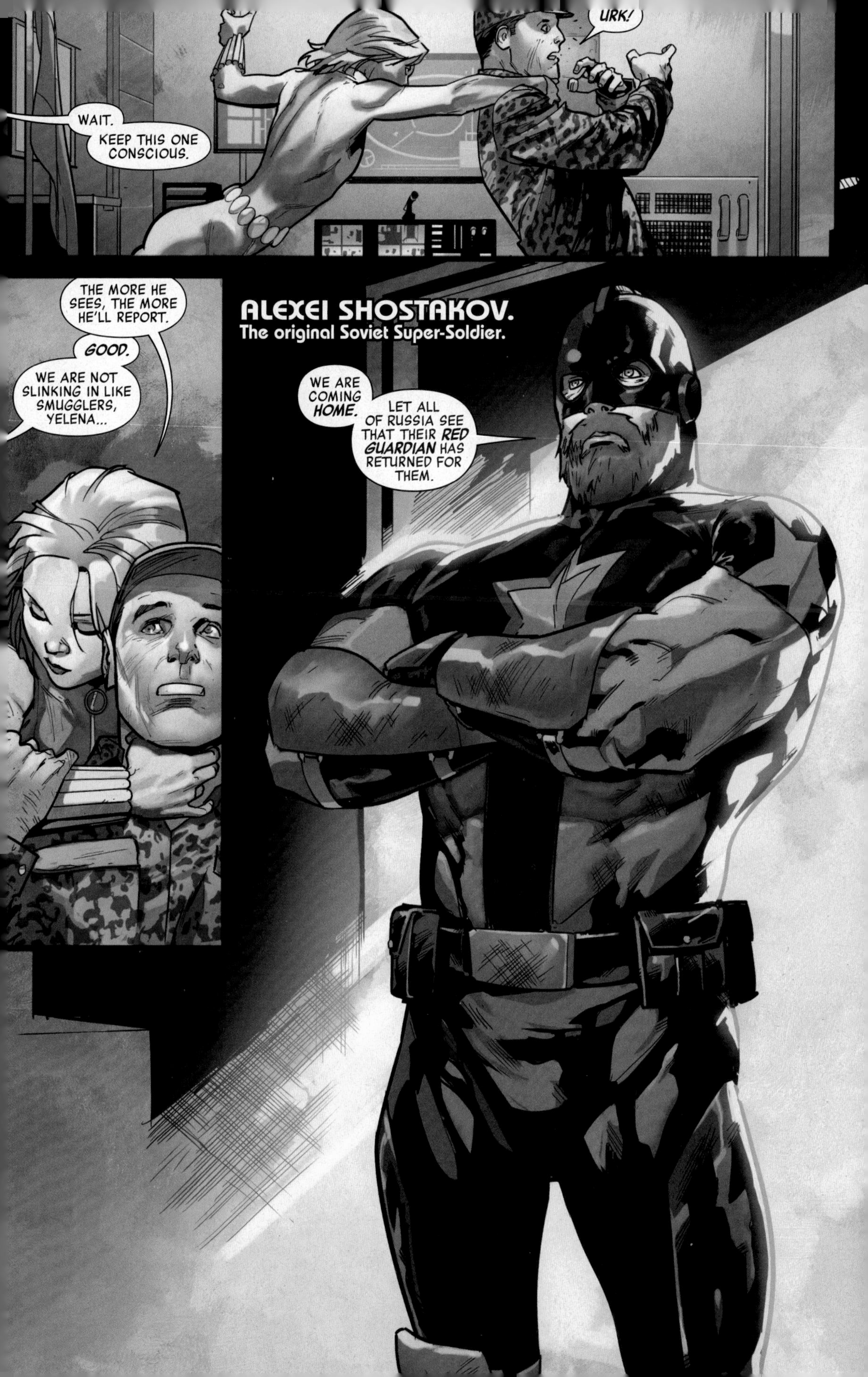
URK!
WAIT. KEEP THIS ONE CONSCIOUS.
THE MORE HE SEES, THE MORE HE'LL REPORT.
GOOD.
WE ARE NOT SLINKING IN LIKE SMUGGLERS, YELENA...
ALEXEI SHOSTAKOV.
The original Soviet Super-Soldier.
WE ARE COMING HOME.
LET ALL OF RUSSIA SEE THAT THEIR RED GUARDIAN HAS RETURNED FOR THEM.

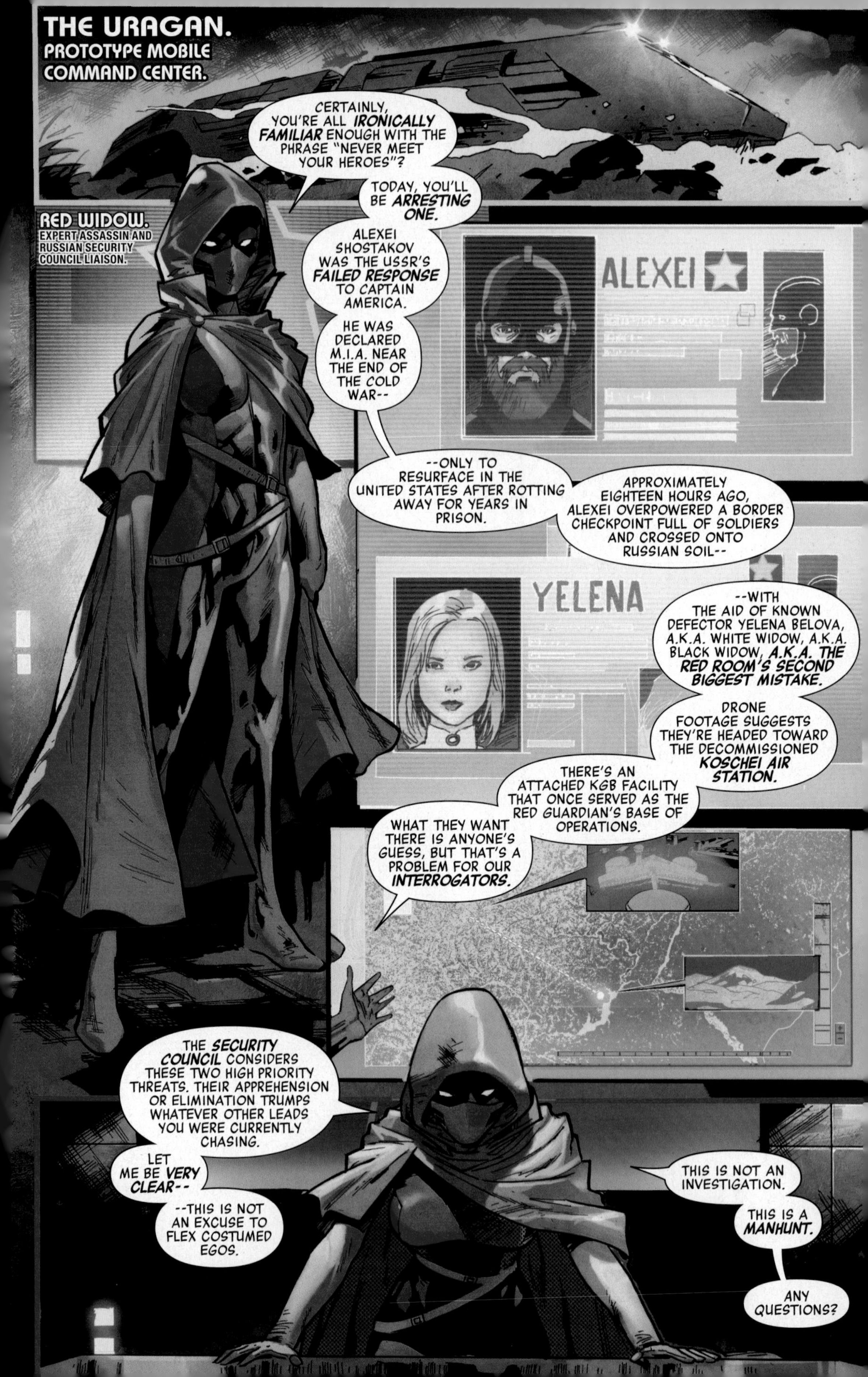

THE URAGAN. PROTOTYPE MOBILE COMMAND CENTER.
CERTAINLY, YOU'RE ALL IRONICALLY FAMILIAR ENOUGH WITH THE PHRASE "NEVER MEET YOUR HEROES"?
TODAY, YOU'LL BE ARRESTING ONE.
RED WIDOW. EXPERT ASSASSIN AND RUSSIAN SECURITY COUNCIL LIAISON.
ALEXEI SHOSTAKOV WAS THE USSR'S FAILED RESPONSE TO CAPTAIN AMERICA.
ALEXEI
HE WAS DECLARED M.I.A. NEAR THE END OF THE COLD WAR--
--ONLY TO RESURFACE IN THE UNITED STATES AFTER ROTTING AWAY FOR YEARS IN PRISON.
APPROXIMATELY EIGHTEEN HOURS AGO, ALEXEI OVERPOWERED A BORDER CHECKPOINT FULL OF SOLDIERS AND CROSSED ONTO RUSSIAN SOIL--
YELENA
--WITH THE AID OF KNOWN DEFECTOR YELENA BELOVA, A.K.A. WHITE WIDOW, A.K.A. BLACK WIDOW, A.K.A. THE RED ROOM'S SECOND BIGGEST MISTAKE.
DRONE FOOTAGE SUGGESTS THEY'RE HEADED TOWARD THE DECOMMISSIONED KOSCHEI AIR STATION.
THERE'S AN ATTACHED KGB FACILITY THAT ONCE SERVED AS THE RED GUARDIAN'S BASE OF OPERATIONS.
WHAT THEY WANT THERE IS ANYONE'S GUESS, BUT THAT'S A PROBLEM FOR OUR INTERROGATORS.
THE SECURITY COUNCIL CONSIDERS THESE TWO HIGH PRIORITY THREATS. THEIR APPREHENSION OR ELIMINATION TRUMPS WHATEVER OTHER LEADS YOU WERE CURRENTLY CHASING.
LET ME BE VERY CLEAR--
--THIS IS NOT AN EXCUSE TO FLEX COSTUMED EGOS.
THIS IS NOT AN INVESTIGATION.
THIS IS A MANHUNT.
ANY QUESTIONS?

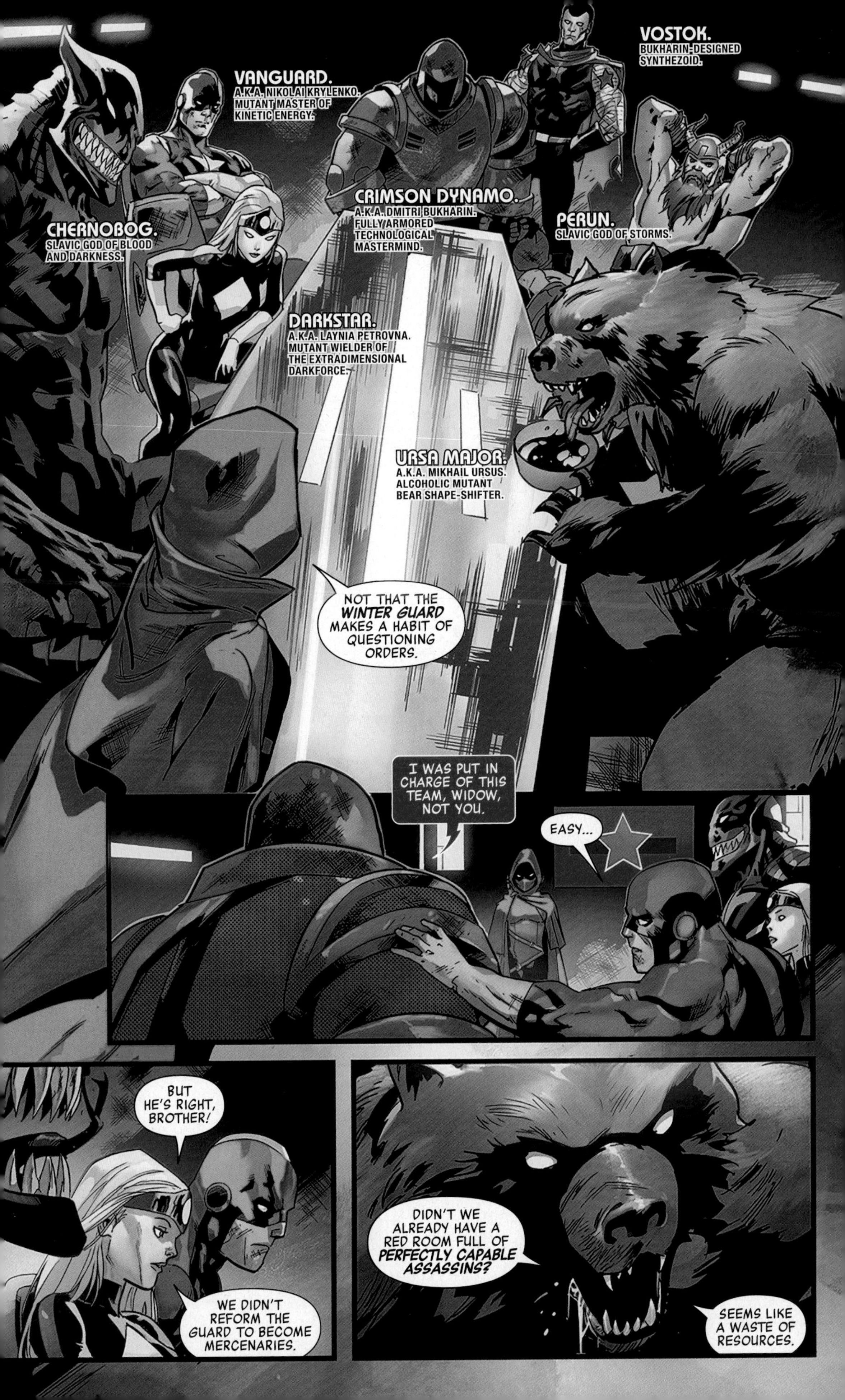
VANGUARD.
A.K.A. NIKOLAI KRYLENKO. MUTANT MASTER OF KINETIC ENERGY.
VOSTOK.
BUKHARIN-DESIGNED SYNTHEZOID.
CHERNOBOG.
SLAVIC GOD OF BLOOD AND DARKNESS.
CRIMSON DYNAMO.
A.K.A. DMITRI BUKHARIN. FULLY ARMORED TECHNOLOGICAL MASTERMIND.
PERUN.
SLAVIC GOD OF STORMS.
DARKSTAR.
A.K.A. LAYNIA PETROVNA. MUTANT WIELDER OF THE EXTRADIMENSIONAL DARKFORCE.
URSA MAJOR.
A.K.A. MIKHAIL URSUS. ALCOHOLIC MUTANT BEAR SHAPE-SHIFTER.
NOT THAT THE WINTER GUARD MAKES A HABIT OF QUESTIONING ORDERS.
I WAS PUT IN CHARGE OF THIS TEAM, WIDOW, NOT YOU.
EASY...
BUT HE'S RIGHT, BROTHER!
WE DIDN'T REFORM THE GUARD TO BECOME MERCENARIES.
DIDN'T WE ALREADY HAVE A RED ROOM FULL OF PERFECTLY CAPABLE ASSASSINS?
SEEMS LIKE A WASTE OF RESOURCES.

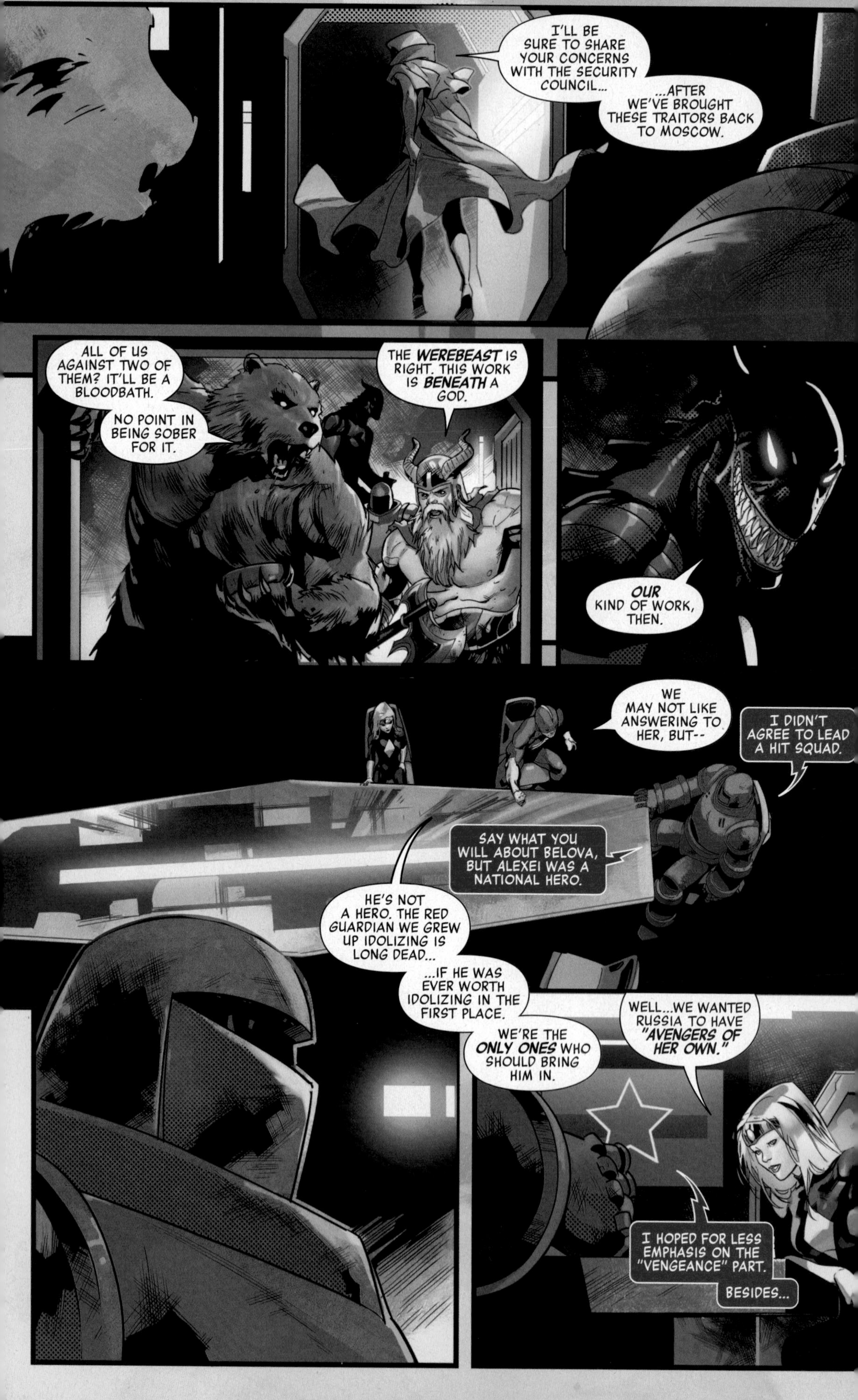

I'LL BE SURE TO SHARE YOUR CONCERNS WITH THE SECURITY COUNCIL...
...AFTER WE'VE BROUGHT THESE TRAITORS BACK TO MOSCOW.
ALL OF US AGAINST TWO OF THEM? IT'LL BE A BLOODBATH.
NO POINT IN BEING SOBER FOR IT.
THE *WEREBEAST* IS RIGHT. THIS WORK IS *BENEATH* A GOD.
OUR KIND OF WORK, THEN.
WE MAY NOT LIKE ANSWERING TO HER, BUT--
I DIDN'T AGREE TO LEAD A HIT SQUAD.
SAY WHAT YOU WILL ABOUT BELOVA, BUT ALEXEI WAS A NATIONAL HERO.
HE'S NOT A HERO. THE RED GUARDIAN WE GREW UP IDOLIZING IS LONG DEAD...
...IF HE WAS EVER WORTH IDOLIZING IN THE FIRST PLACE.
WE'RE THE *ONLY ONES* WHO SHOULD BRING HIM IN.
WELL...WE WANTED RUSSIA TO HAVE *"AVENGERS OF HER OWN."*
I HOPED FOR LESS EMPHASIS ON THE "VENGEANCE" PART.
BESIDES...

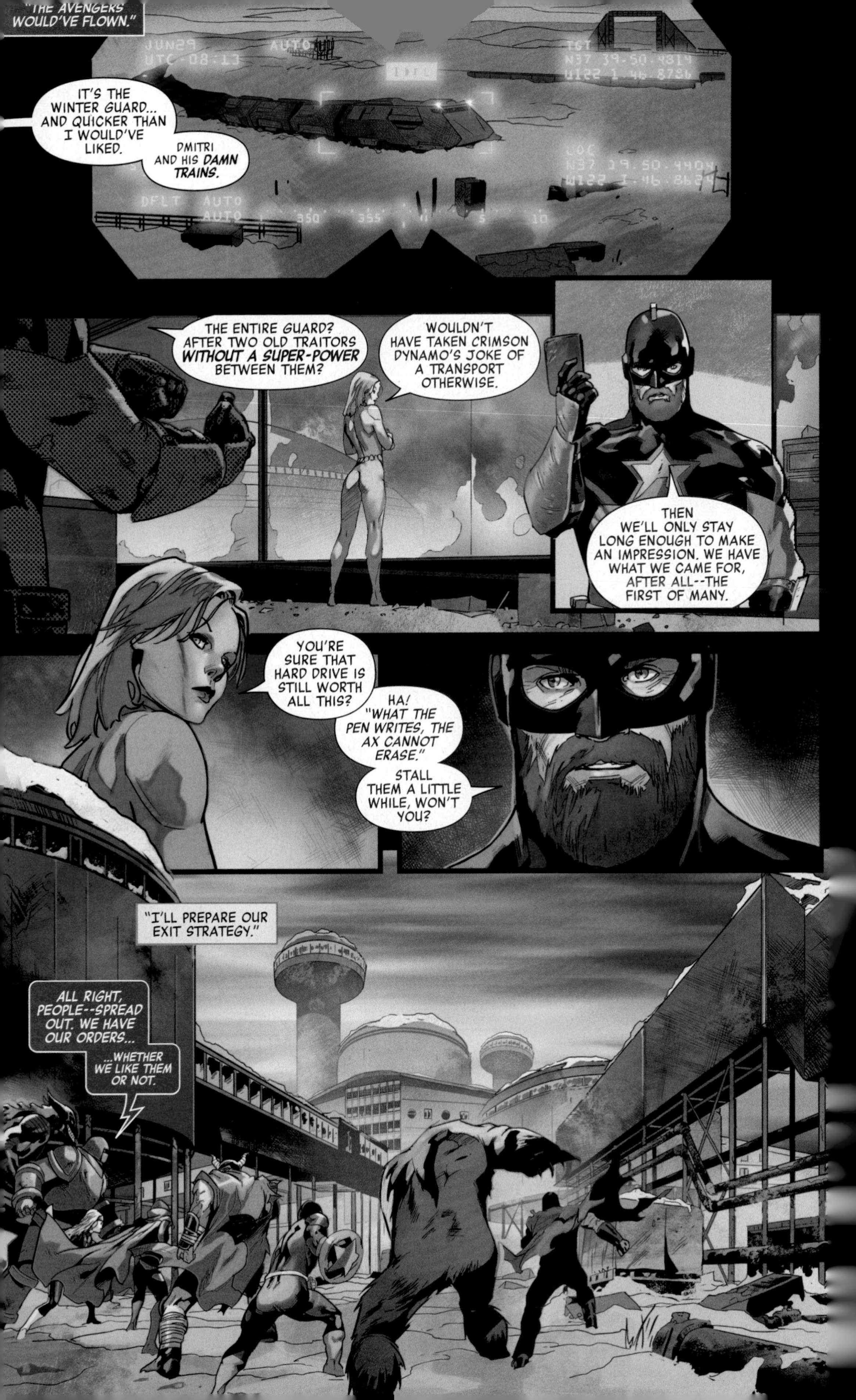
"THE AVENGERS WOULD'VE FLOWN."
IT'S THE WINTER GUARD... AND QUICKER THAN I WOULD'VE LIKED.
DMITRI AND HIS DAMN TRAINS.
THE ENTIRE GUARD? AFTER TWO OLD TRAITORS WITHOUT A SUPER-POWER BETWEEN THEM?
WOULDN'T HAVE TAKEN CRIMSON DYNAMO'S JOKE OF A TRANSPORT OTHERWISE.
THEN WE'LL ONLY STAY LONG ENOUGH TO MAKE AN IMPRESSION. WE HAVE WHAT WE CAME FOR, AFTER ALL--THE FIRST OF MANY.
YOU'RE SURE THAT HARD DRIVE IS STILL WORTH ALL THIS?
HA! "WHAT THE PEN WRITES, THE AX CANNOT ERASE."
STALL THEM A LITTLE WHILE, WON'T YOU?
"I'LL PREPARE OUR EXIT STRATEGY."
ALL RIGHT, PEOPLE--SPREAD OUT. WE HAVE OUR ORDERS...
...WHETHER WE LIKE THEM OR NOT.

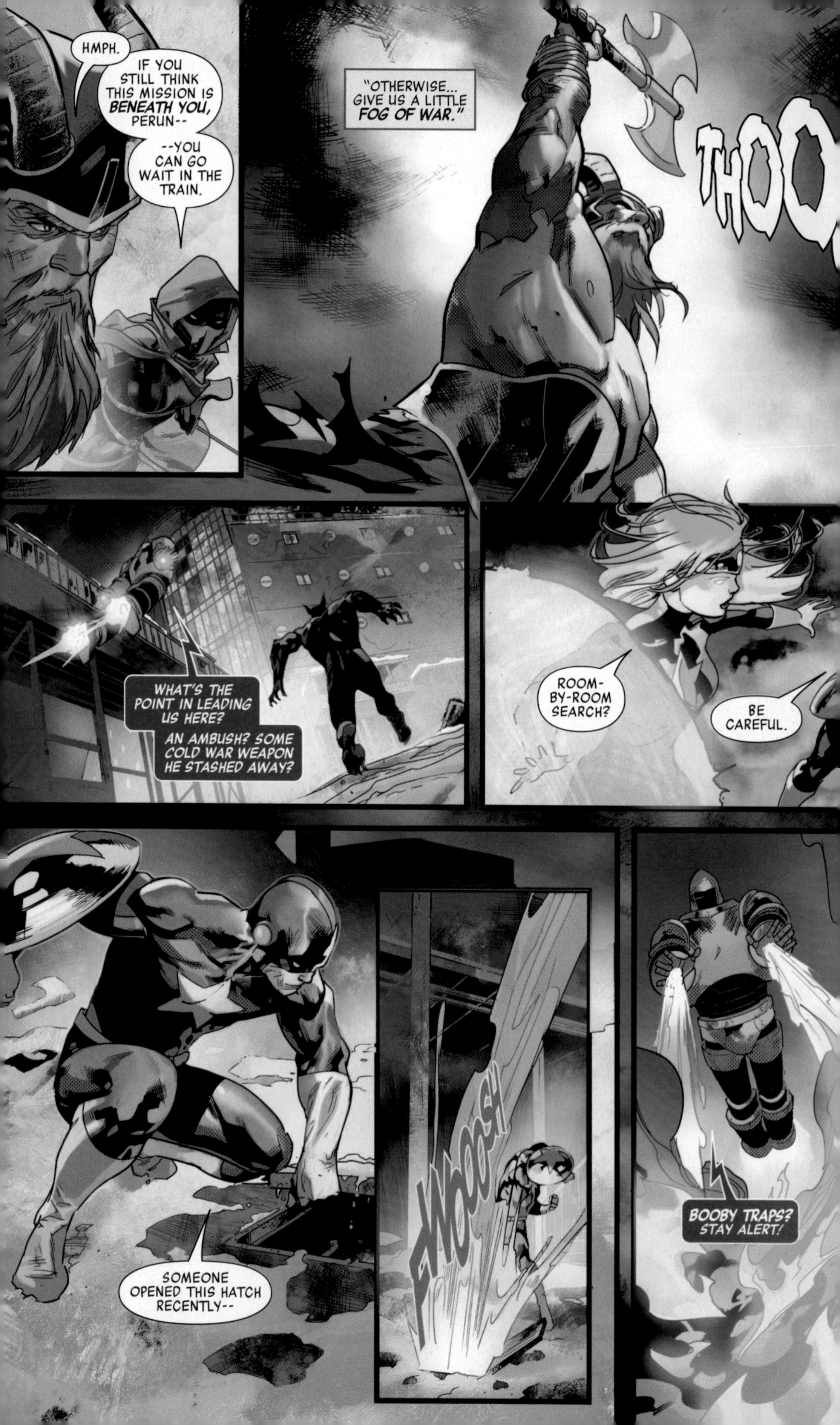
HMPH.
IF YOU STILL THINK THIS MISSION IS **BENEATH YOU,** PERUN--
--YOU CAN GO WAIT IN THE TRAIN.
"OTHERWISE... GIVE US A LITTLE **FOG OF WAR.**"
THOO
WHAT'S THE POINT IN LEADING US HERE?
AN AMBUSH? SOME COLD WAR WEAPON HE STASHED AWAY?
ROOM-BY-ROOM SEARCH?
BE CAREFUL.
SOMEONE OPENED THIS HATCH RECENTLY--
FWOOSH
BOOBY TRAPS? STAY ALERT!

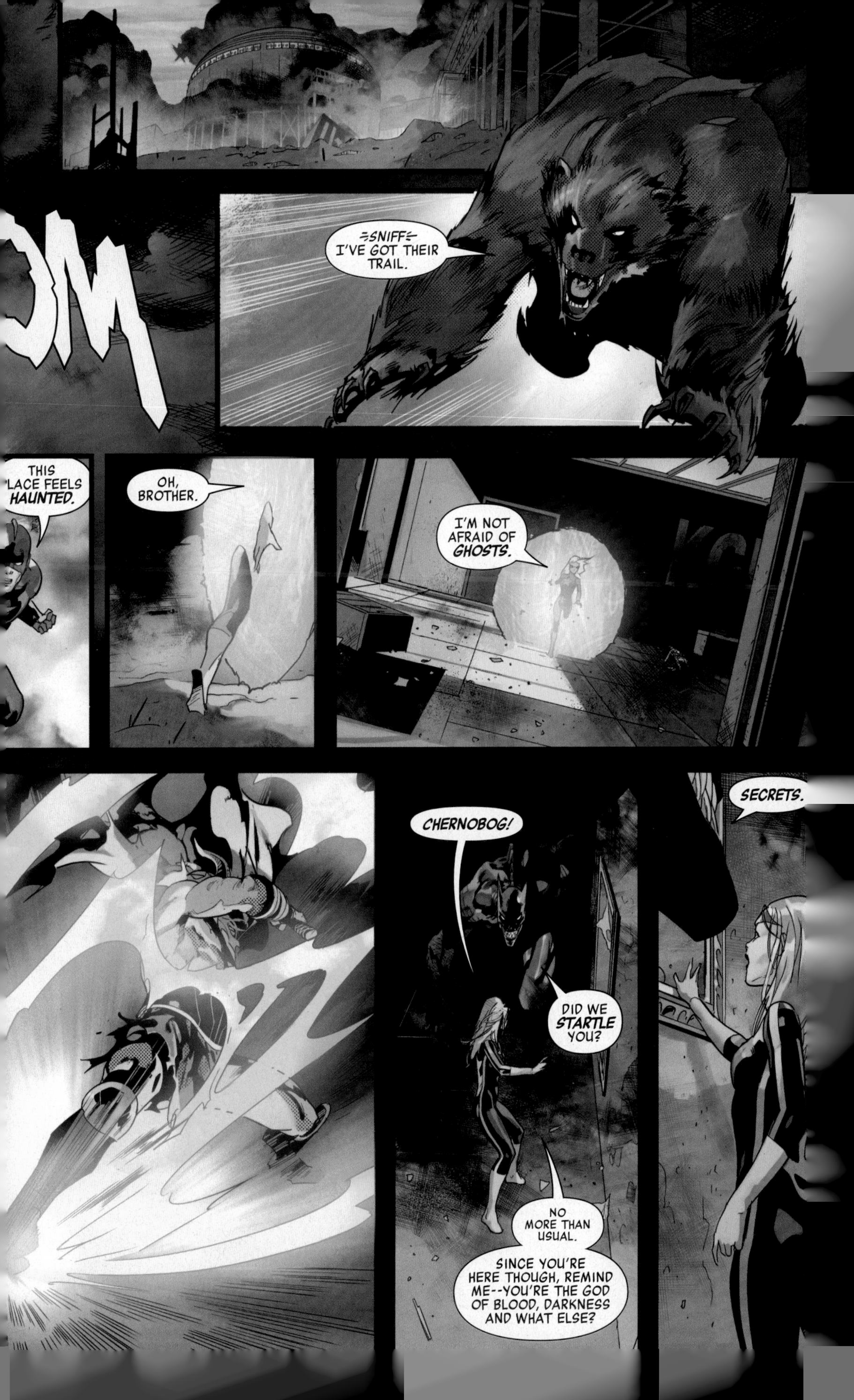

=SNIFF=
I'VE GOT THEIR TRAIL.
THIS LACE FEELS HAUNTED.
OH, BROTHER.
I'M NOT AFRAID OF GHOSTS.
CHERNOBOG!
DID WE STARTLE YOU?
NO MORE THAN USUAL.
SINCE YOU'RE HERE THOUGH, REMIND ME--YOU'RE THE GOD OF BLOOD, DARKNESS AND WHAT ELSE?
SECRETS.

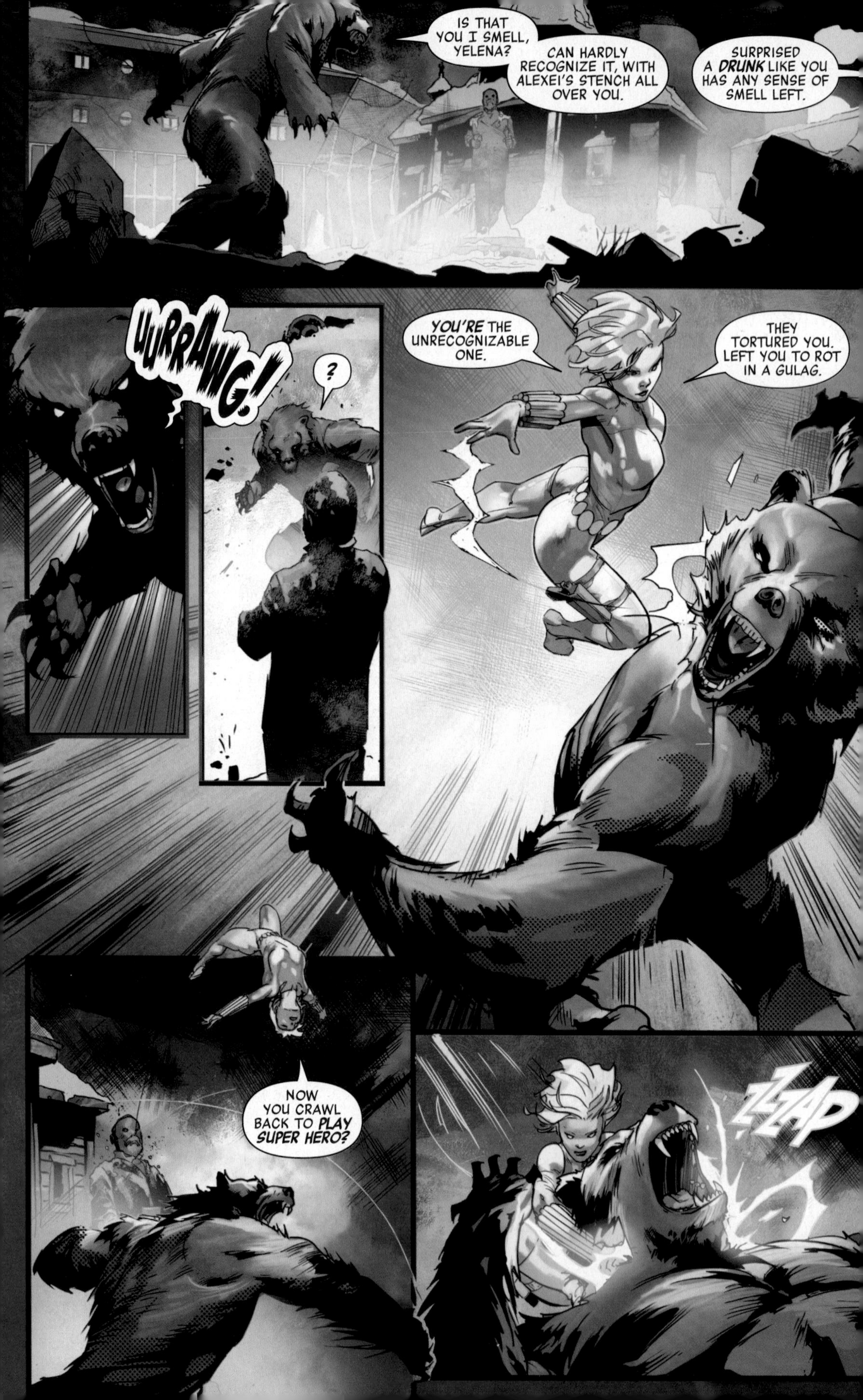
IS THAT YOU I SMELL, YELENA?
CAN HARDLY RECOGNIZE IT, WITH ALEXEI'S STENCH ALL OVER YOU.
SURPRISED A DRUNK LIKE YOU HAS ANY SENSE OF SMELL LEFT.
UURRAWG!
?
YOU'RE THE UNRECOGNIZABLE ONE.
THEY TORTURED YOU. LEFT YOU TO ROT IN A GULAG.
NOW YOU CRAWL BACK TO PLAY SUPER HERO?
ZZZAP

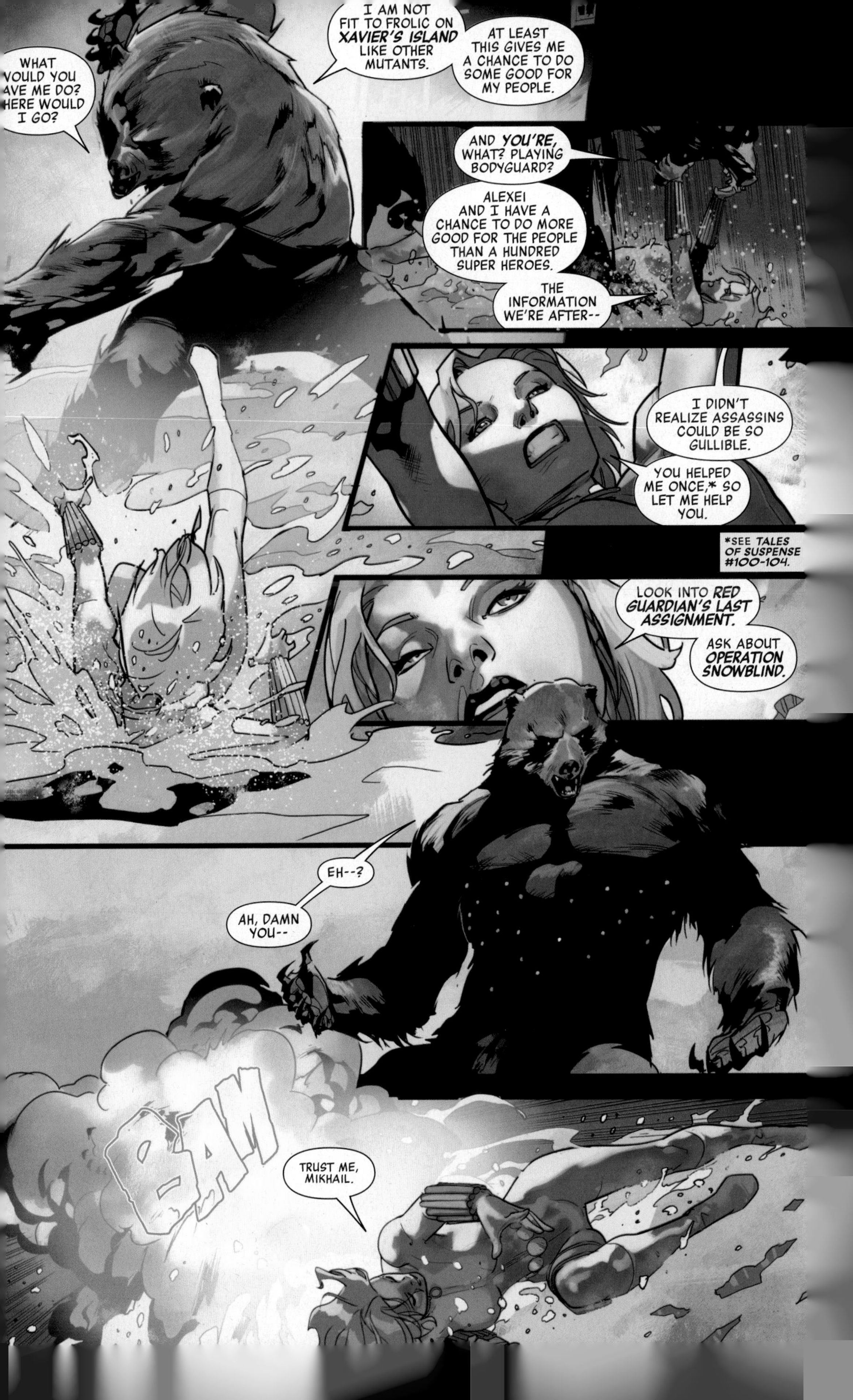
WHAT WOULD YOU HAVE ME DO? WHERE WOULD I GO?
I AM NOT FIT TO FROLIC ON XAVIER'S ISLAND LIKE OTHER MUTANTS.
AT LEAST THIS GIVES ME A CHANCE TO DO SOME GOOD FOR MY PEOPLE.
AND YOU'RE, WHAT? PLAYING BODYGUARD?
ALEXEI AND I HAVE A CHANCE TO DO MORE GOOD FOR THE PEOPLE THAN A HUNDRED SUPER HEROES.
THE INFORMATION WE'RE AFTER--
I DIDN'T REALIZE ASSASSINS COULD BE SO GULLIBLE.
YOU HELPED ME ONCE,* SO LET ME HELP YOU.
*SEE TALES OF SUSPENSE #100-104.
LOOK INTO RED GUARDIAN'S LAST ASSIGNMENT.
ASK ABOUT OPERATION SNOWBLIND.
EH--?
AH, DAMN YOU--
BAM
TRUST ME, MIKHAIL.

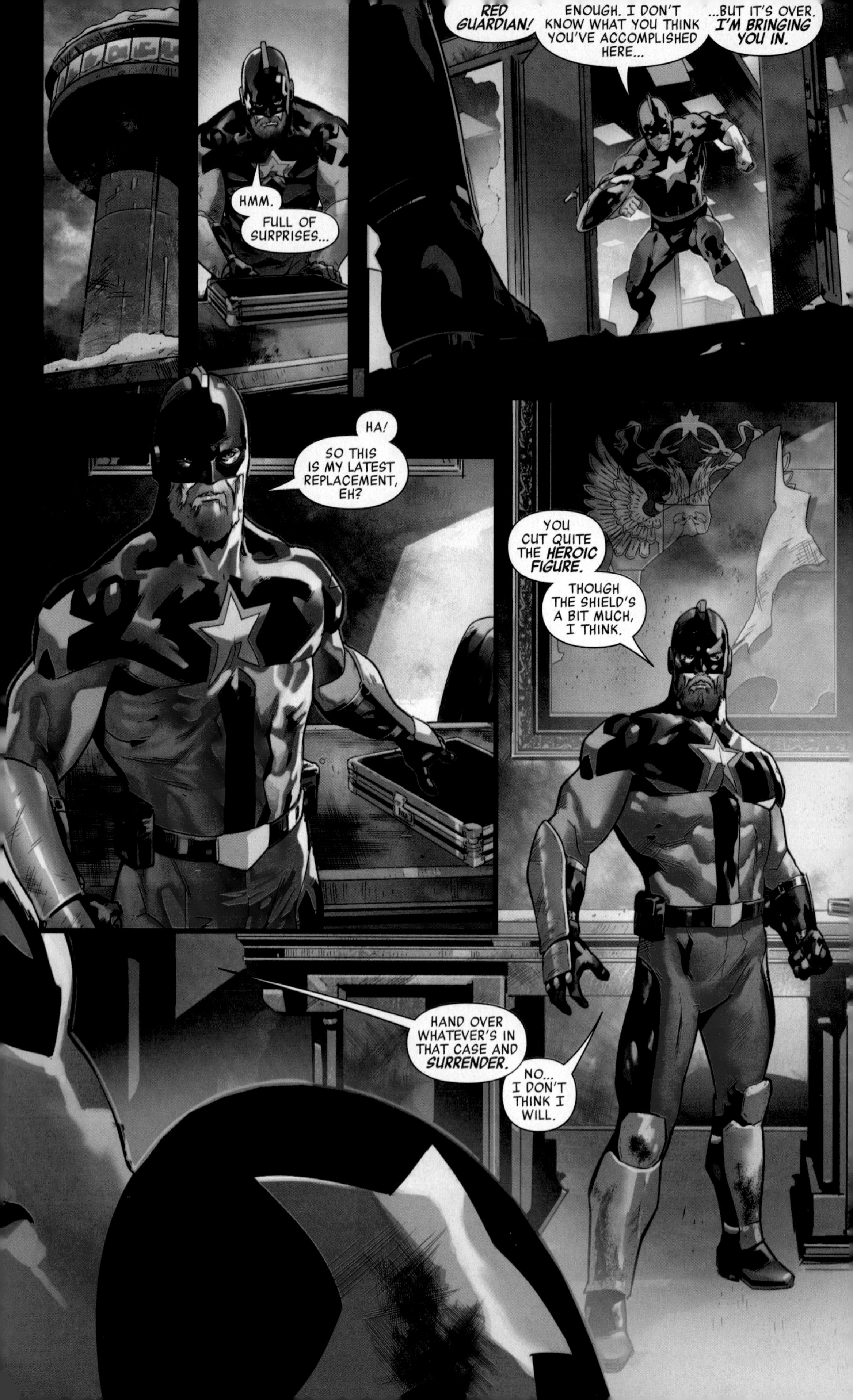
HMM.
FULL OF SURPRISES...
RED GUARDIAN!
ENOUGH. I DON'T KNOW WHAT YOU THINK YOU'VE ACCOMPLISHED HERE...
...BUT IT'S OVER. I'M BRINGING YOU IN.
HA!
SO THIS IS MY LATEST REPLACEMENT, EH?
YOU CUT QUITE THE HEROIC FIGURE.
THOUGH THE SHIELD'S A BIT MUCH, I THINK.
HAND OVER WHATEVER'S IN THAT CASE AND SURRENDER.
NO... I DON'T THINK I WILL.

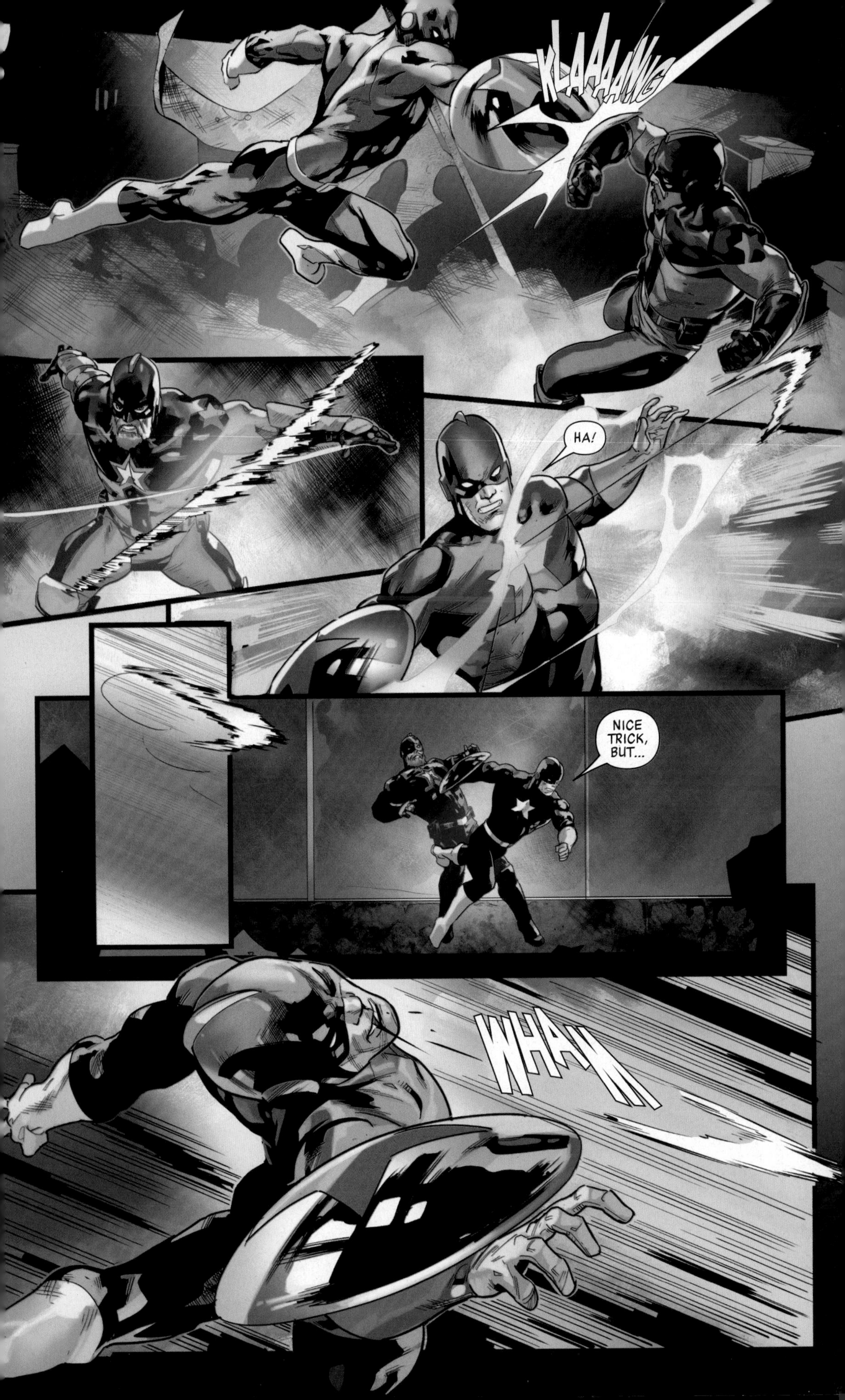
KLAAAANG
HA!
NICE TRICK, BUT...
WHAK

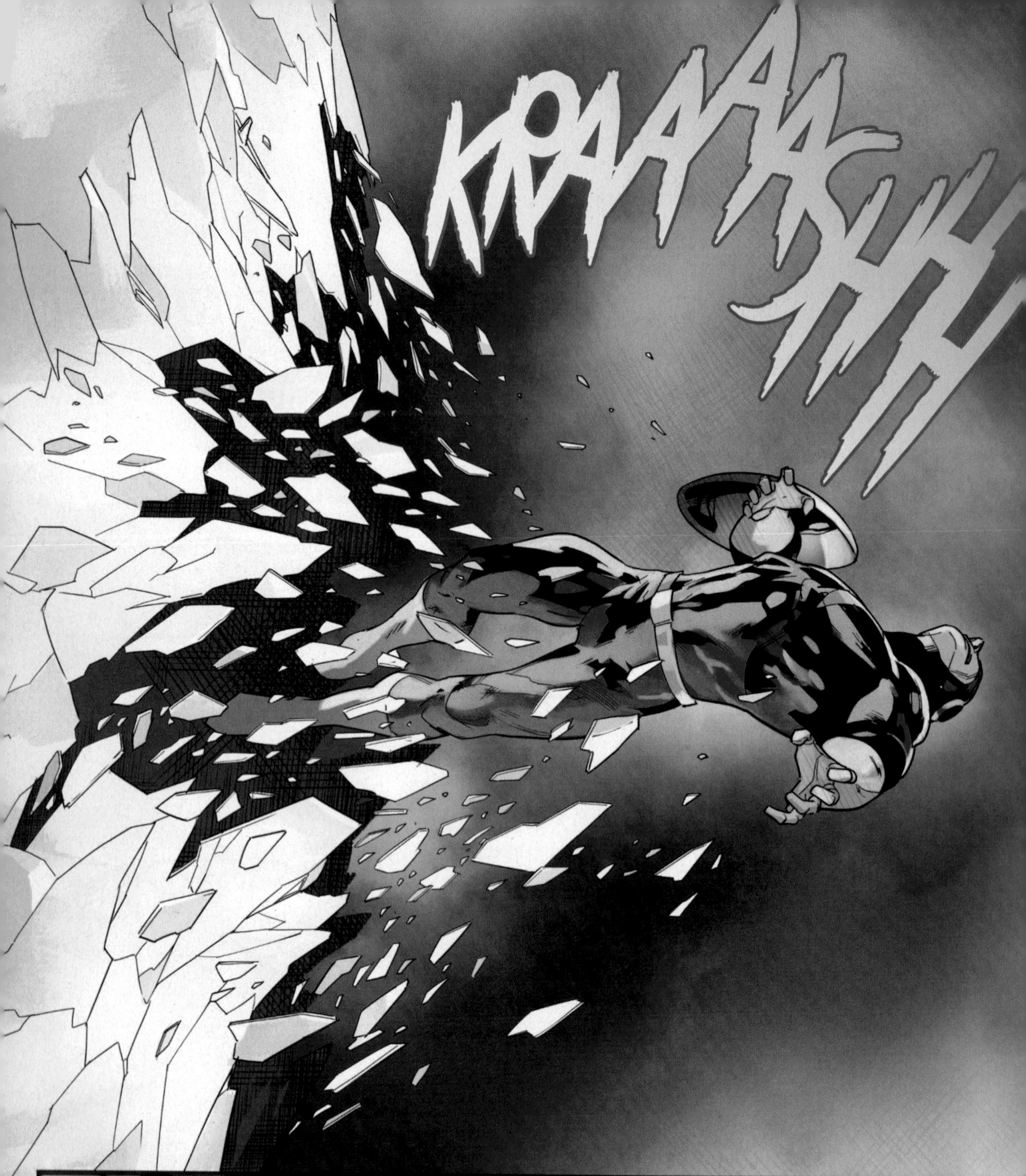
KRAAAASHH

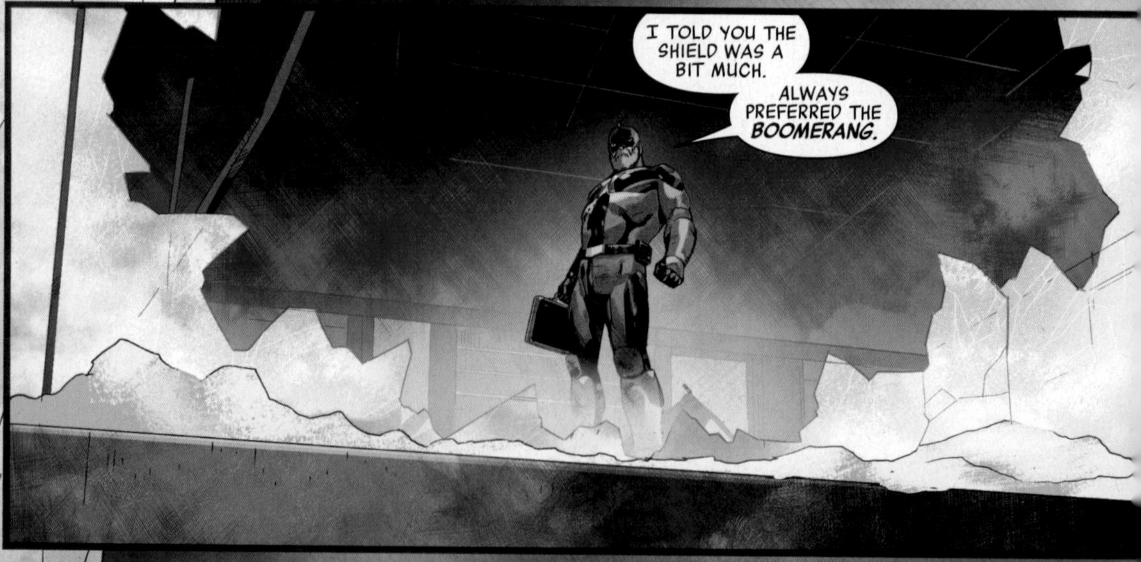
I TOLD YOU THE SHIELD WAS A BIT MUCH.
ALWAYS PREFERRED THE *BOOMERANG.*

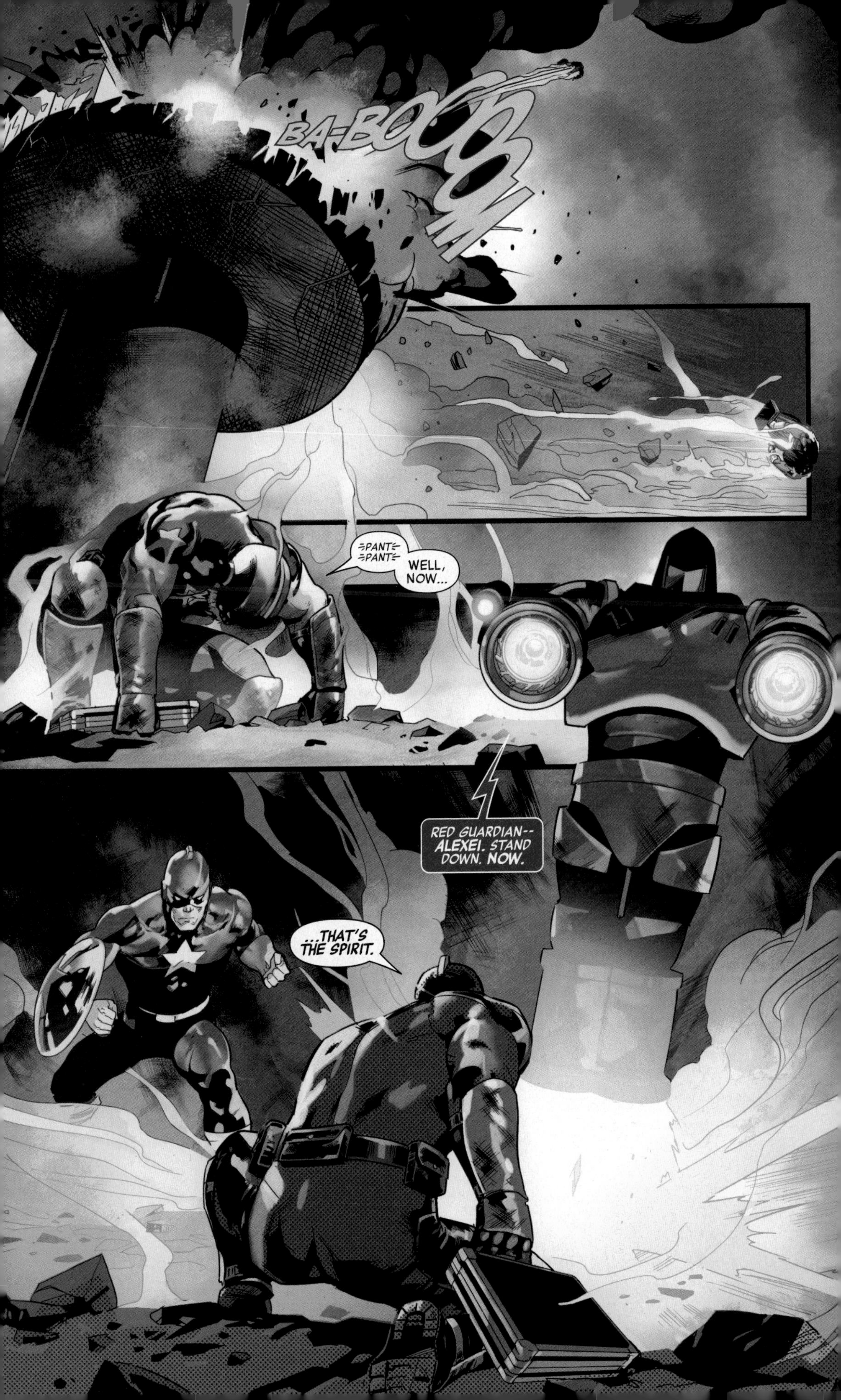
BA-BOOOOM
PANT PANT
WELL, NOW...
RED GUARDIAN-- ALEXEI. STAND DOWN. NOW.
...THAT'S THE SPIRIT.

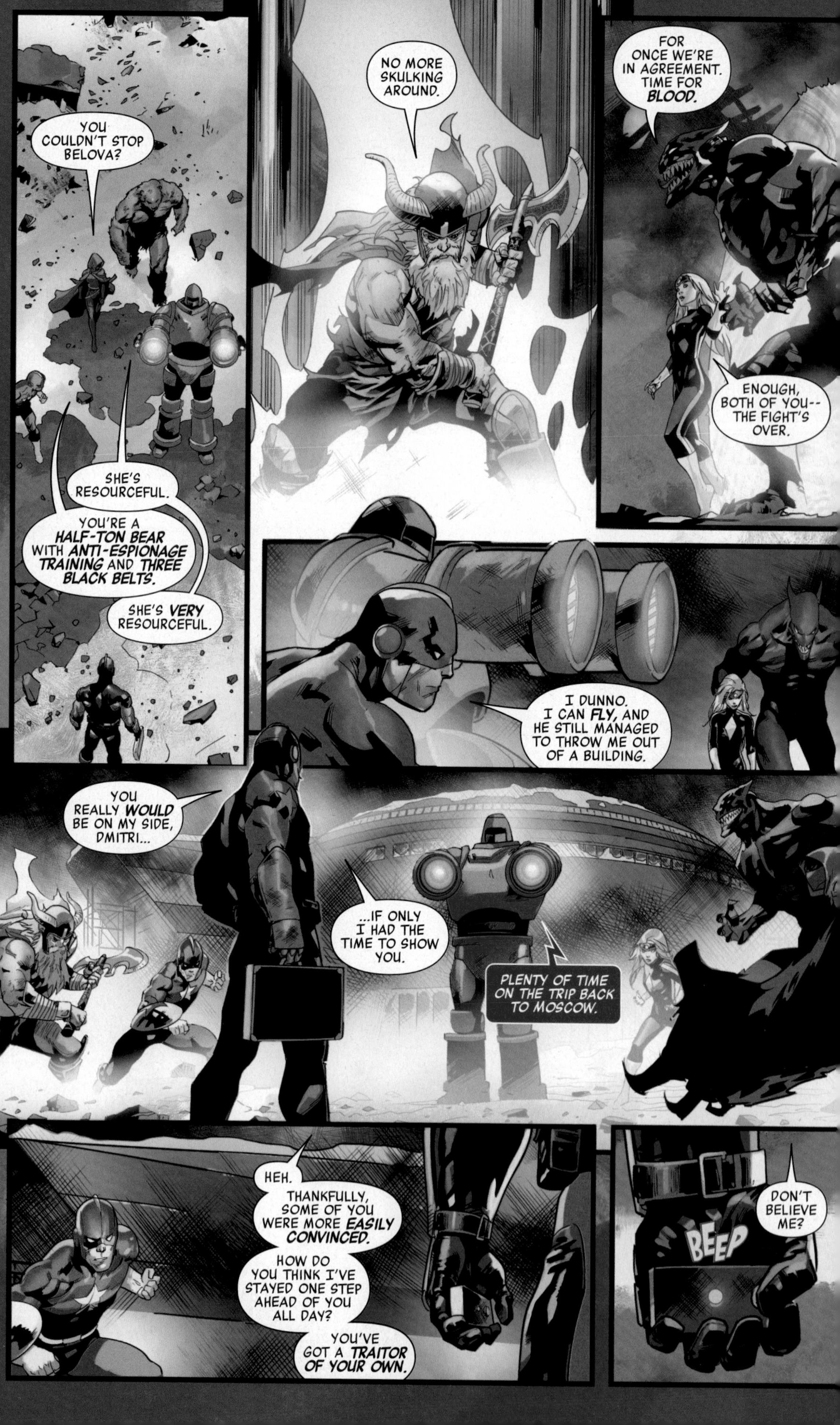
YOU COULDN'T STOP BELOVA?
SHE'S RESOURCEFUL.
YOU'RE A HALF-TON BEAR WITH ANTI-ESPIONAGE TRAINING AND THREE BLACK BELTS.
SHE'S VERY RESOURCEFUL.
NO MORE SKULKING AROUND.
FOR ONCE WE'RE IN AGREEMENT. TIME FOR BLOOD.
ENOUGH, BOTH OF YOU-- THE FIGHT'S OVER.
I DUNNO. I CAN FLY, AND HE STILL MANAGED TO THROW ME OUT OF A BUILDING.
YOU REALLY WOULD BE ON MY SIDE, DMITRI...
...IF ONLY I HAD THE TIME TO SHOW YOU.
PLENTY OF TIME ON THE TRIP BACK TO MOSCOW.
HEH.
THANKFULLY, SOME OF YOU WERE MORE EASILY CONVINCED.
HOW DO YOU THINK I'VE STAYED ONE STEP AHEAD OF YOU ALL DAY?
YOU'VE GOT A TRAITOR OF YOUR OWN.
DON'T BELIEVE ME?
BEEP

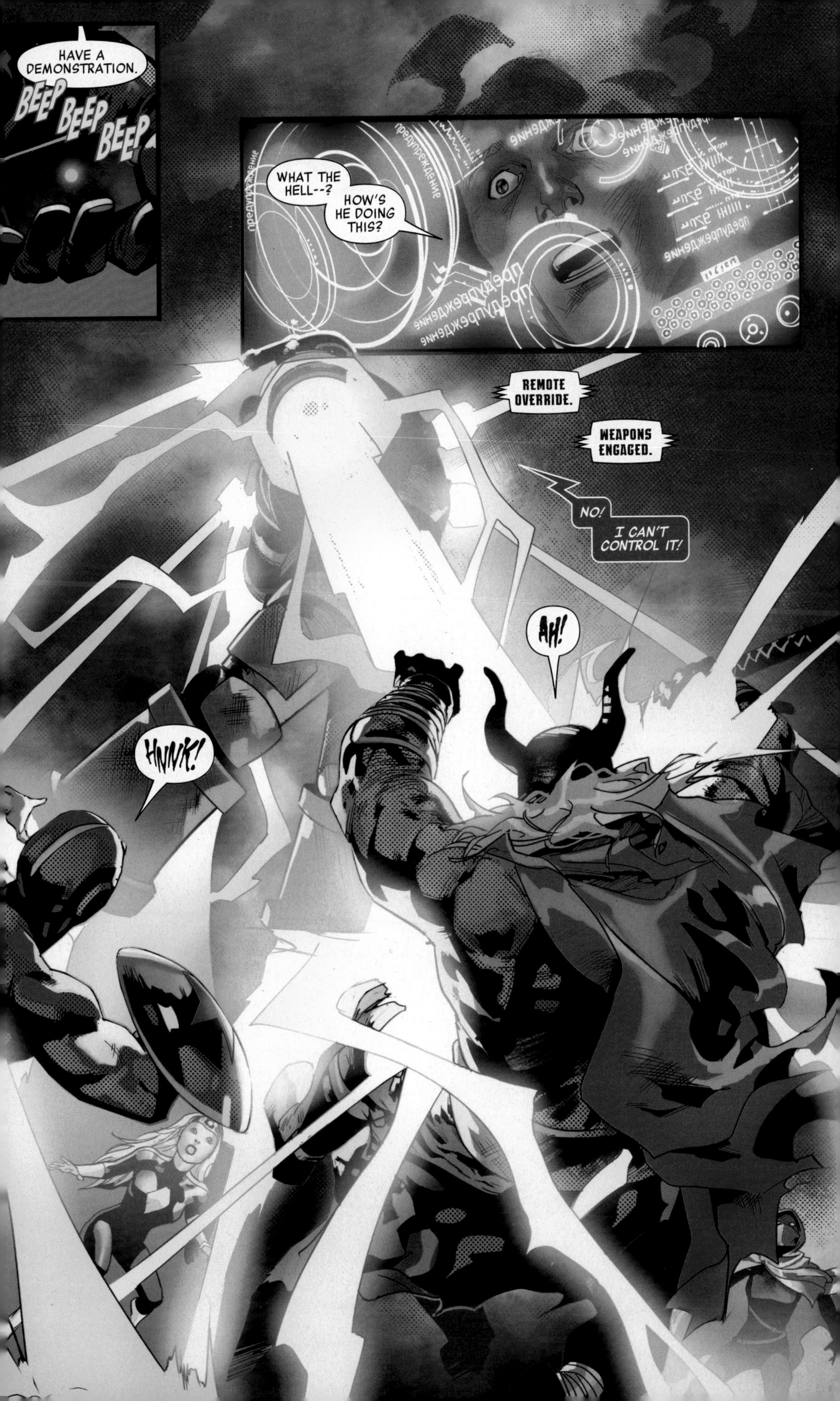
HAVE A DEMONSTRATION.
BEEP BEEP BEEP
WHAT THE HELL--?
HOW'S HE DOING THIS?
REMOTE OVERRIDE.
WEAPONS ENGAGED.
NO!
I CAN'T CONTROL IT!
AH!
HNNK!

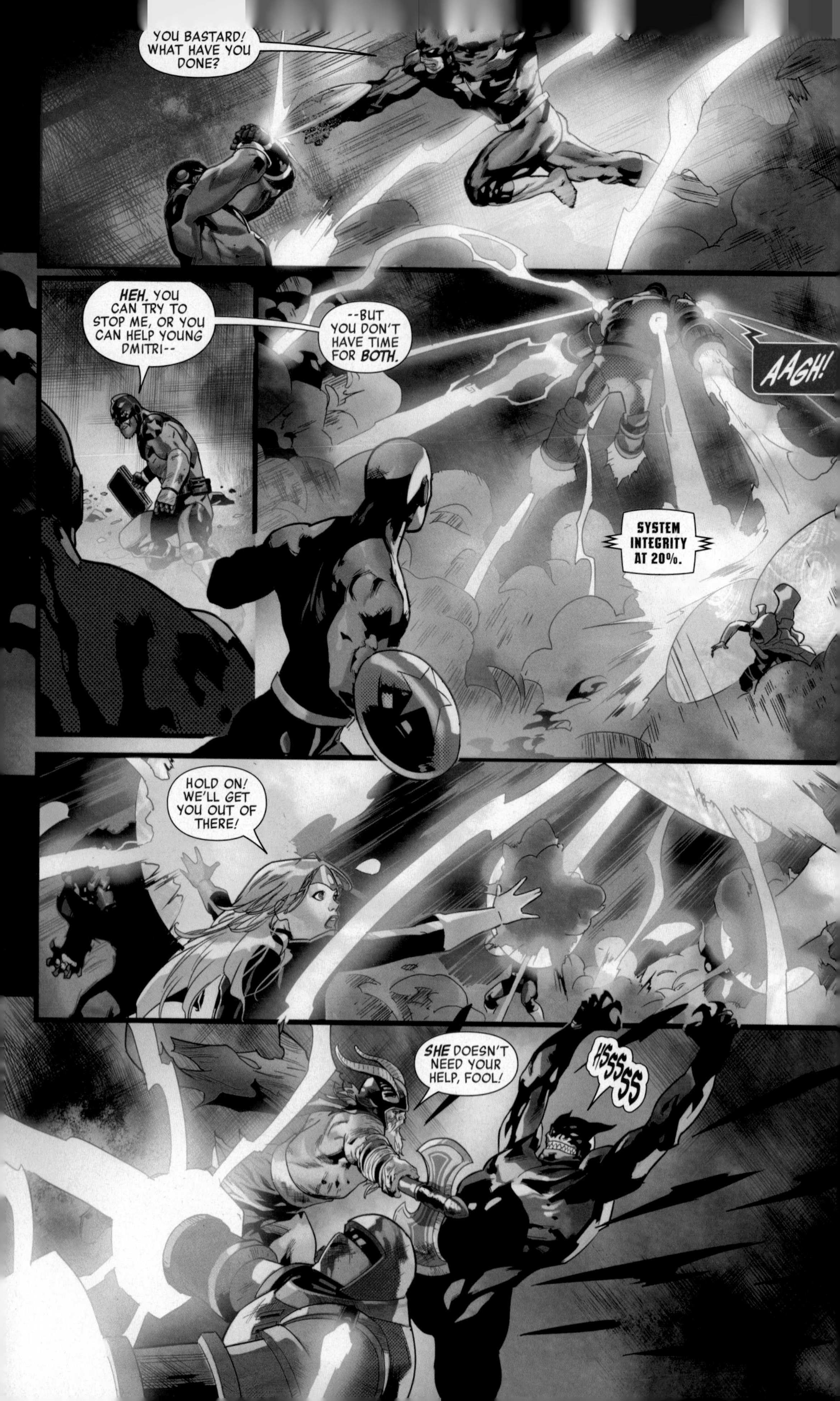
YOU BASTARD! WHAT HAVE YOU DONE?
HEH. YOU CAN TRY TO STOP ME, OR YOU CAN HELP YOUNG DMITRI--
--BUT YOU DON'T HAVE TIME FOR BOTH.
AAGH!
SYSTEM INTEGRITY AT 20%.
HOLD ON! WE'LL GET YOU OUT OF THERE!
SHE DOESN'T NEED YOUR HELP, FOOL!
HSSSSS

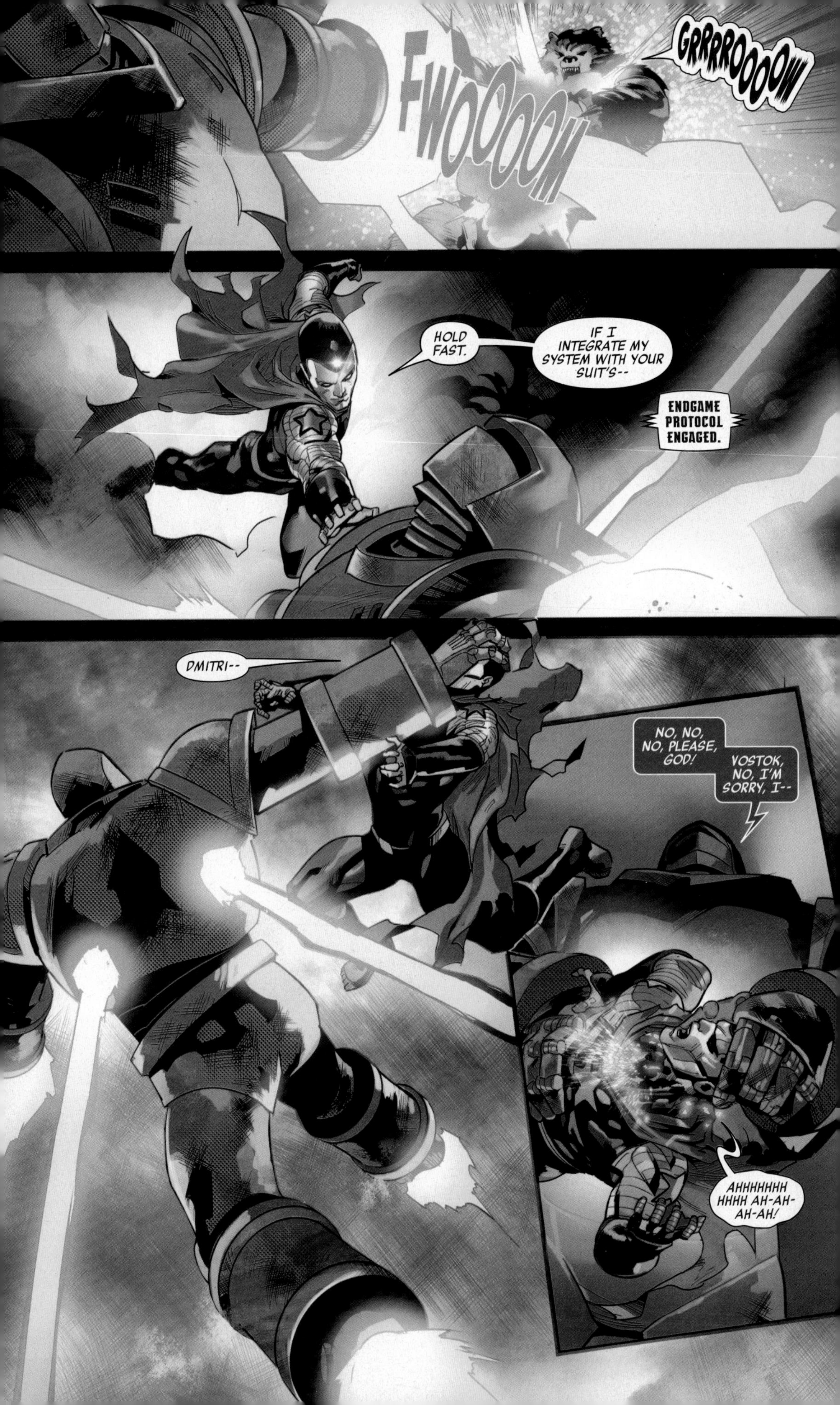
FWOOOOM
GRRRROOOOW
HOLD FAST.
IF I INTEGRATE MY SYSTEM WITH YOUR SUIT'S--
ENDGAME PROTOCOL ENGAGED.
DMITRI--
NO, NO, NO, PLEASE, GOD!
VOSTOK, NO, I'M SORRY, I--
AHHHHHHH HHHH AH-AH-AH-AH!

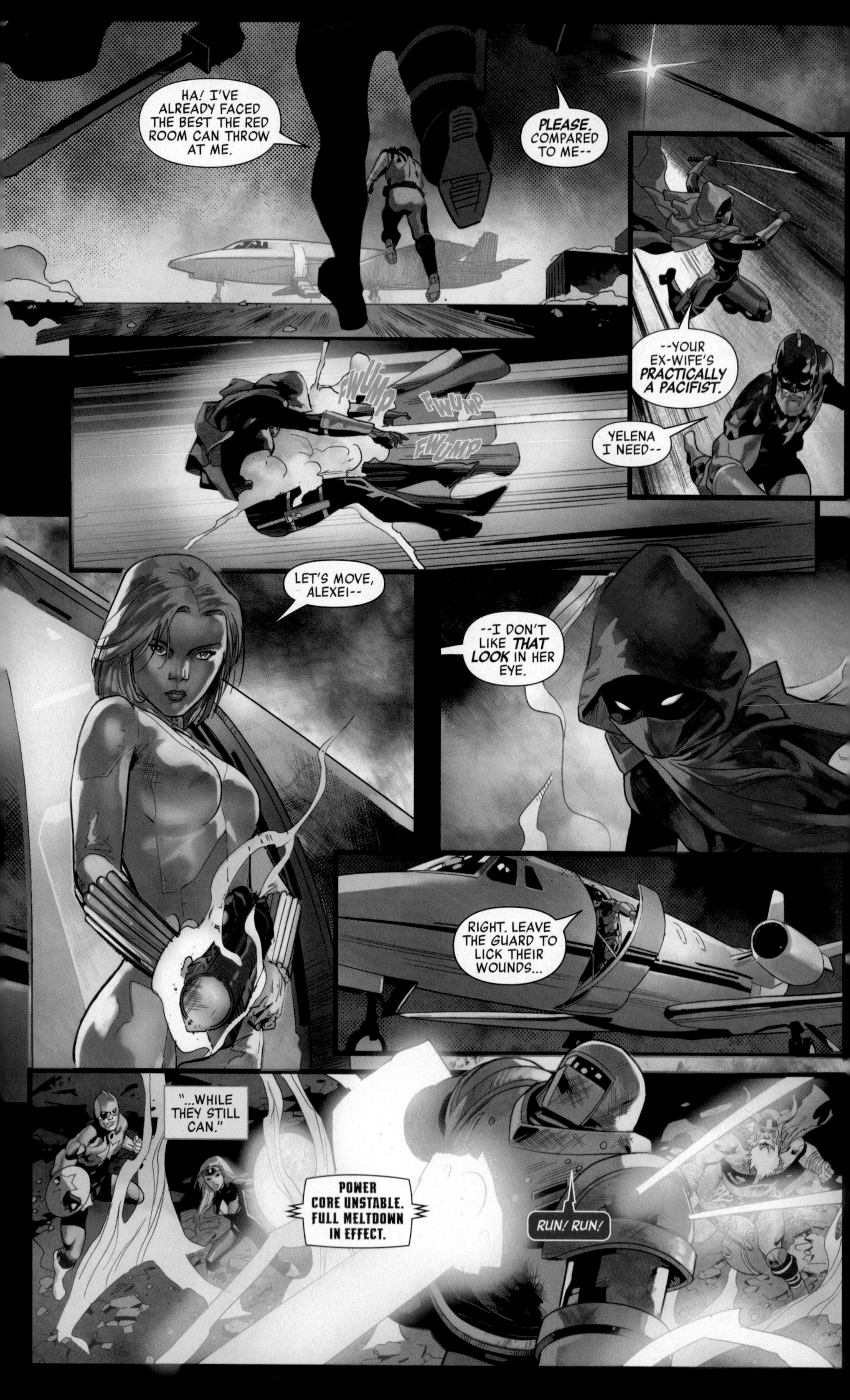
HA! I'VE ALREADY FACED THE BEST THE RED ROOM CAN THROW AT ME.
PLEASE. COMPARED TO ME--
--YOUR EX-WIFE'S PRACTICALLY A PACIFIST.
YELENA I NEED--
FWUMP
FWUMP
FWUMP
LET'S MOVE, ALEXEI--
--I DON'T LIKE THAT LOOK IN HER EYE.
RIGHT. LEAVE THE GUARD TO LICK THEIR WOUNDS...
"...WHILE THEY STILL CAN."
POWER CORE UNSTABLE. FULL MELTDOWN IN EFFECT.
RUN! RUN!

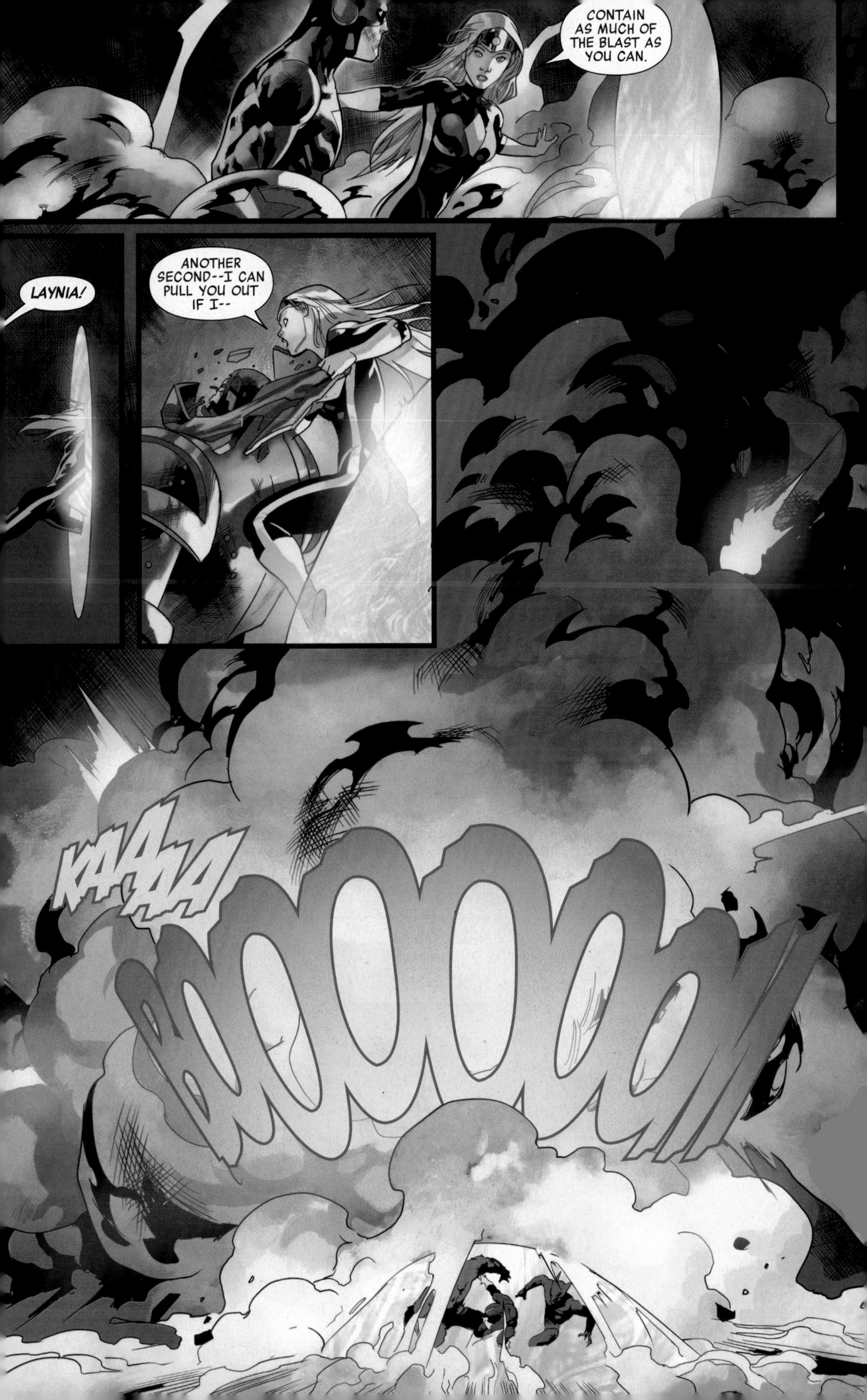

CONTAIN AS MUCH OF THE BLAST AS YOU CAN.
LAYNIA!
ANOTHER SECOND--I CAN PULL YOU OUT IF I--
KAAAA
BOOOOOOM

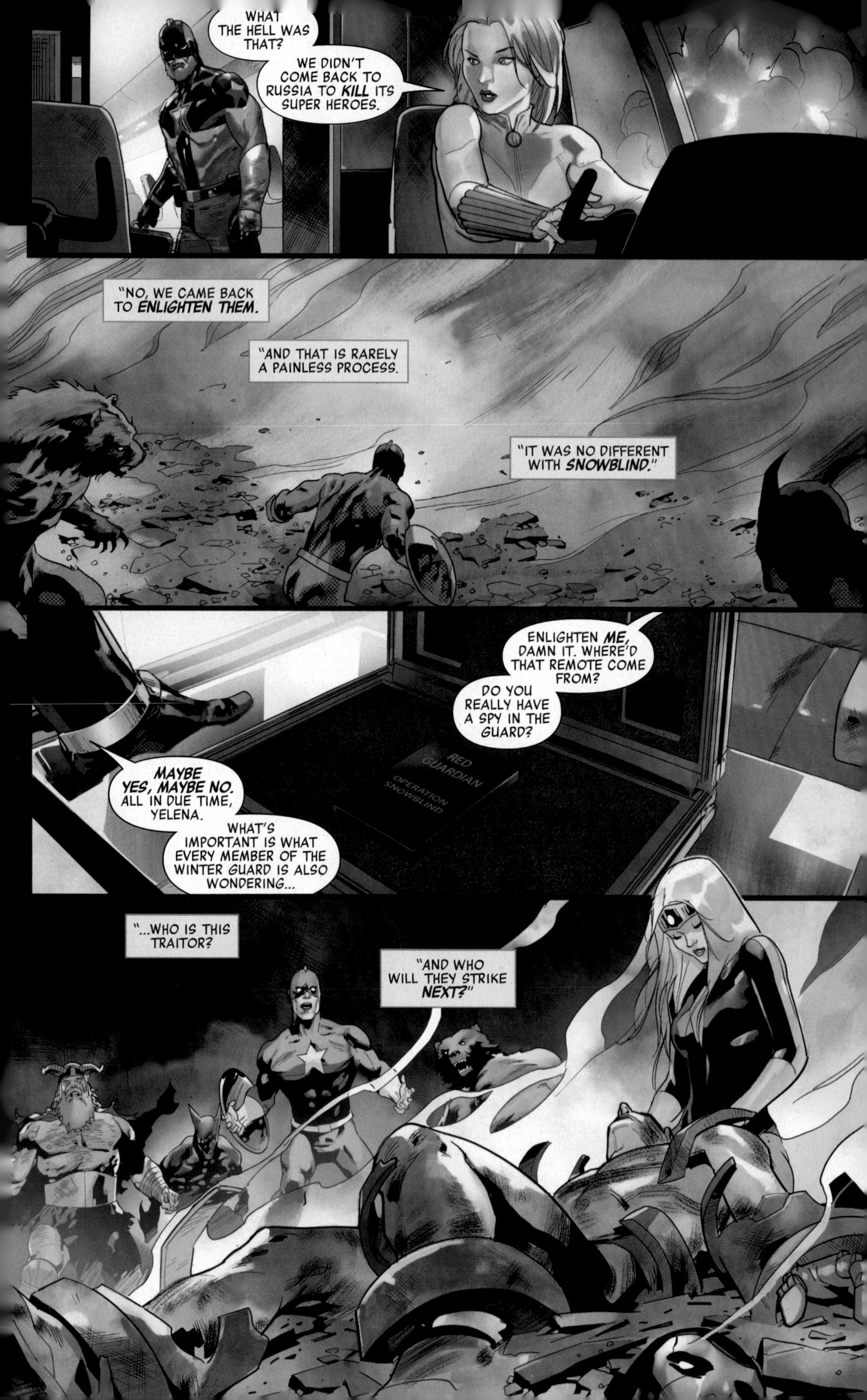
WHAT THE HELL WAS THAT?
WE DIDN'T COME BACK TO RUSSIA TO KILL ITS SUPER HEROES.
"NO, WE CAME BACK TO ENLIGHTEN THEM.
"AND THAT IS RARELY A PAINLESS PROCESS.
"IT WAS NO DIFFERENT WITH SNOWBLIND."
ENLIGHTEN ME, DAMN IT. WHERE'D THAT REMOTE COME FROM?
DO YOU REALLY HAVE A SPY IN THE GUARD?
RED GUARDIAN
OPERATION SNOWBLIND
MAYBE YES, MAYBE NO. ALL IN DUE TIME, YELENA.
WHAT'S IMPORTANT IS WHAT EVERY MEMBER OF THE WINTER GUARD IS ALSO WONDERING...
"...WHO IS THIS TRAITOR?
"AND WHO WILL THEY STRIKE NEXT?"

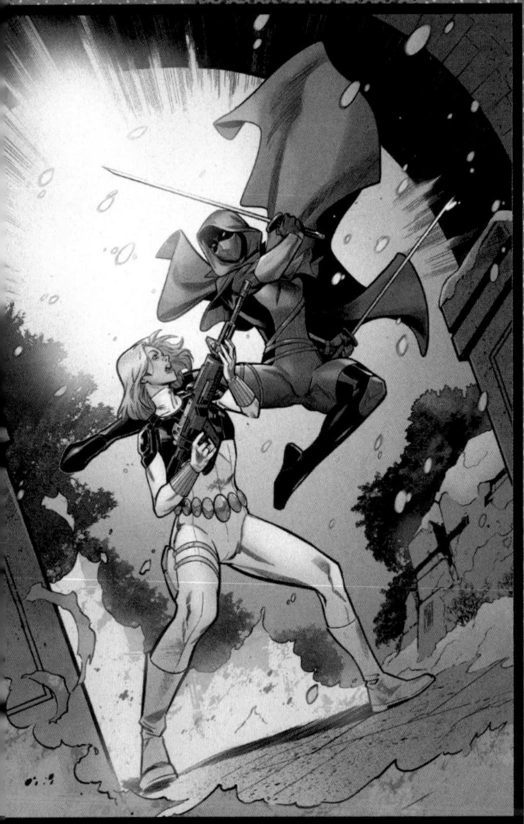

Winter Guard #1 Variant
BY KEN LASHLEY & JUAN FERNANDEZ

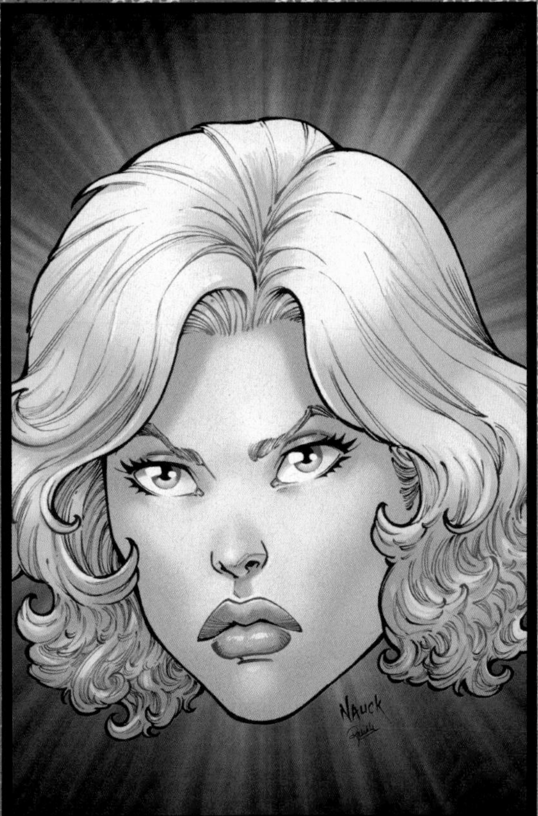
NAUCK

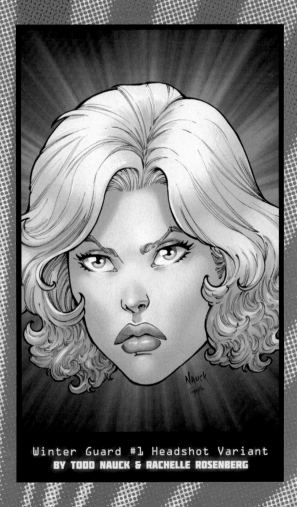

Winter Guard #1 Headshot Variant
BY TODD NAUCK & RACHELLE ROSENBERG

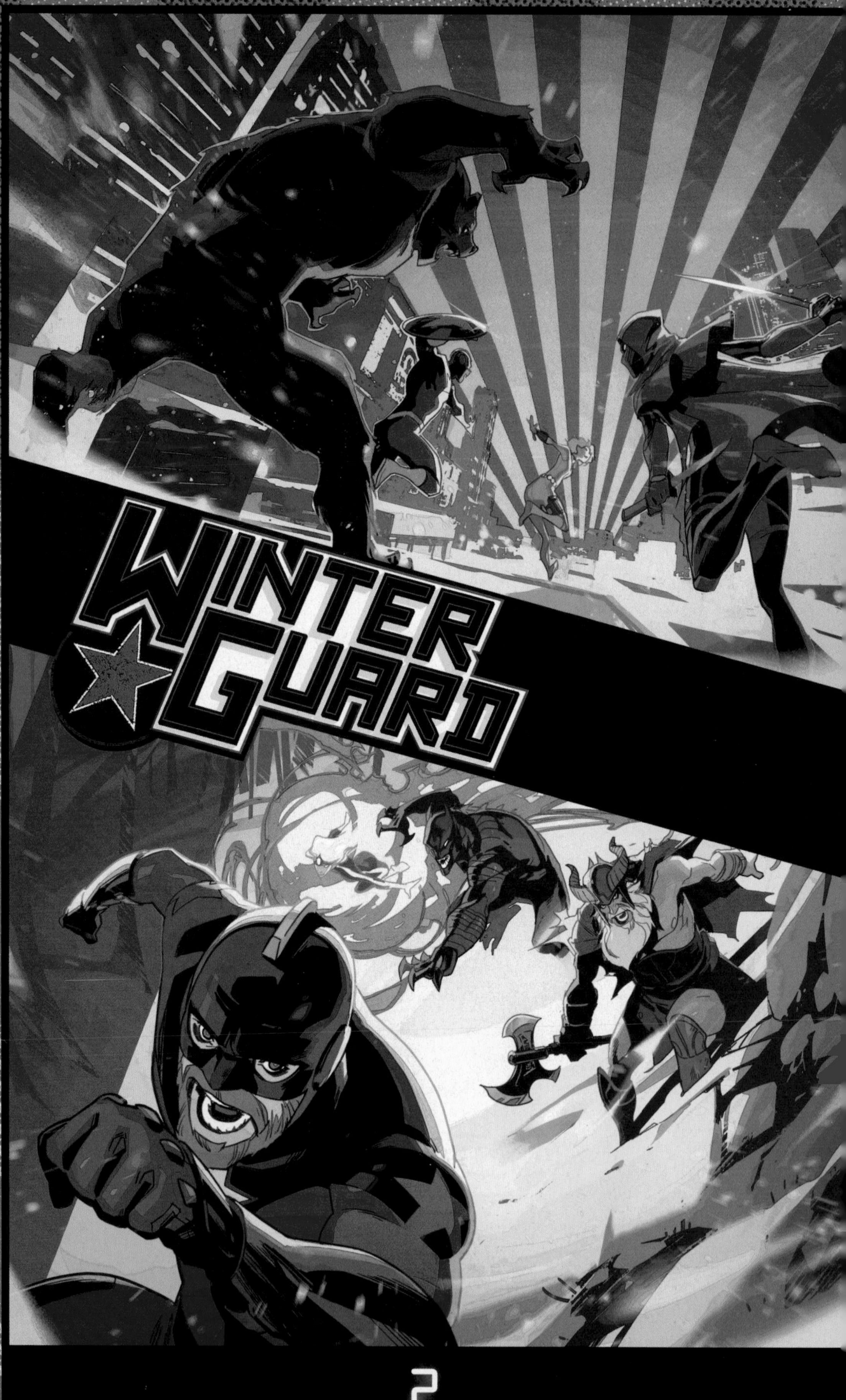
WINTER GUARD
2

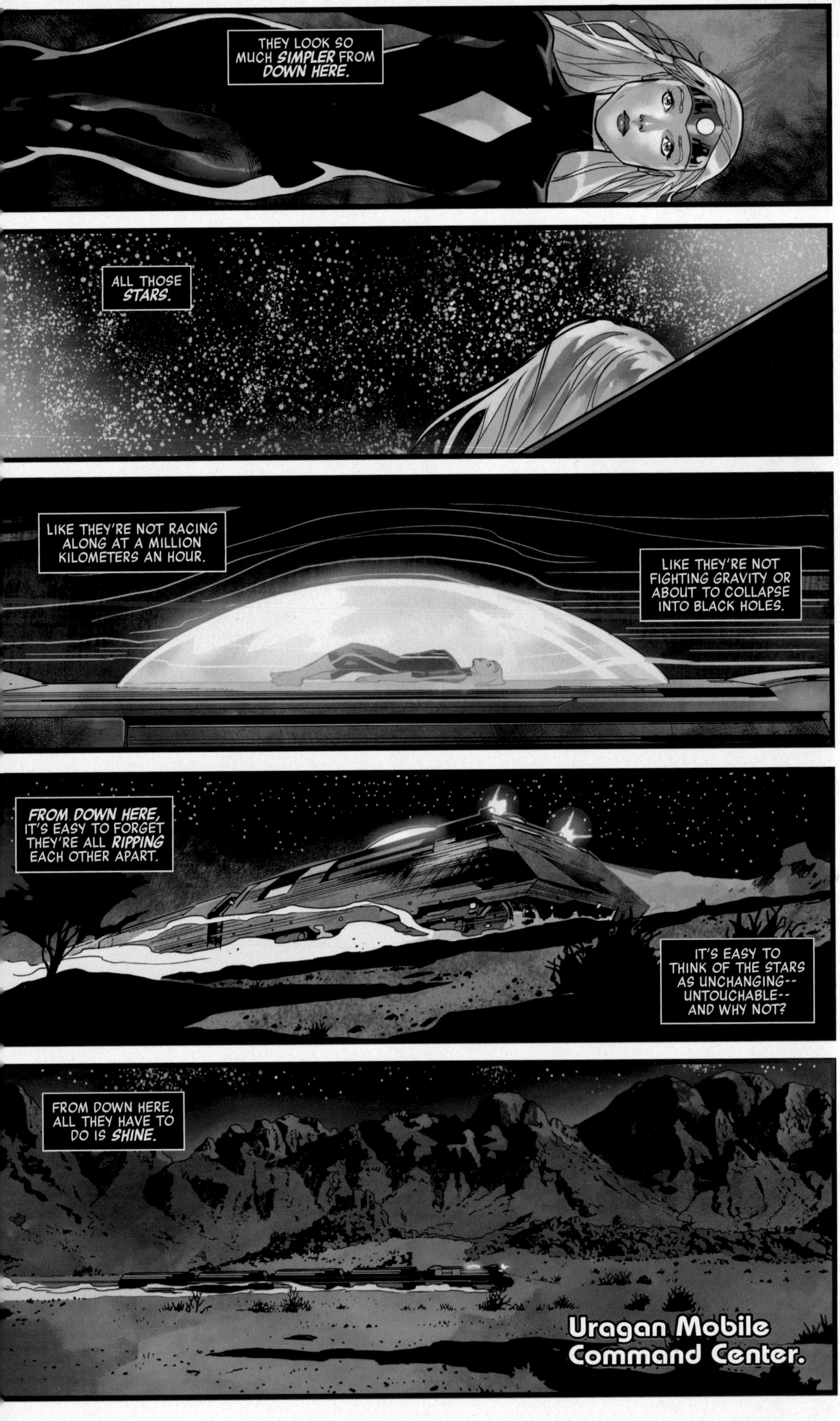

THEY LOOK SO MUCH SIMPLER FROM DOWN HERE.
ALL THOSE STARS.
LIKE THEY'RE NOT RACING ALONG AT A MILLION KILOMETERS AN HOUR.
LIKE THEY'RE NOT FIGHTING GRAVITY OR ABOUT TO COLLAPSE INTO BLACK HOLES.
FROM DOWN HERE, IT'S EASY TO FORGET THEY'RE ALL RIPPING EACH OTHER APART.
IT'S EASY TO THINK OF THE STARS AS UNCHANGING-- UNTOUCHABLE-- AND WHY NOT?
FROM DOWN HERE, ALL THEY HAVE TO DO IS SHINE.
Uragan Mobile Command Center.

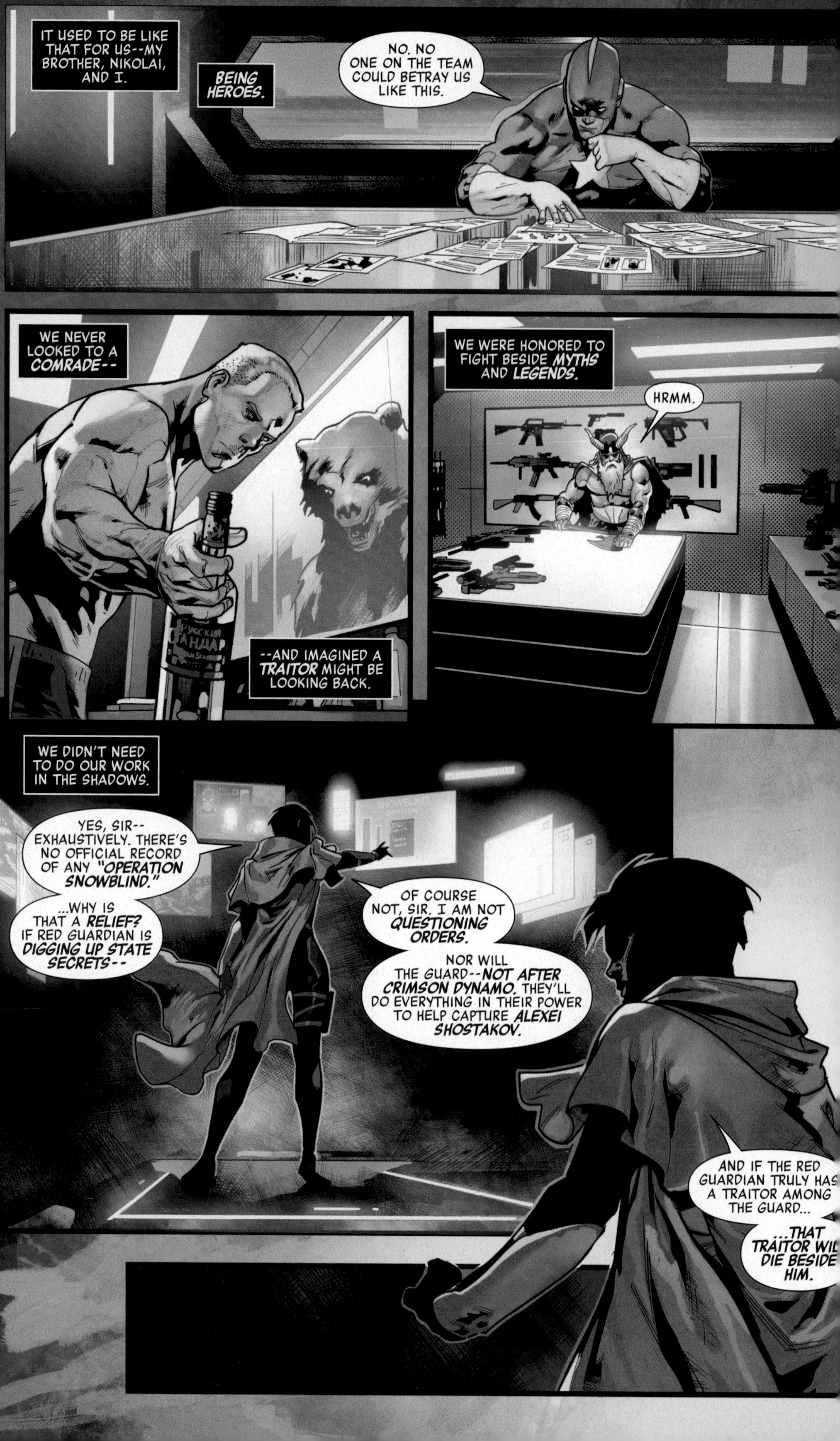
IT USED TO BE LIKE THAT FOR US--MY BROTHER, NIKOLAI, AND I.
BEING HEROES.
NO. NO ONE ON THE TEAM COULD BETRAY US LIKE THIS.
WE NEVER LOOKED TO A COMRADE--
--AND IMAGINED A TRAITOR MIGHT BE LOOKING BACK.
WE WERE HONORED TO FIGHT BESIDE MYTHS AND LEGENDS.
HRMM.
WE DIDN'T NEED TO DO OUR WORK IN THE SHADOWS.
YES, SIR-- EXHAUSTIVELY. THERE'S NO OFFICIAL RECORD OF ANY "OPERATION SNOWBLIND."
...WHY IS THAT A RELIEF? IF RED GUARDIAN IS DIGGING UP STATE SECRETS--
OF COURSE NOT, SIR. I AM NOT QUESTIONING ORDERS.
NOR WILL THE GUARD--NOT AFTER CRIMSON DYNAMO. THEY'LL DO EVERYTHING IN THEIR POWER TO HELP CAPTURE ALEXEI SHOSTAKOV.
AND IF THE RED GUARDIAN TRULY HAS A TRAITOR AMONG THE GUARD...
...THAT TRAITOR WIL DIE BESIDE HIM.

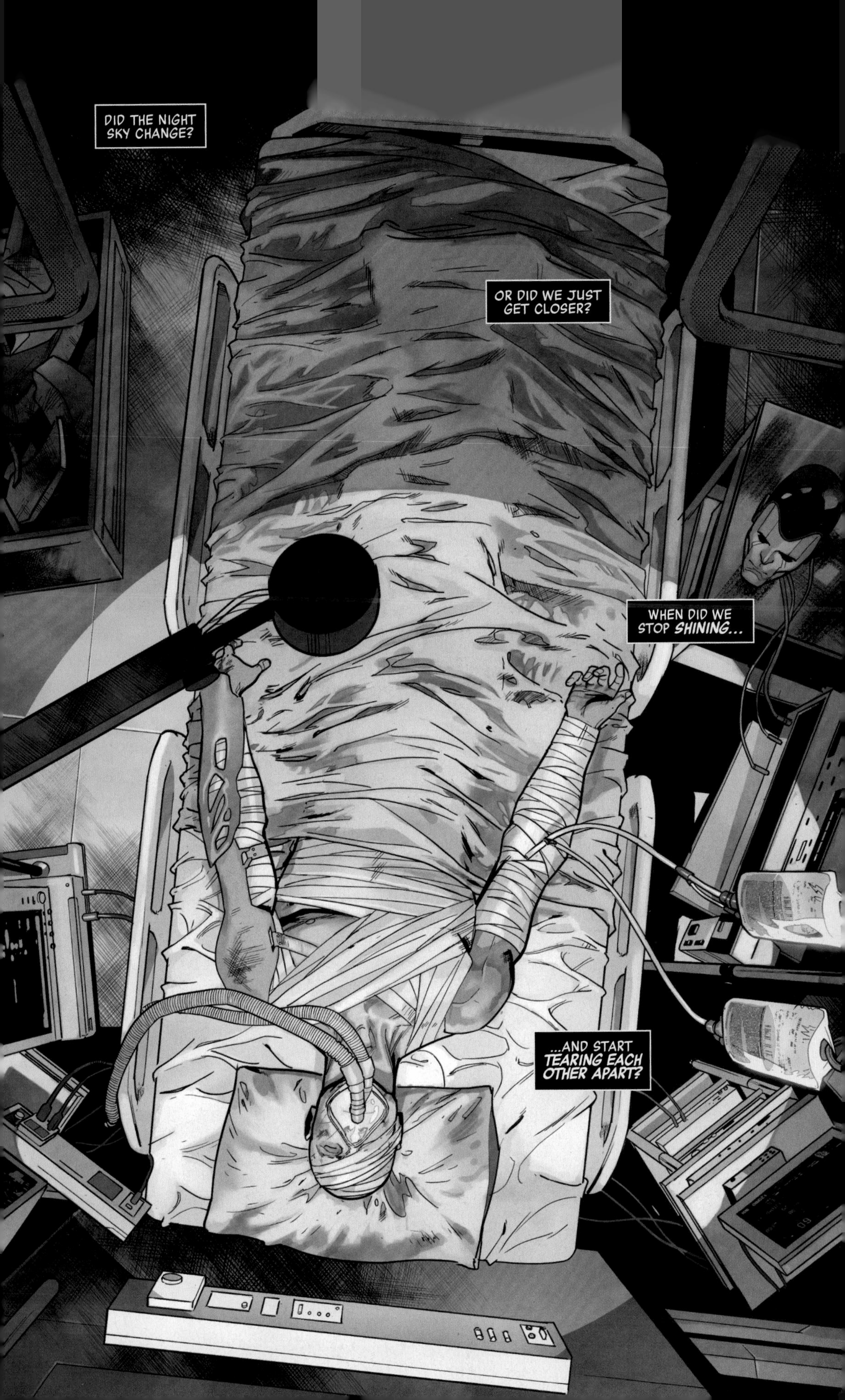
DID THE NIGHT SKY CHANGE?
OR DID WE JUST GET CLOSER?
WHEN DID WE STOP SHINING...
...AND START TEARING EACH OTHER APART?

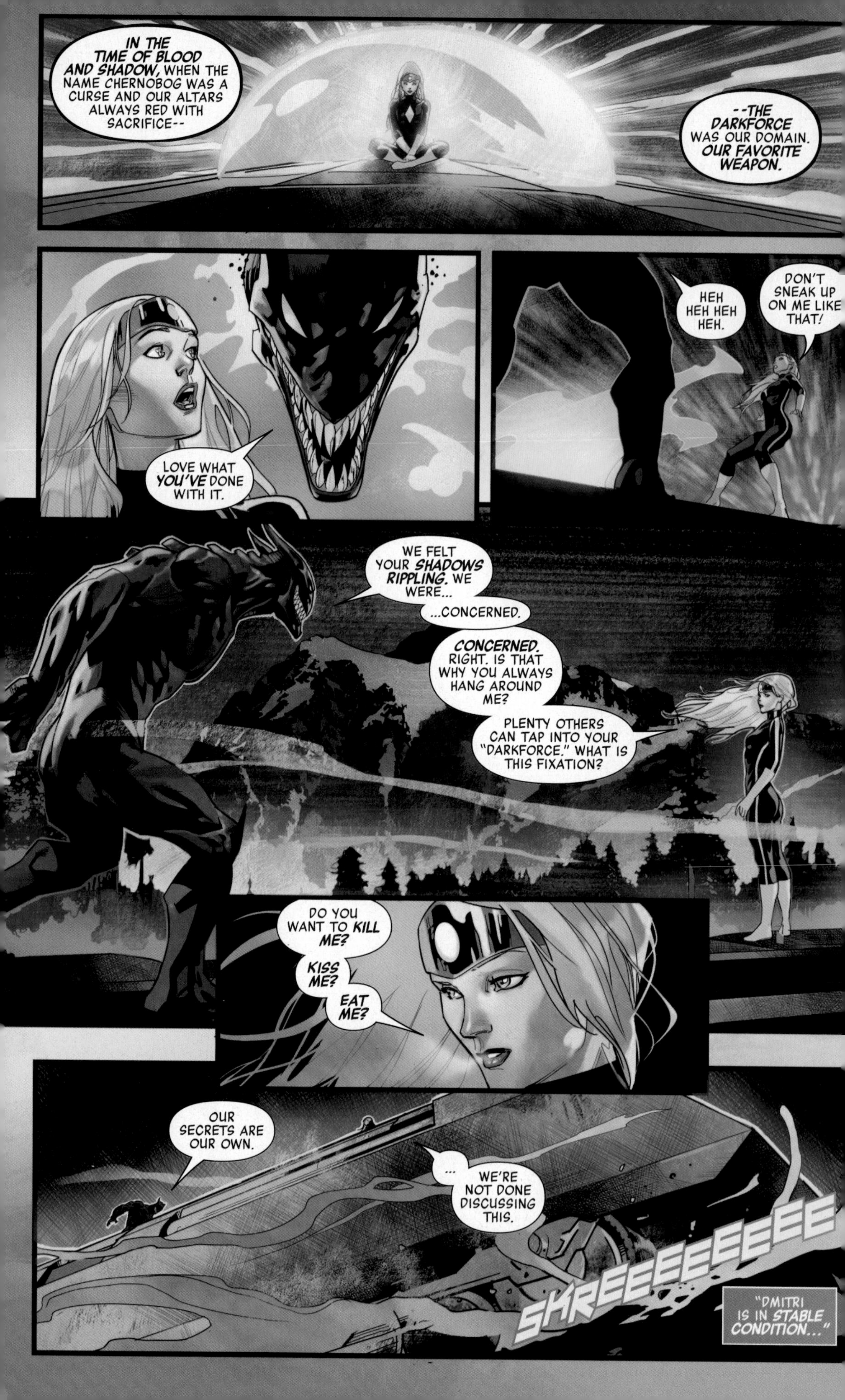
IN THE TIME OF BLOOD AND SHADOW, WHEN THE NAME CHERNOBOG WAS A CURSE AND OUR ALTARS ALWAYS RED WITH SACRIFICE--
--THE DARKFORCE WAS OUR DOMAIN. OUR FAVORITE WEAPON.
LOVE WHAT YOU'VE DONE WITH IT.
HEH HEH HEH HEH.
DON'T SNEAK UP ON ME LIKE THAT!
WE FELT YOUR SHADOWS RIPPLING. WE WERE...
...CONCERNED.
CONCERNED. RIGHT. IS THAT WHY YOU ALWAYS HANG AROUND ME?
PLENTY OTHERS CAN TAP INTO YOUR "DARKFORCE." WHAT IS THIS FIXATION?
DO YOU WANT TO KILL ME?
KISS ME?
EAT ME?
OUR SECRETS ARE OUR OWN.
...
WE'RE NOT DONE DISCUSSING THIS.
SKREEEEEEEEE
"DMITRI IS IN STABLE CONDITION..."

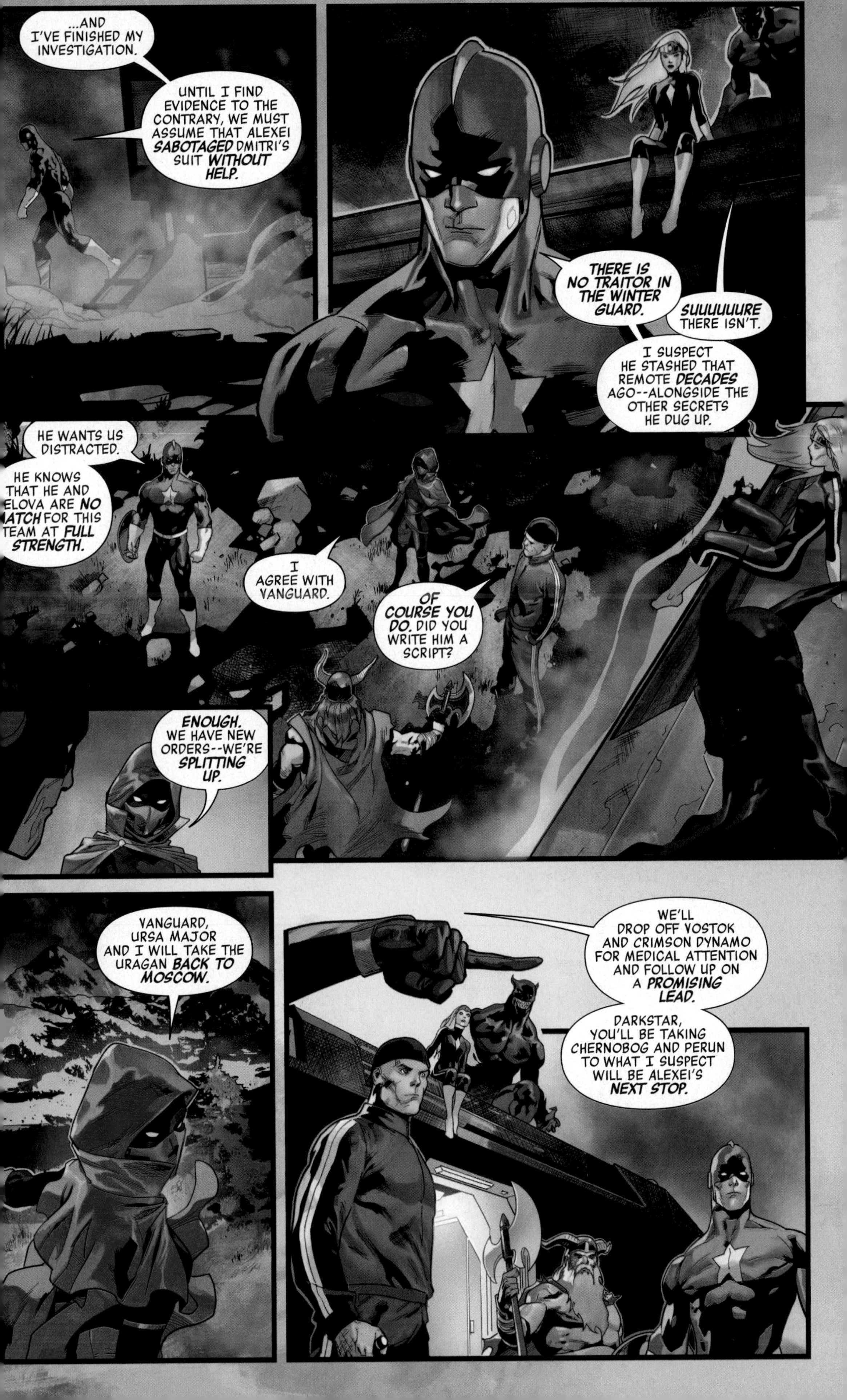

...AND I'VE FINISHED MY INVESTIGATION.
UNTIL I FIND EVIDENCE TO THE CONTRARY, WE MUST ASSUME THAT ALEXEI SABOTAGED DMITRI'S SUIT WITHOUT HELP.
THERE IS NO TRAITOR IN THE WINTER GUARD.
SUUUUUURE THERE ISN'T.
I SUSPECT HE STASHED THAT REMOTE DECADES AGO--ALONGSIDE THE OTHER SECRETS HE DUG UP.
HE WANTS US DISTRACTED.
HE KNOWS THAT HE AND ELOVA ARE NO MATCH FOR THIS TEAM AT FULL STRENGTH.
I AGREE WITH VANGUARD.
OF COURSE YOU DO. DID YOU WRITE HIM A SCRIPT?
ENOUGH. WE HAVE NEW ORDERS--WE'RE SPLITTING UP.
VANGUARD, URSA MAJOR AND I WILL TAKE THE URAGAN BACK TO MOSCOW.
WE'LL DROP OFF VOSTOK AND CRIMSON DYNAMO FOR MEDICAL ATTENTION AND FOLLOW UP ON A PROMISING LEAD.
DARKSTAR, YOU'LL BE TAKING CHERNOBOG AND PERUN TO WHAT I SUSPECT WILL BE ALEXEI'S NEXT STOP.

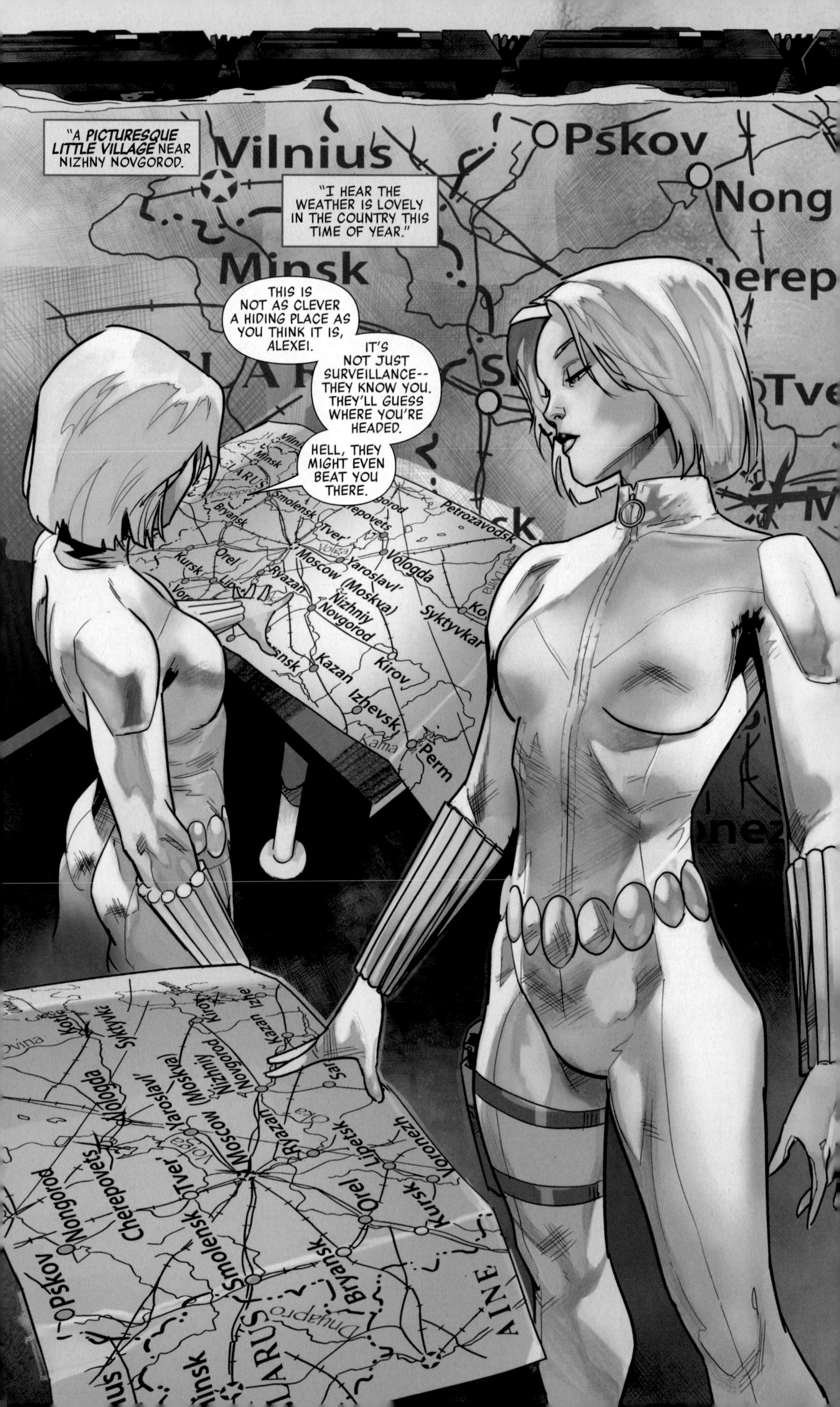
"A PICTURESQUE LITTLE VILLAGE NEAR NIZHNY NOVGOROD.
"I HEAR THE WEATHER IS LOVELY IN THE COUNTRY THIS TIME OF YEAR."
THIS IS NOT AS CLEVER A HIDING PLACE AS YOU THINK IT IS, ALEXEI.
IT'S NOT JUST SURVEILLANCE-- THEY KNOW YOU. THEY'LL GUESS WHERE YOU'RE HEADED.
HELL, THEY MIGHT EVEN BEAT YOU THERE.
Vilnius
Pskov
Minsk
Nong
Smolensk
Tver'
Moscow (Moskva)
Yaroslavl'
Vologda
Nizhniy Novgorod
Ryazan
Kazan
Kirov
Izhevsk
Perm
Syktyvkar
Petrozavodsk
Bryansk
Orel
Kursk
Cherepovets
Voronezh
Lipetsk
Dnyapro

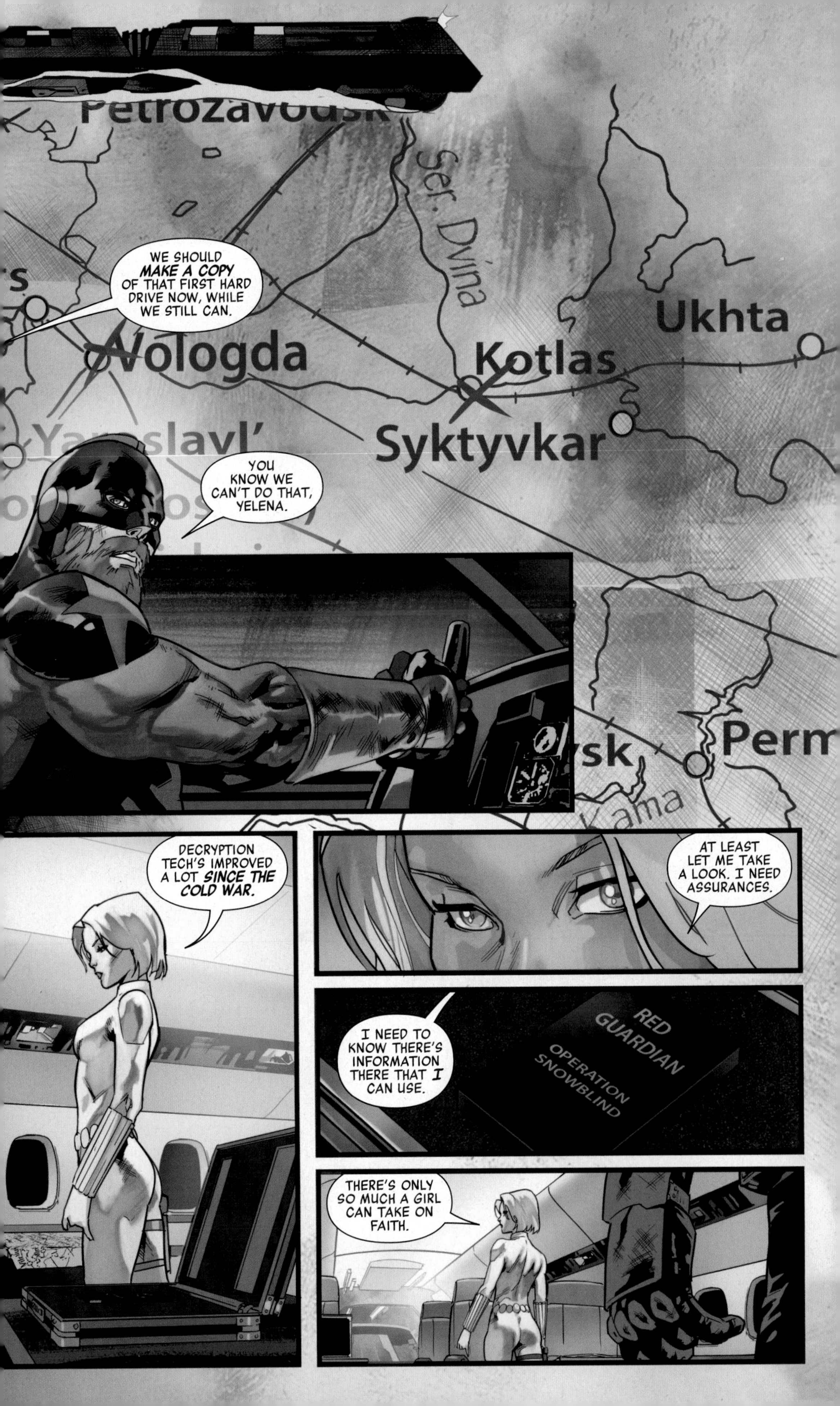
Petrozavodsk
Ser. Dvina
WE SHOULD MAKE A COPY OF THAT FIRST HARD DRIVE NOW, WHILE WE STILL CAN.
Ukhta
Vologda
Kotlas
Syktyvkar
YOU KNOW WE CAN'T DO THAT, YELENA.
Perm
Kama
DECRYPTION TECH'S IMPROVED A LOT SINCE THE COLD WAR.
AT LEAST LET ME TAKE A LOOK. I NEED ASSURANCES.
I NEED TO KNOW THERE'S INFORMATION THERE THAT I CAN USE.
RED GUARDIAN
OPERATION SNOWBLIND
THERE'S ONLY SO MUCH A GIRL CAN TAKE ON FAITH.

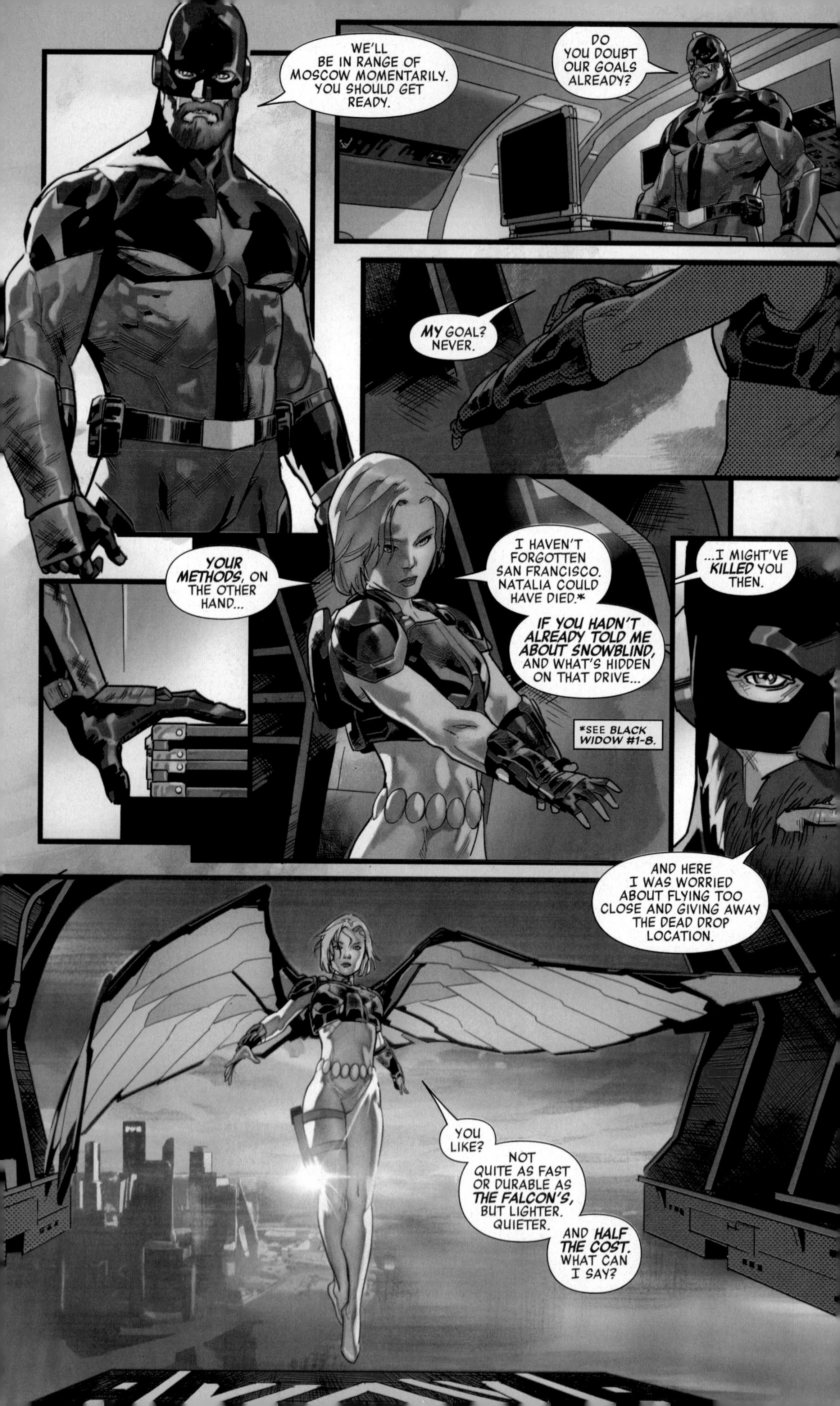
WE'LL BE IN RANGE OF MOSCOW MOMENTARILY. YOU SHOULD GET READY.
DO YOU DOUBT OUR GOALS ALREADY?
MY GOAL? NEVER.
YOUR METHODS, ON THE OTHER HAND...
I HAVEN'T FORGOTTEN SAN FRANCISCO. NATALIA COULD HAVE DIED.*
IF YOU HADN'T ALREADY TOLD ME ABOUT SNOWBLIND, AND WHAT'S HIDDEN ON THAT DRIVE...
...I MIGHT'VE KILLED YOU THEN.
*SEE BLACK WIDOW #1-8.
AND HERE I WAS WORRIED ABOUT FLYING TOO CLOSE AND GIVING AWAY THE DEAD DROP LOCATION.
YOU LIKE?
NOT QUITE AS FAST OR DURABLE AS THE FALCON'S, BUT LIGHTER. QUIETER.
AND HALF THE COST. WHAT CAN I SAY?

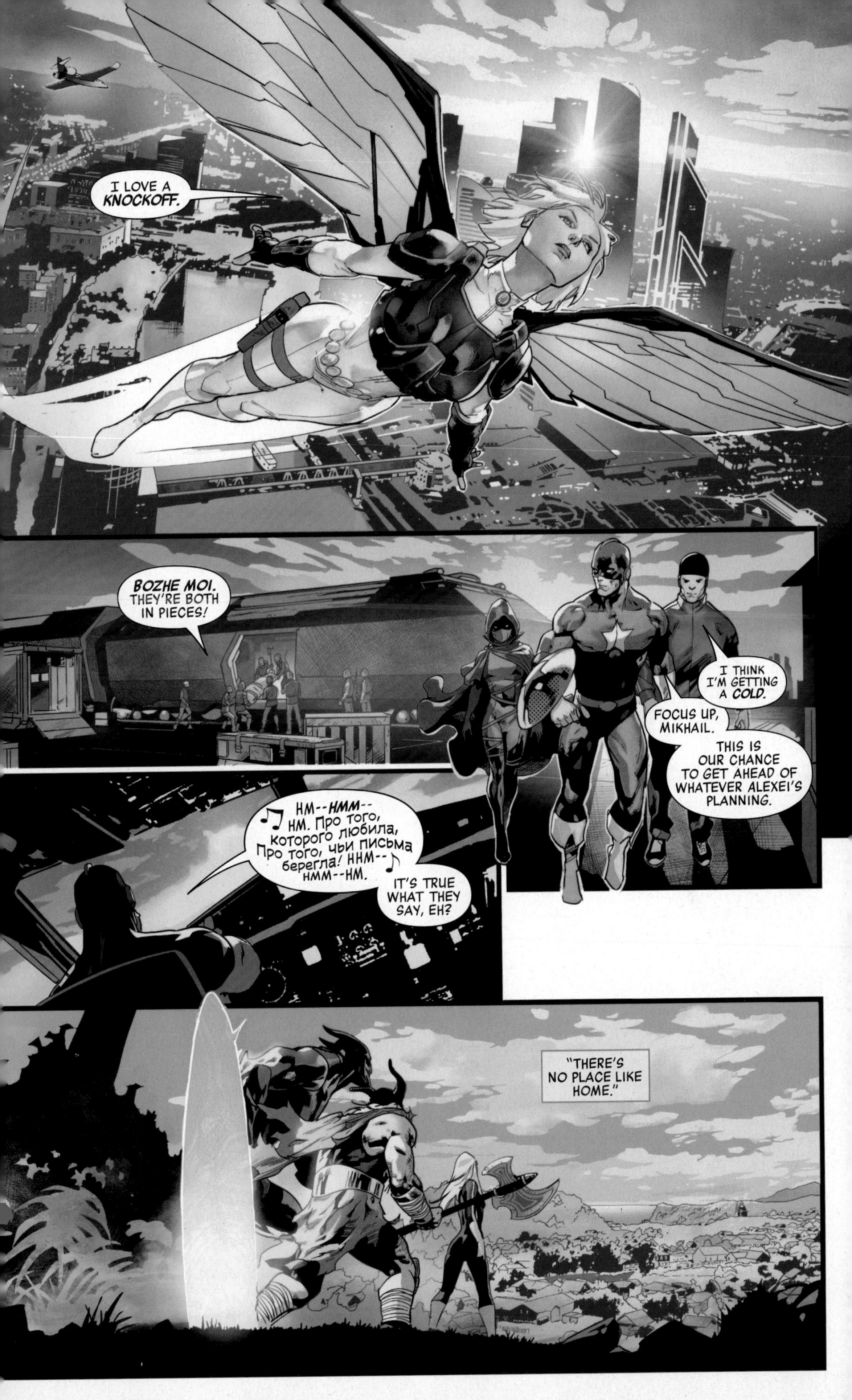
I LOVE A KNOCKOFF.
BOZHE MOI. THEY'RE BOTH IN PIECES!
I THINK I'M GETTING A COLD.
FOCUS UP, MIKHAIL.
THIS IS OUR CHANCE TO GET AHEAD OF WHATEVER ALEXEI'S PLANNING.
HM--HMM--HM. Про того, которого любила, Про того, чьи письма берегла! HHM--HMM--HM.
IT'S TRUE WHAT THEY SAY, EH?
"THERE'S NO PLACE LIKE HOME."

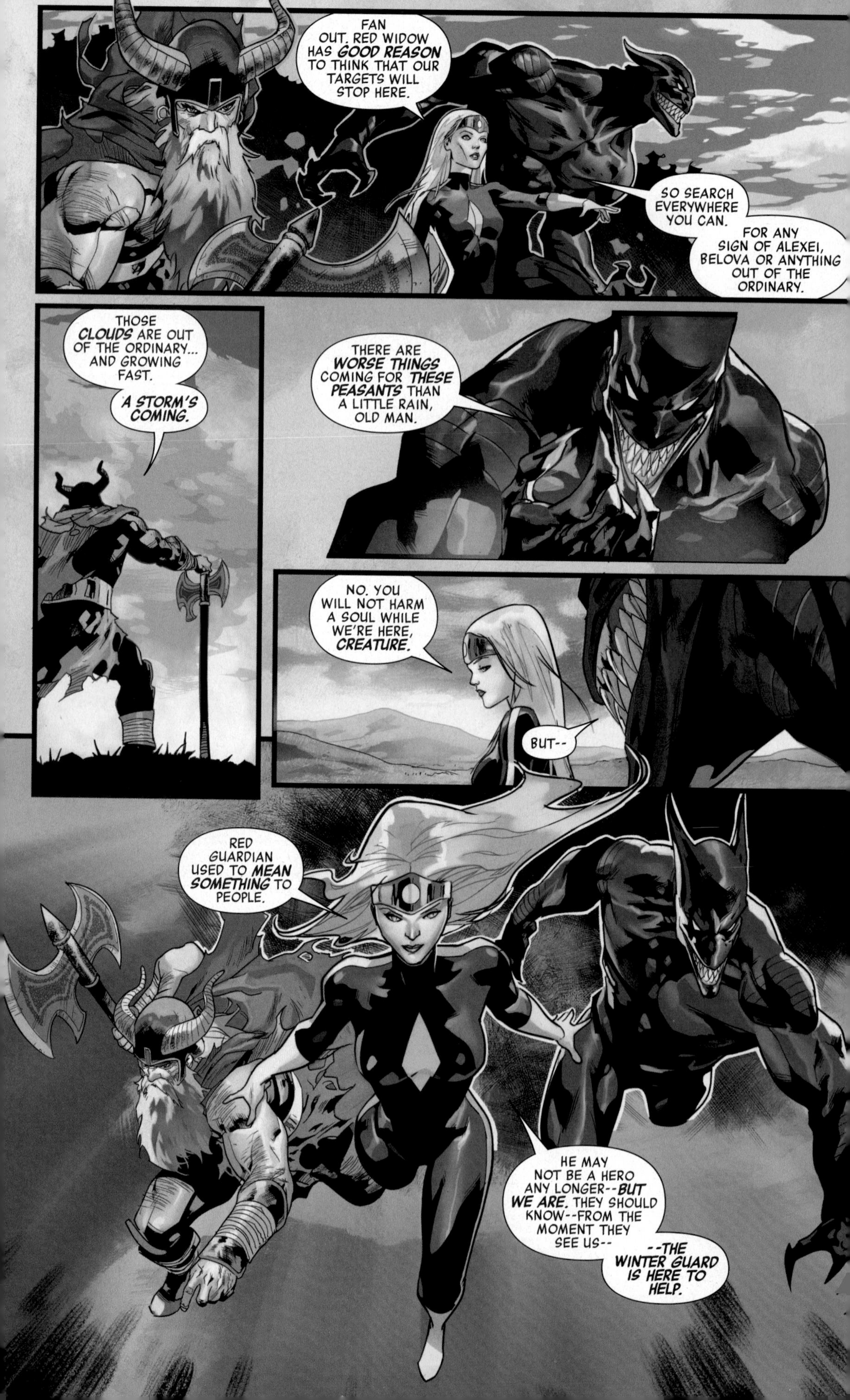
FAN OUT. RED WIDOW HAS GOOD REASON TO THINK THAT OUR TARGETS WILL STOP HERE.
SO SEARCH EVERYWHERE YOU CAN.
FOR ANY SIGN OF ALEXEI, BELOVA OR ANYTHING OUT OF THE ORDINARY.
THOSE CLOUDS ARE OUT OF THE ORDINARY... AND GROWING FAST.
A STORM'S COMING.
THERE ARE WORSE THINGS COMING FOR THESE PEASANTS THAN A LITTLE RAIN, OLD MAN.
NO. YOU WILL NOT HARM A SOUL WHILE WE'RE HERE, CREATURE.
BUT--
RED GUARDIAN USED TO MEAN SOMETHING TO PEOPLE.
HE MAY NOT BE A HERO ANY LONGER--BUT WE ARE. THEY SHOULD KNOW--FROM THE MOMENT THEY SEE US--
--THE WINTER GUARD IS HERE TO HELP.

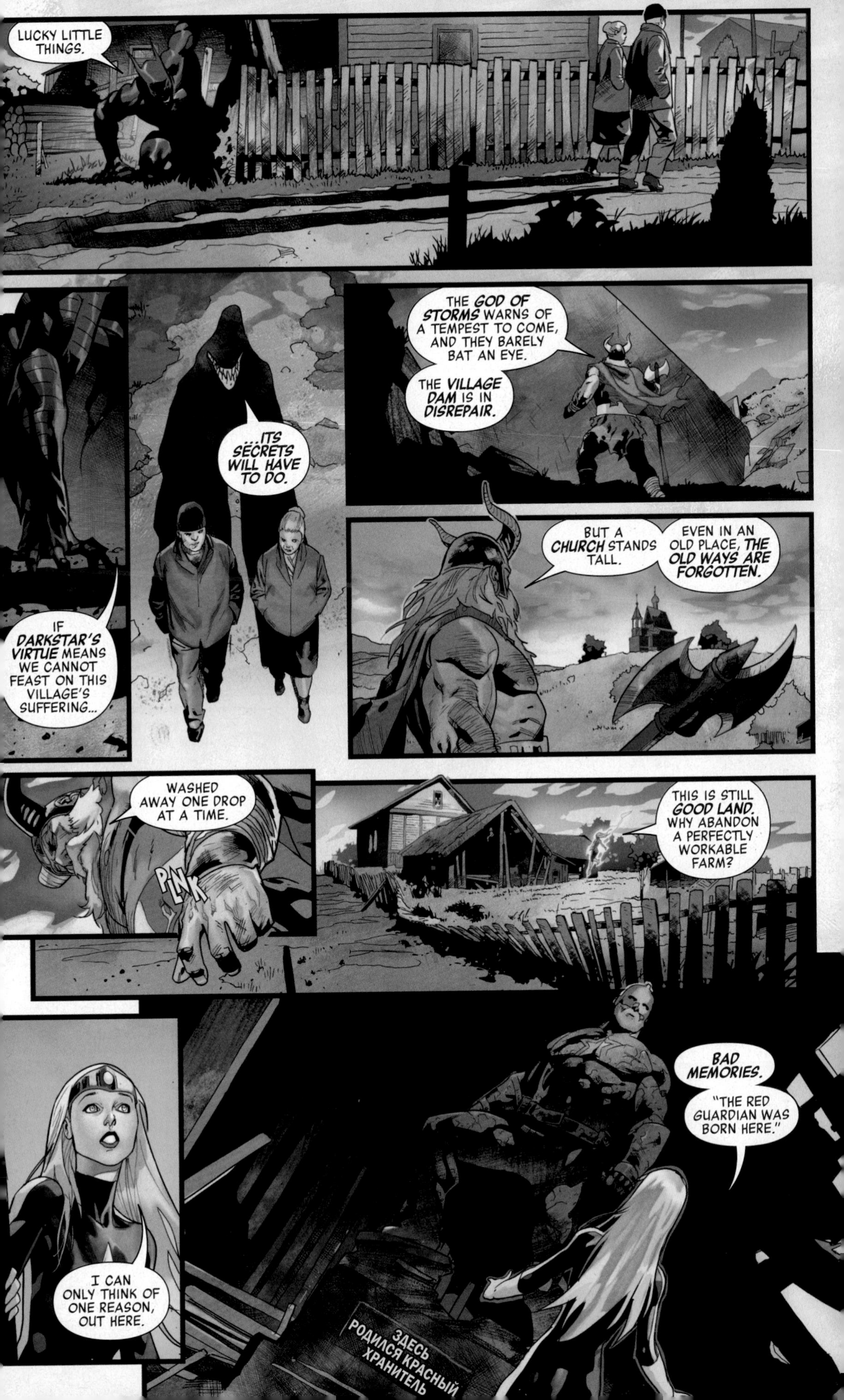

LUCKY LITTLE THINGS.
IF DARKSTAR'S VIRTUE MEANS WE CANNOT FEAST ON THIS VILLAGE'S SUFFERING...
...ITS SECRETS WILL HAVE TO DO.
THE GOD OF STORMS WARNS OF A TEMPEST TO COME, AND THEY BARELY BAT AN EYE.
THE VILLAGE DAM IS IN DISREPAIR.
BUT A CHURCH STANDS TALL.
EVEN IN AN OLD PLACE, THE OLD WAYS ARE FORGOTTEN.
WASHED AWAY ONE DROP AT A TIME.
PLINK
THIS IS STILL GOOD LAND. WHY ABANDON A PERFECTLY WORKABLE FARM?
I CAN ONLY THINK OF ONE REASON, OUT HERE.
BAD MEMORIES.
"THE RED GUARDIAN WAS BORN HERE."
ЗДЕСЬ РОДИЛСЯ КРАСНЫЙ ХРАНИТЕЛЬ

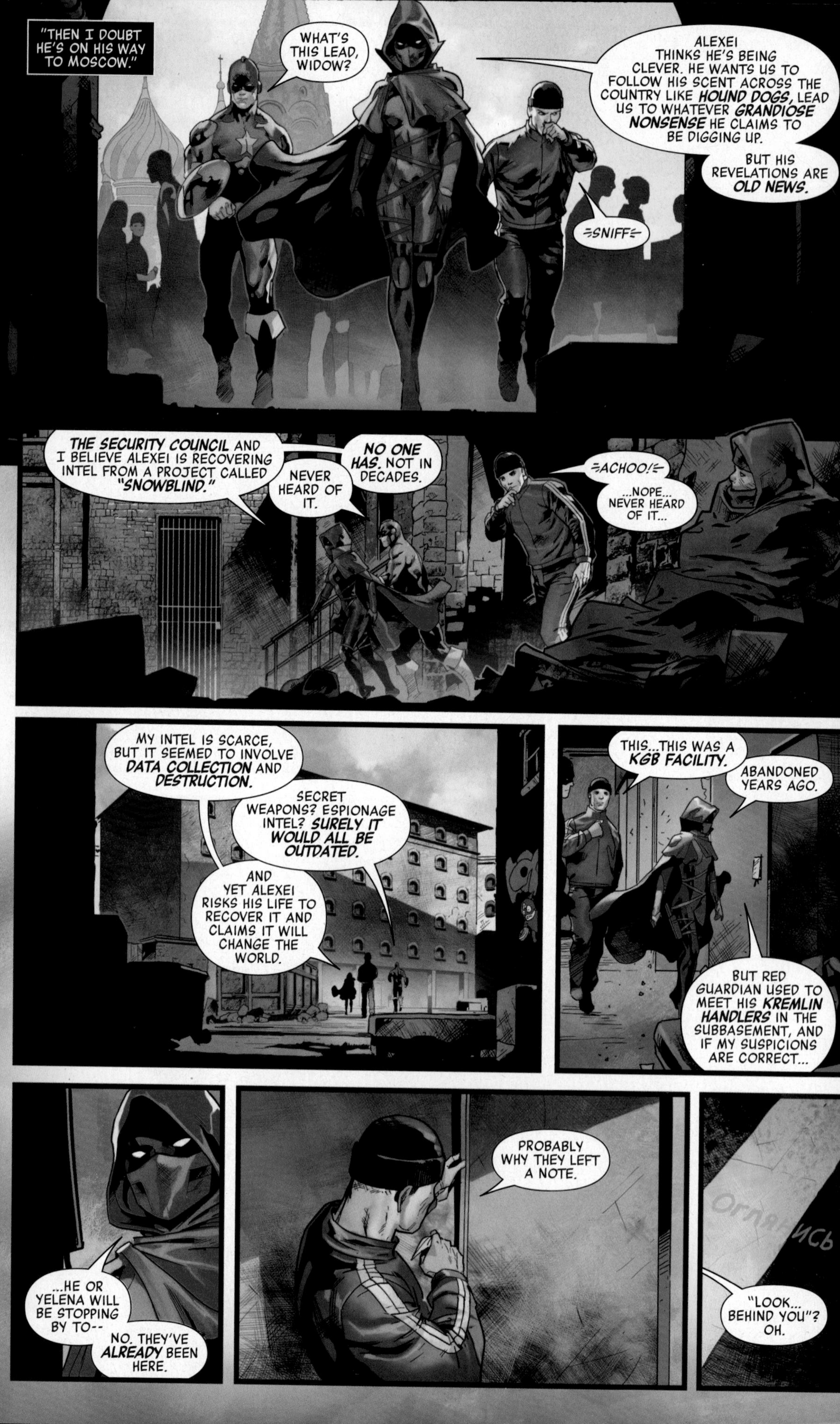
"THEN I DOUBT HE'S ON HIS WAY TO MOSCOW."
WHAT'S THIS LEAD, WIDOW?
ALEXEI THINKS HE'S BEING CLEVER. HE WANTS US TO FOLLOW HIS SCENT ACROSS THE COUNTRY LIKE HOUND DOGS, LEAD US TO WHATEVER GRANDIOSE NONSENSE HE CLAIMS TO BE DIGGING UP.
BUT HIS REVELATIONS ARE OLD NEWS.
SNIFF
THE SECURITY COUNCIL AND I BELIEVE ALEXEI IS RECOVERING INTEL FROM A PROJECT CALLED "SNOWBLIND."
NEVER HEARD OF IT.
NO ONE HAS. NOT IN DECADES.
ACHOO!
...NOPE... NEVER HEARD OF IT...
MY INTEL IS SCARCE, BUT IT SEEMED TO INVOLVE DATA COLLECTION AND DESTRUCTION.
SECRET WEAPONS? ESPIONAGE INTEL? SURELY IT WOULD ALL BE OUTDATED.
AND YET ALEXEI RISKS HIS LIFE TO RECOVER IT AND CLAIMS IT WILL CHANGE THE WORLD.
THIS...THIS WAS A KGB FACILITY.
ABANDONED YEARS AGO.
BUT RED GUARDIAN USED TO MEET HIS KREMLIN HANDLERS IN THE SUBBASEMENT, AND IF MY SUSPICIONS ARE CORRECT...
...HE OR YELENA WILL BE STOPPING BY TO--
NO. THEY'VE ALREADY BEEN HERE.
PROBABLY WHY THEY LEFT A NOTE.
Оглянись
"LOOK... BEHIND YOU"? OH.

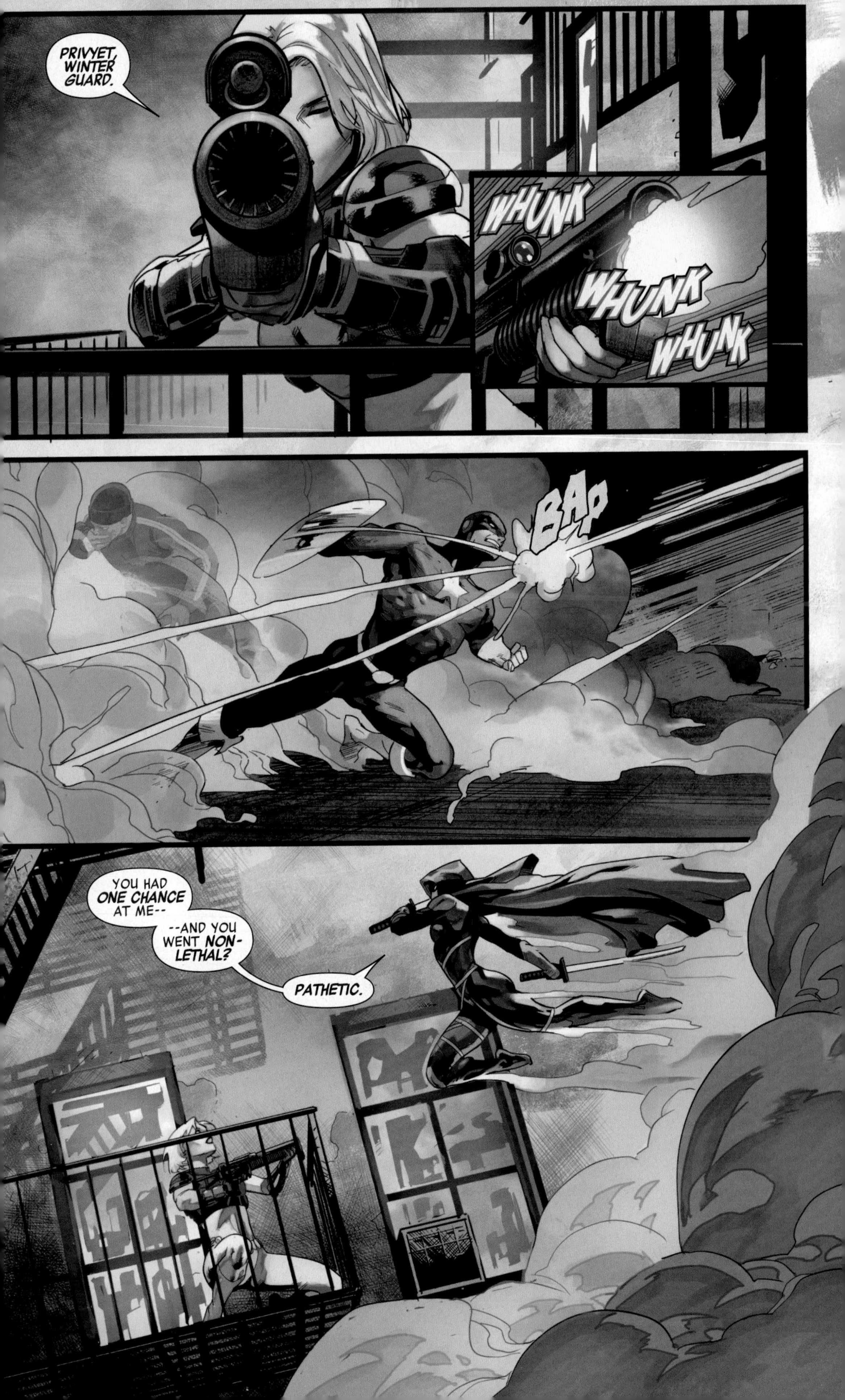

PRIVYET, WINTER GUARD.
WHUNK
WHUNK
WHUNK
BAP
YOU HAD ONE CHANCE AT ME--
--AND YOU WENT NON-LETHAL?
PATHETIC.

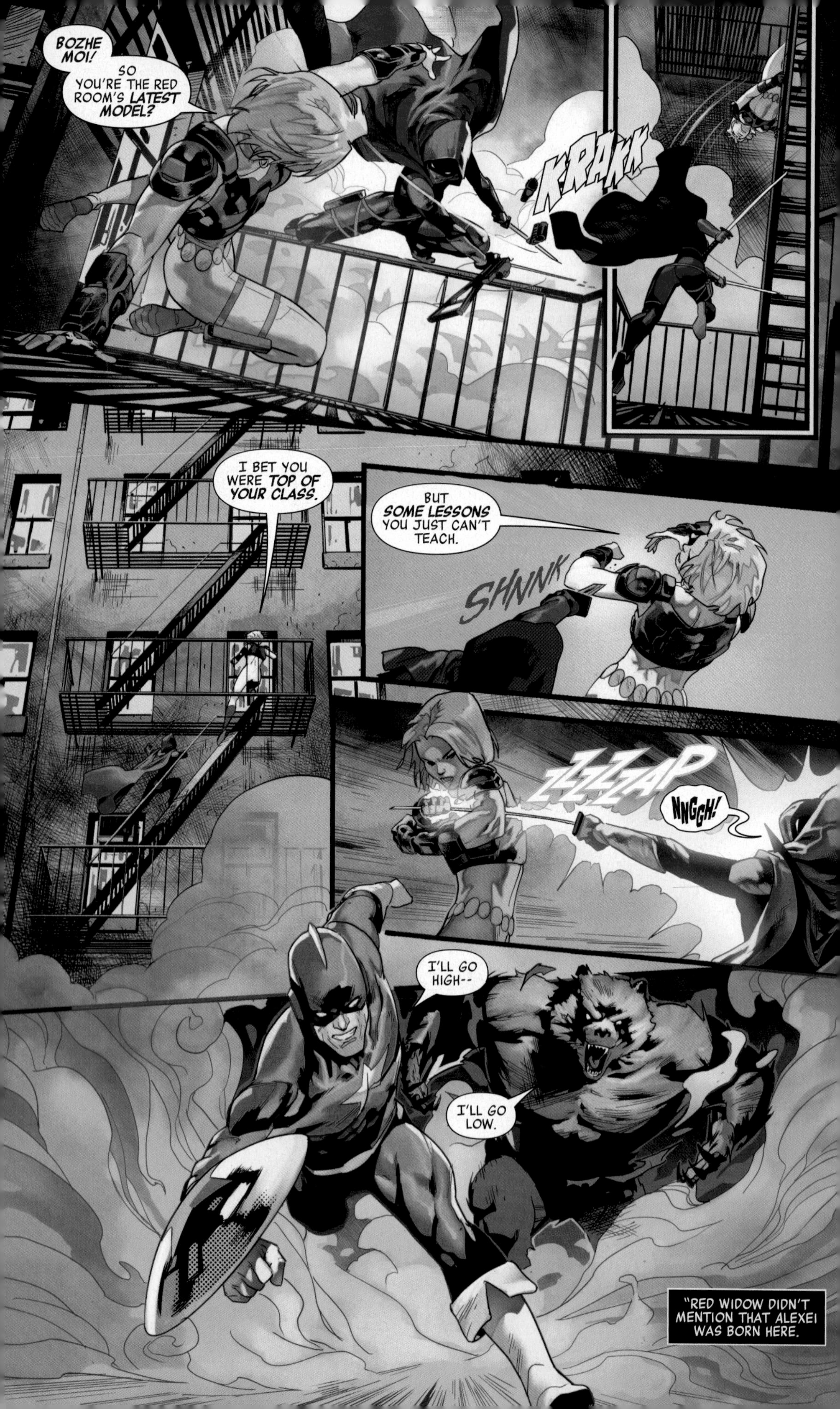
BOZHE MOI!
SO YOU'RE THE RED ROOM'S LATEST MODEL?
KRAKK
I BET YOU WERE TOP OF YOUR CLASS.
BUT SOME LESSONS YOU JUST CAN'T TEACH.
SHNNK
ZZZZZAP
NNGGH!
I'LL GO HIGH--
I'LL GO LOW.
"RED WIDOW DIDN'T MENTION THAT ALEXEI WAS BORN HERE.

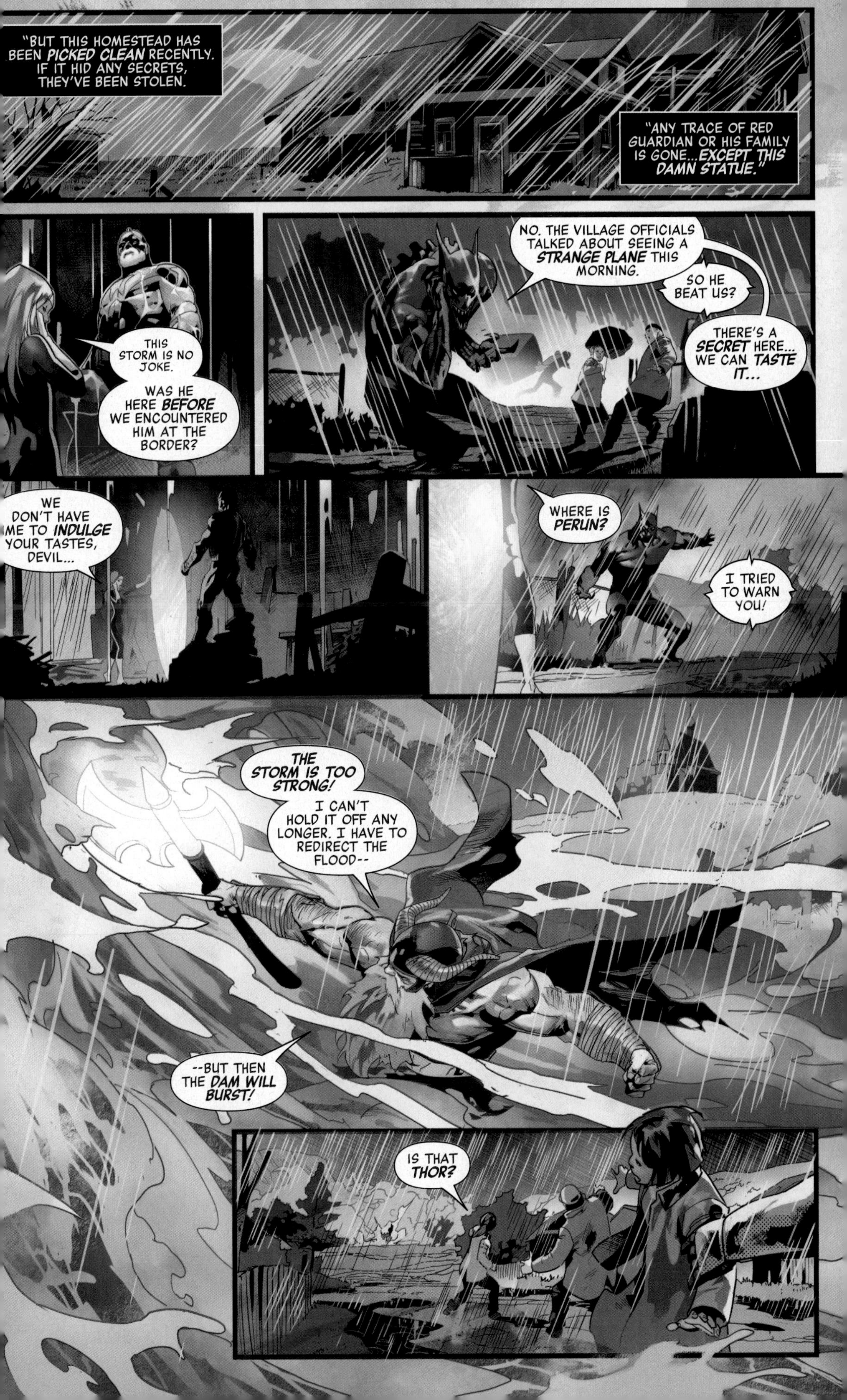
"BUT THIS HOMESTEAD HAS BEEN PICKED CLEAN RECENTLY. IF IT HID ANY SECRETS, THEY'VE BEEN STOLEN.
"ANY TRACE OF RED GUARDIAN OR HIS FAMILY IS GONE...EXCEPT THIS DAMN STATUE."
THIS STORM IS NO JOKE.
WAS HE HERE BEFORE WE ENCOUNTERED HIM AT THE BORDER?
NO. THE VILLAGE OFFICIALS TALKED ABOUT SEEING A STRANGE PLANE THIS MORNING.
SO HE BEAT US?
THERE'S A SECRET HERE... WE CAN TASTE IT...
WE DON'T HAVE ME TO INDULGE YOUR TASTES, DEVIL...
WHERE IS PERUN?
I TRIED TO WARN YOU!
THE STORM IS TOO STRONG!
I CAN'T HOLD IT OFF ANY LONGER. I HAVE TO REDIRECT THE FLOOD--
--BUT THEN THE DAM WILL BURST!
IS THAT THOR?

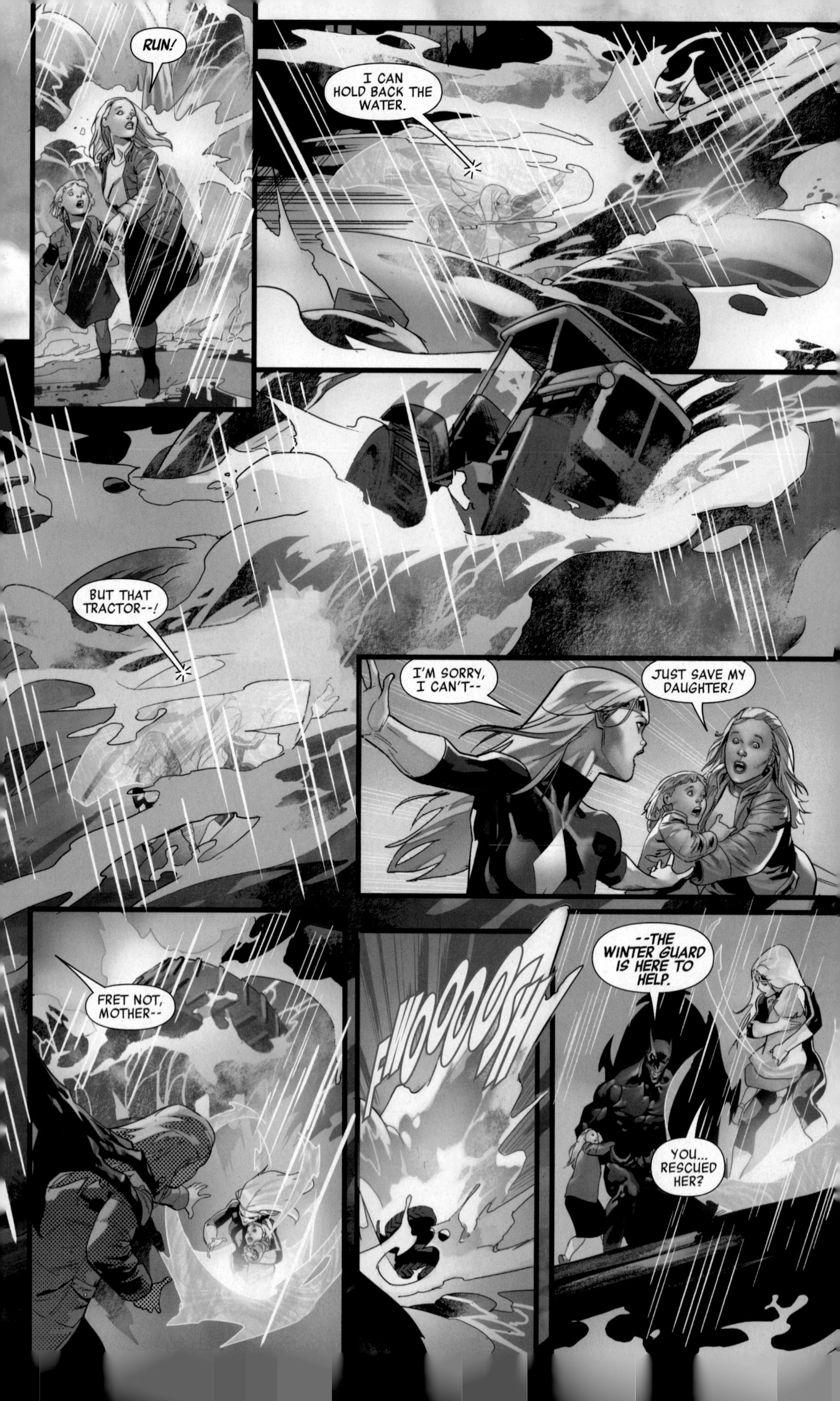

RUN!
I CAN HOLD BACK THE WATER.
BUT THAT TRACTOR--!
I'M SORRY, I CAN'T--
JUST SAVE MY DAUGHTER!
FRET NOT, MOTHER--
FWOOOOSH
--THE WINTER GUARD IS HERE TO HELP.
YOU... RESCUED HER?

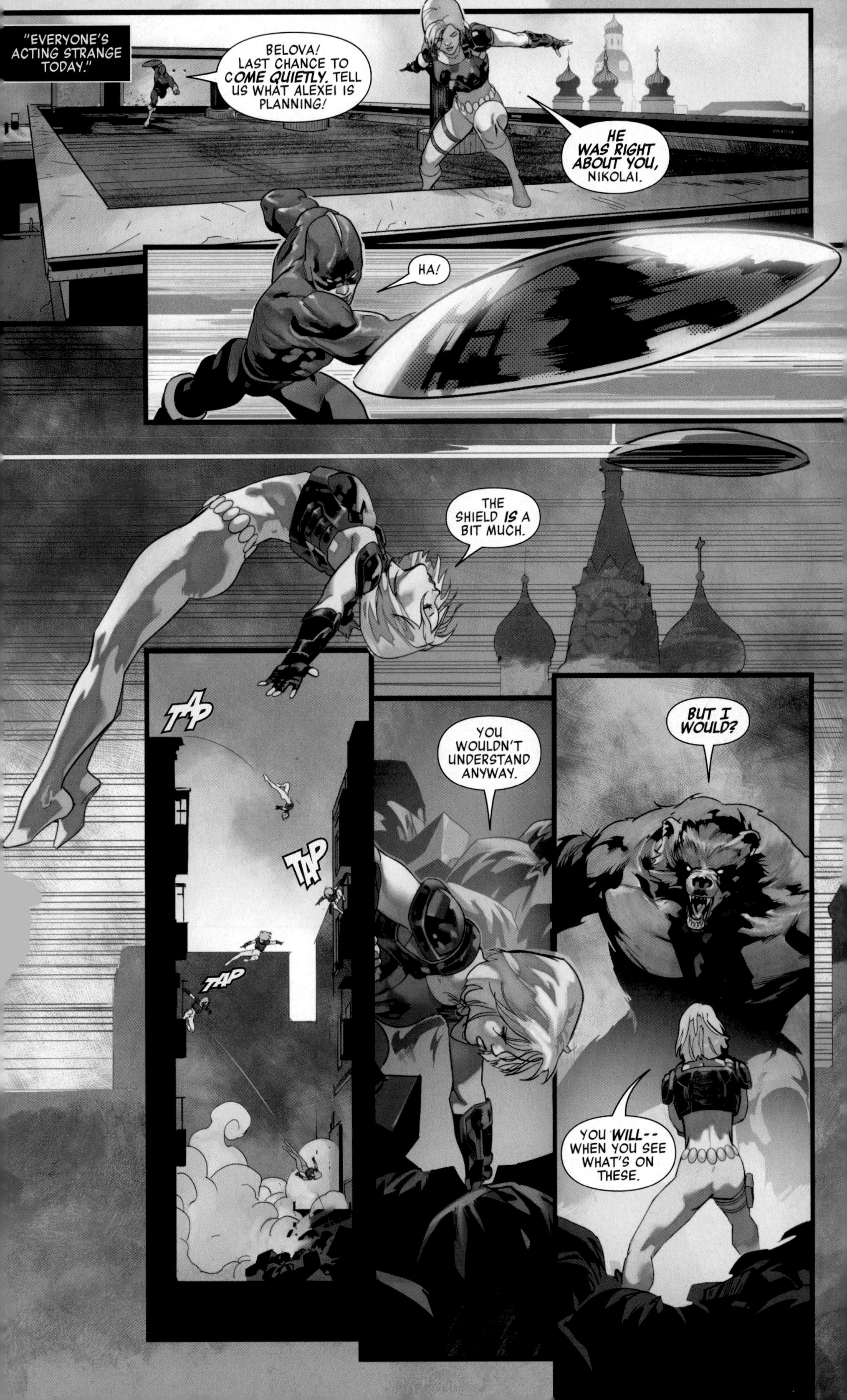
"EVERYONE'S ACTING STRANGE TODAY."
BELOVA! LAST CHANCE TO COME QUIETLY. TELL US WHAT ALEXEI IS PLANNING!
HE WAS RIGHT ABOUT YOU, NIKOLAI.
HA!
THE SHIELD IS A BIT MUCH.
TAP
TAP
TAP
YOU WOULDN'T UNDERSTAND ANYWAY.
BUT I WOULD?
YOU WILL-- WHEN YOU SEE WHAT'S ON THESE.

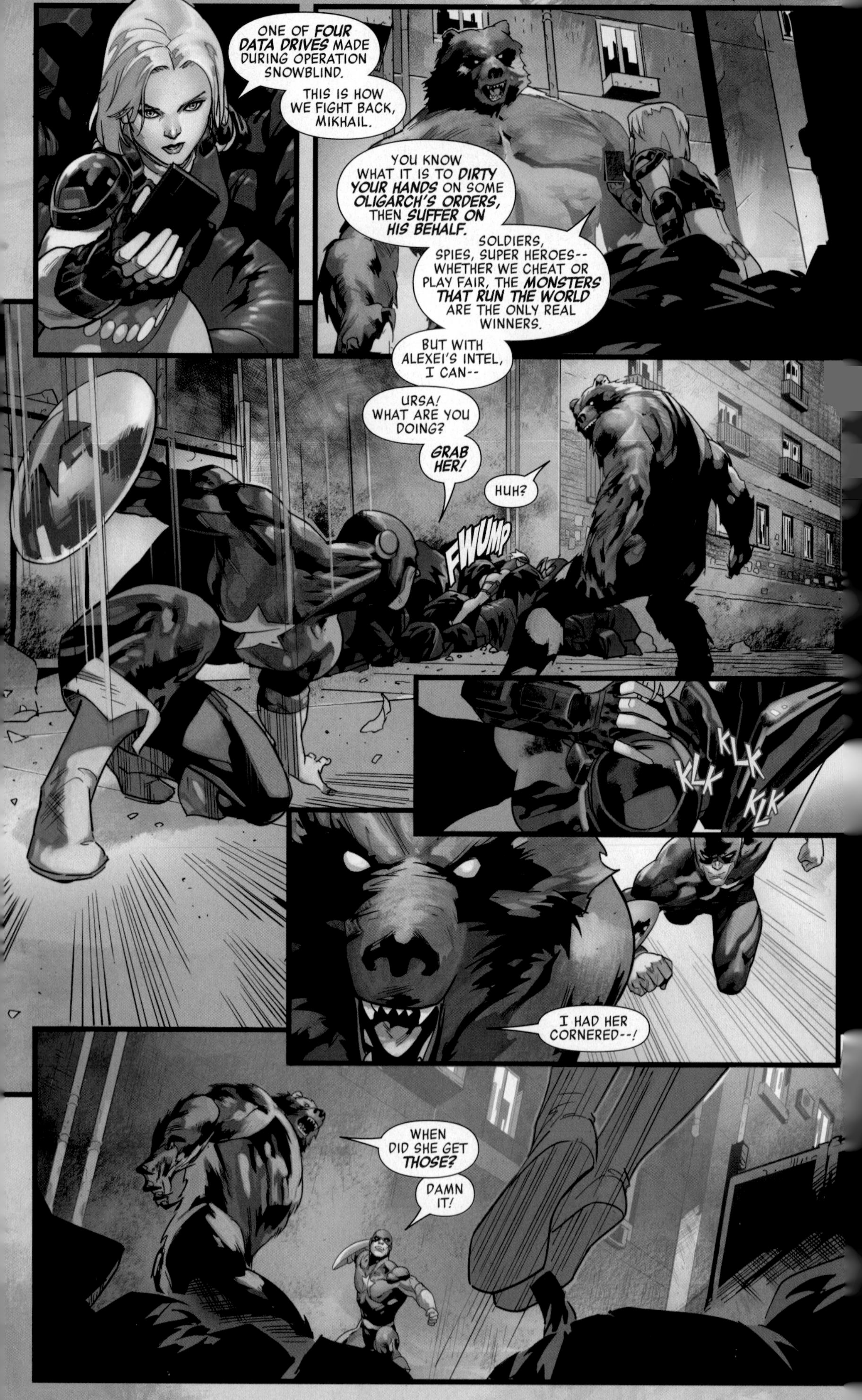

ONE OF FOUR DATA DRIVES MADE DURING OPERATION SNOWBLIND.
THIS IS HOW WE FIGHT BACK, MIKHAIL.
YOU KNOW WHAT IT IS TO DIRTY YOUR HANDS ON SOME OLIGARCH'S ORDERS, THEN SUFFER ON HIS BEHALF.
SOLDIERS, SPIES, SUPER HEROES--WHETHER WE CHEAT OR PLAY FAIR, THE MONSTERS THAT RUN THE WORLD ARE THE ONLY REAL WINNERS.
BUT WITH ALEXEI'S INTEL, I CAN--
URSA! WHAT ARE YOU DOING?
GRAB HER!
HUH?
FWUMP
KLK
KLK
KLK
I HAD HER CORNERED--!
WHEN DID SHE GET THOSE?
DAMN IT!

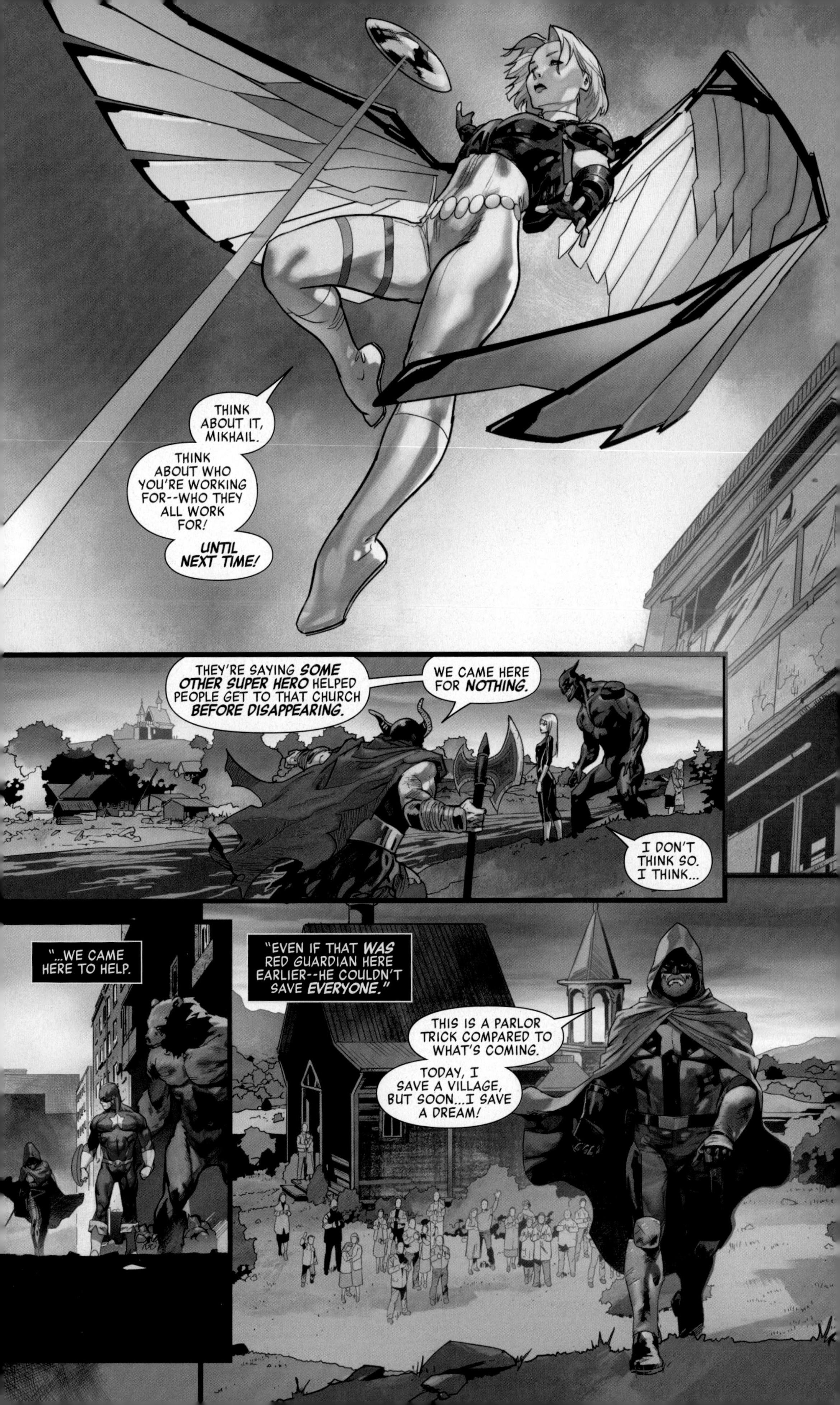

THINK ABOUT IT, MIKHAIL.
THINK ABOUT WHO YOU'RE WORKING FOR--WHO THEY ALL WORK FOR!
UNTIL NEXT TIME!
THEY'RE SAYING SOME OTHER SUPER HERO HELPED PEOPLE GET TO THAT CHURCH BEFORE DISAPPEARING.
WE CAME HERE FOR NOTHING.
I DON'T THINK SO. I THINK...
"...WE CAME HERE TO HELP.
"EVEN IF THAT WAS RED GUARDIAN HERE EARLIER--HE COULDN'T SAVE EVERYONE."
THIS IS A PARLOR TRICK COMPARED TO WHAT'S COMING.
TODAY, I SAVE A VILLAGE, BUT SOON...I SAVE A DREAM!

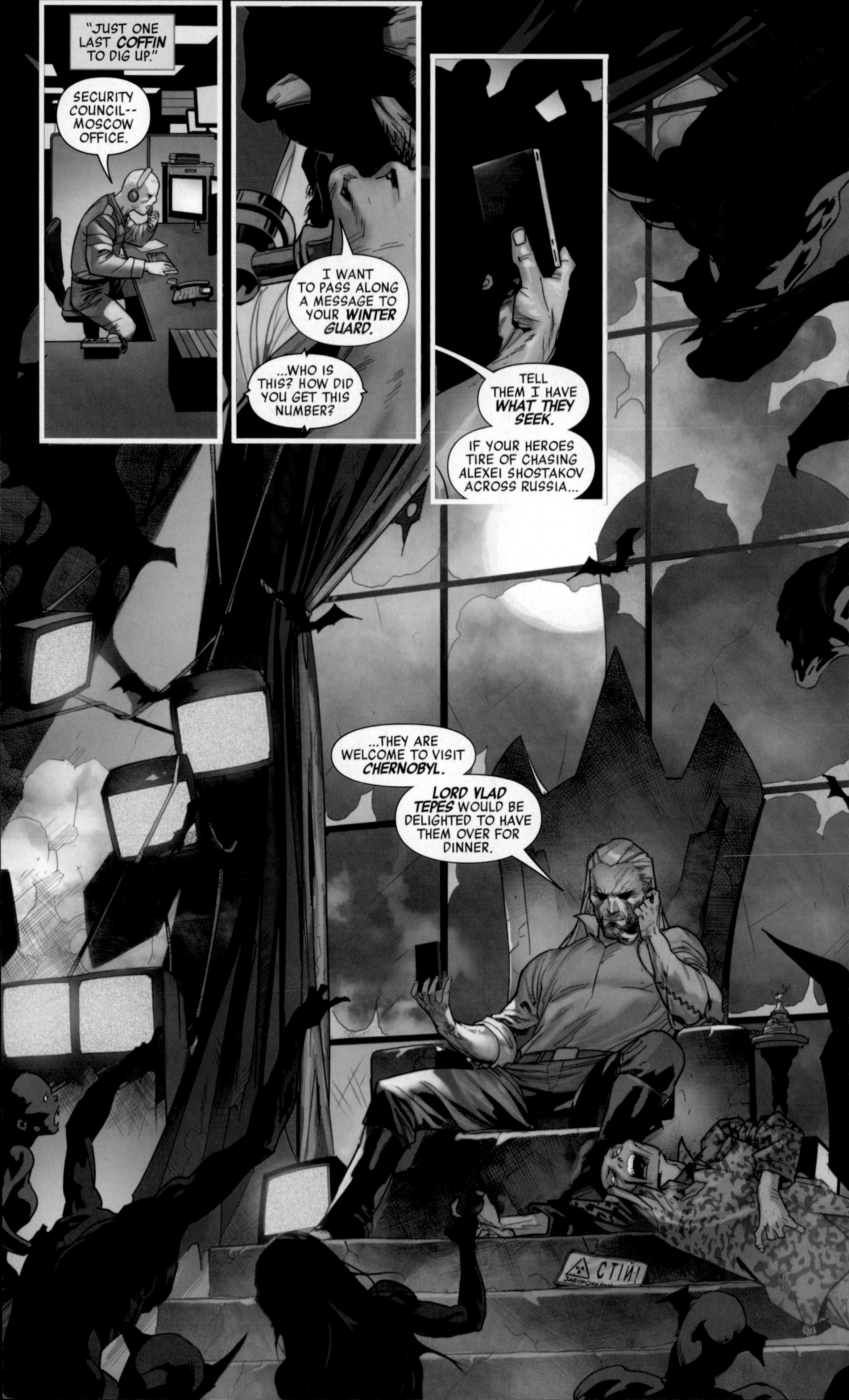
"JUST ONE LAST COFFIN TO DIG UP."
SECURITY COUNCIL-- MOSCOW OFFICE.
I WANT TO PASS ALONG A MESSAGE TO YOUR WINTER GUARD.
...WHO IS THIS? HOW DID YOU GET THIS NUMBER?
TELL THEM I HAVE WHAT THEY SEEK.
IF YOUR HEROES TIRE OF CHASING ALEXEI SHOSTAKOV ACROSS RUSSIA...
...THEY ARE WELCOME TO VISIT CHERNOBYL.
LORD VLAD TEPES WOULD BE DELIGHTED TO HAVE THEM OVER FOR DINNER.
СТІЙ!

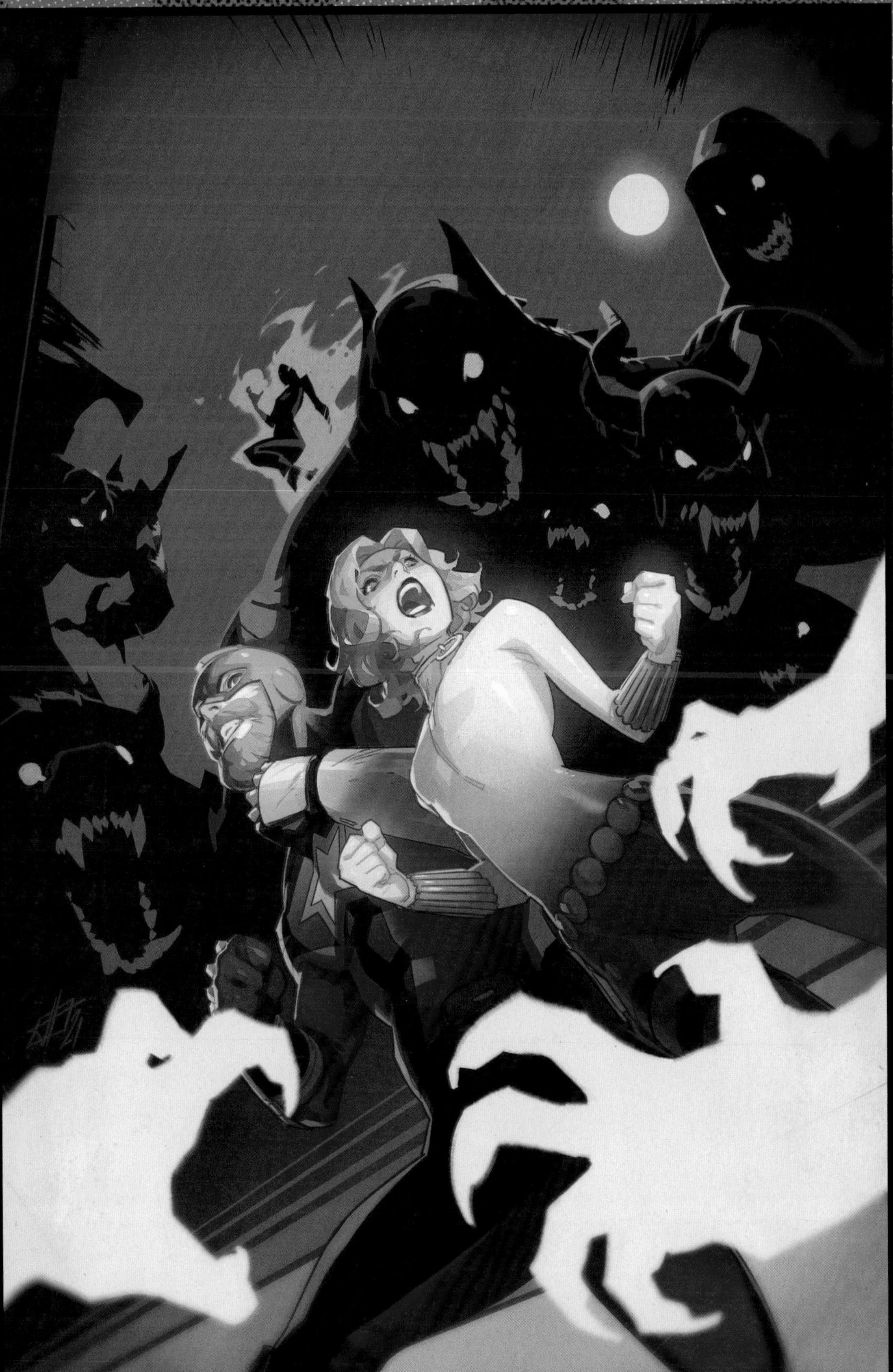

3

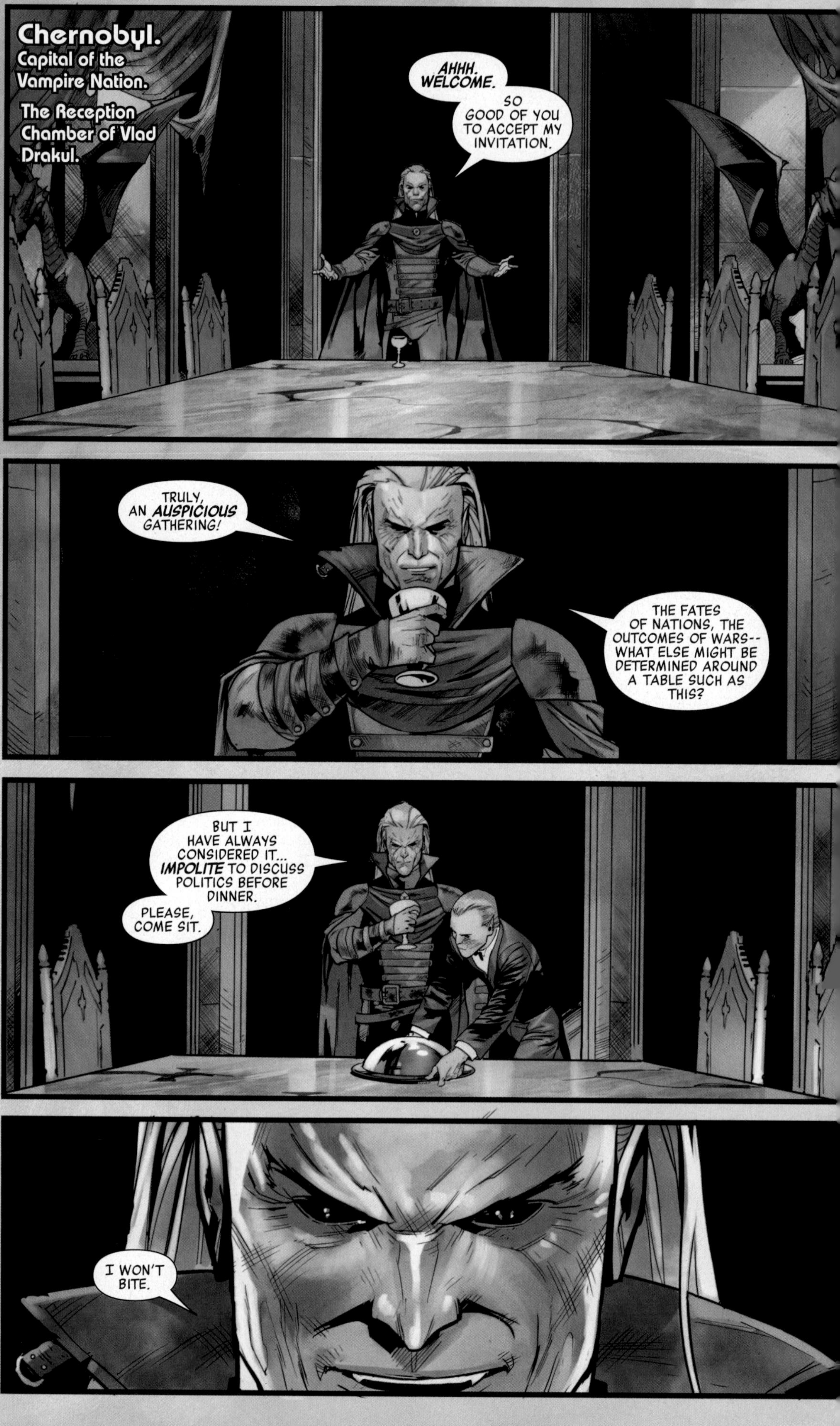
Chernobyl.
Capital of the Vampire Nation.
The Reception Chamber of Vlad Drakul.
AHHH. WELCOME.
SO GOOD OF YOU TO ACCEPT MY INVITATION.
TRULY, AN AUSPICIOUS GATHERING!
THE FATES OF NATIONS, THE OUTCOMES OF WARS-- WHAT ELSE MIGHT BE DETERMINED AROUND A TABLE SUCH AS THIS?
BUT I HAVE ALWAYS CONSIDERED IT... IMPOLITE TO DISCUSS POLITICS BEFORE DINNER.
PLEASE, COME SIT.
I WON'T BITE.

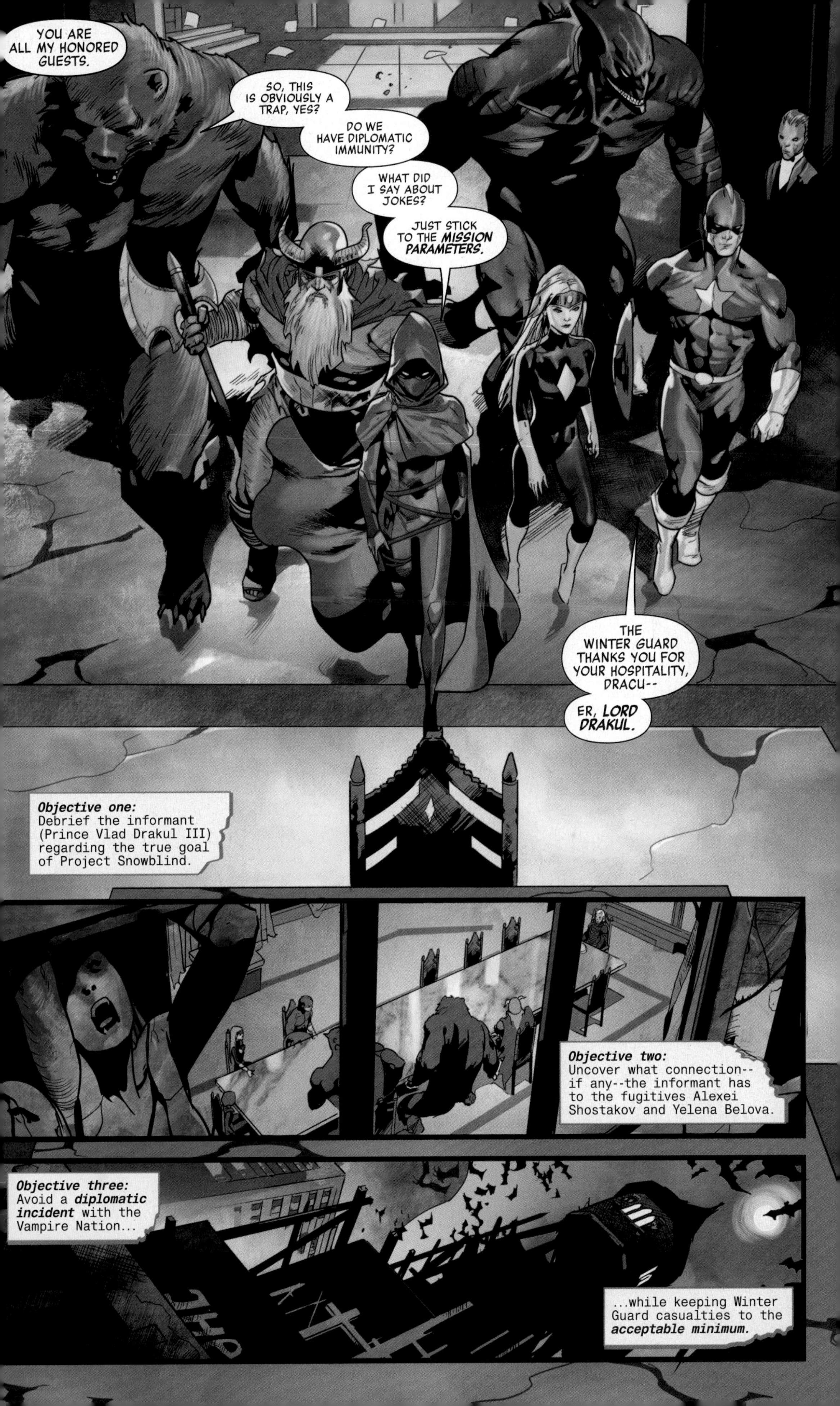
YOU ARE ALL MY HONORED GUESTS.
SO, THIS IS OBVIOUSLY A TRAP, YES?
DO WE HAVE DIPLOMATIC IMMUNITY?
WHAT DID I SAY ABOUT JOKES?
JUST STICK TO THE MISSION PARAMETERS.
THE WINTER GUARD THANKS YOU FOR YOUR HOSPITALITY, DRACU--
ER, LORD DRAKUL.
Objective one: Debrief the informant (Prince Vlad Drakul III) regarding the true goal of Project Snowblind.
Objective two: Uncover what connection--if any--the informant has to the fugitives Alexei Shostakov and Yelena Belova.
Objective three: Avoid a diplomatic incident with the Vampire Nation...
...while keeping Winter Guard casualties to the acceptable minimum.

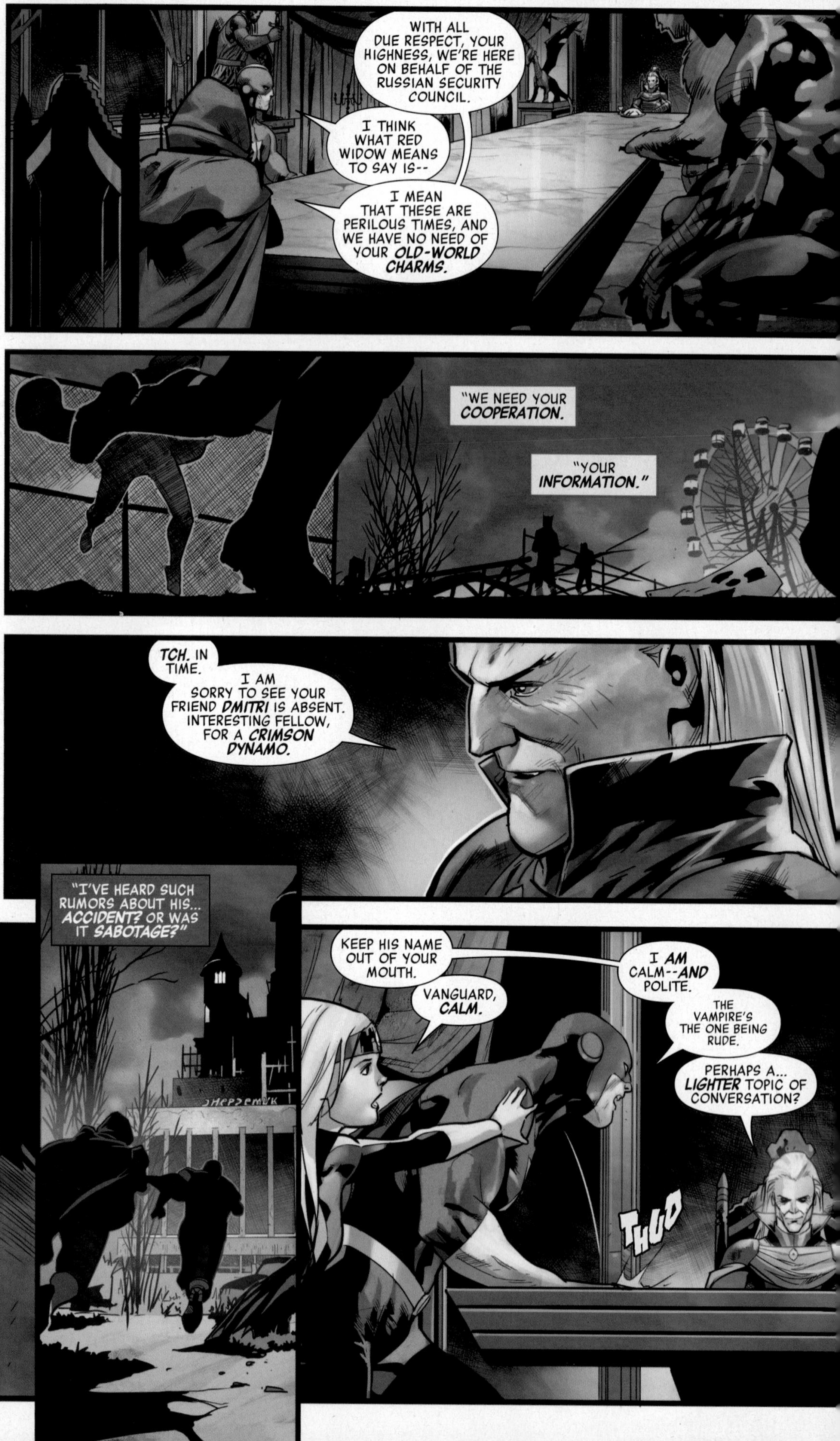
WITH ALL DUE RESPECT, YOUR HIGHNESS, WE'RE HERE ON BEHALF OF THE RUSSIAN SECURITY COUNCIL.
I THINK WHAT RED WIDOW MEANS TO SAY IS--
I MEAN THAT THESE ARE PERILOUS TIMES, AND WE HAVE NO NEED OF YOUR OLD-WORLD CHARMS.
"WE NEED YOUR COOPERATION.
"YOUR INFORMATION."
TCH. IN TIME.
I AM SORRY TO SEE YOUR FRIEND DMITRI IS ABSENT. INTERESTING FELLOW, FOR A CRIMSON DYNAMO.
"I'VE HEARD SUCH RUMORS ABOUT HIS... ACCIDENT? OR WAS IT SABOTAGE?"
KEEP HIS NAME OUT OF YOUR MOUTH.
VANGUARD, CALM.
I AM CALM--AND POLITE.
THE VAMPIRE'S THE ONE BEING RUDE.
PERHAPS A... LIGHTER TOPIC OF CONVERSATION?
THUD

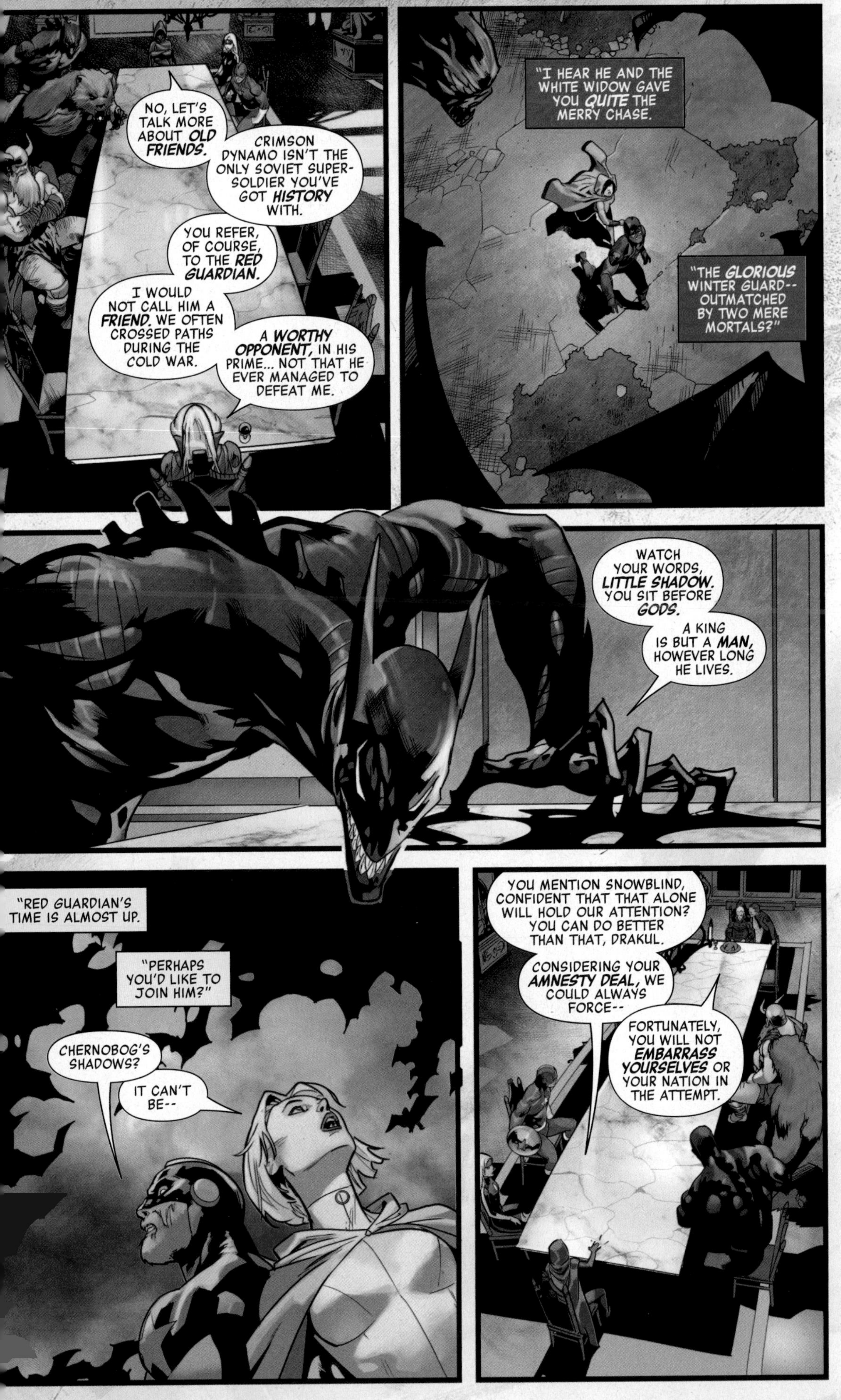
NO, LET'S TALK MORE ABOUT OLD FRIENDS.
CRIMSON DYNAMO ISN'T THE ONLY SOVIET SUPER-SOLDIER YOU'VE GOT HISTORY WITH.
YOU REFER, OF COURSE, TO THE RED GUARDIAN.
I WOULD NOT CALL HIM A FRIEND. WE OFTEN CROSSED PATHS DURING THE COLD WAR.
A WORTHY OPPONENT, IN HIS PRIME... NOT THAT HE EVER MANAGED TO DEFEAT ME.
"I HEAR HE AND THE WHITE WIDOW GAVE YOU QUITE THE MERRY CHASE.
"THE GLORIOUS WINTER GUARD--OUTMATCHED BY TWO MERE MORTALS?"
WATCH YOUR WORDS, LITTLE SHADOW. YOU SIT BEFORE GODS.
A KING IS BUT A MAN, HOWEVER LONG HE LIVES.
"RED GUARDIAN'S TIME IS ALMOST UP.
"PERHAPS YOU'D LIKE TO JOIN HIM?"
CHERNOBOG'S SHADOWS?
IT CAN'T BE--
YOU MENTION SNOWBLIND, CONFIDENT THAT THAT ALONE WILL HOLD OUR ATTENTION? YOU CAN DO BETTER THAN THAT, DRAKUL.
CONSIDERING YOUR AMNESTY DEAL, WE COULD ALWAYS FORCE--
FORTUNATELY, YOU WILL NOT EMBARRASS YOURSELVES OR YOUR NATION IN THE ATTEMPT.

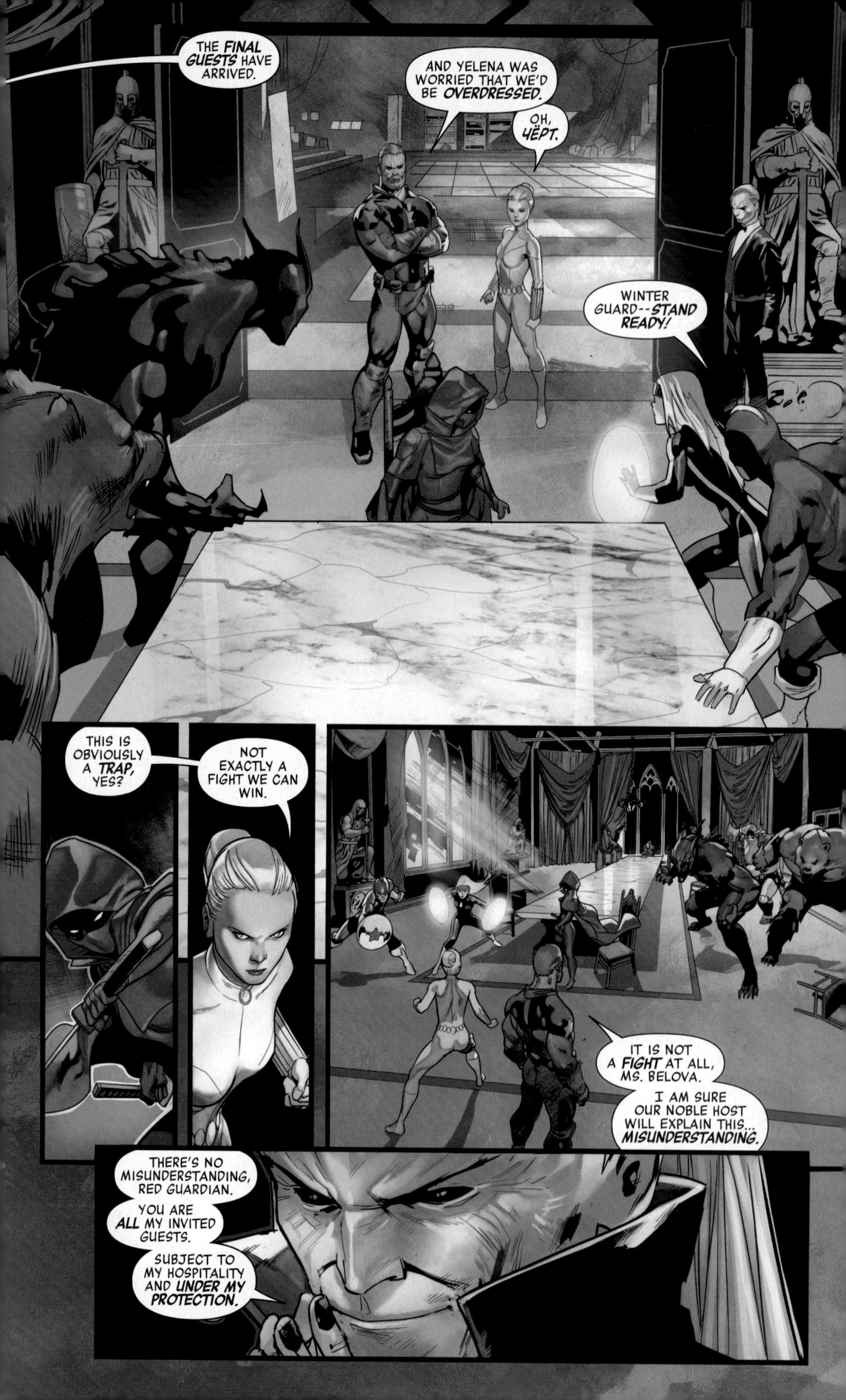
THE FINAL GUESTS HAVE ARRIVED.
AND YELENA WAS WORRIED THAT WE'D BE OVERDRESSED.
OH, ЧЁРТ.
WINTER GUARD--STAND READY!
THIS IS OBVIOUSLY A TRAP, YES?
NOT EXACTLY A FIGHT WE CAN WIN.
IT IS NOT A FIGHT AT ALL, MS. BELOVA.
I AM SURE OUR NOBLE HOST WILL EXPLAIN THIS... MISUNDERSTANDING.
THERE'S NO MISUNDERSTANDING, RED GUARDIAN.
YOU ARE ALL MY INVITED GUESTS.
SUBJECT TO MY HOSPITALITY AND UNDER MY PROTECTION.

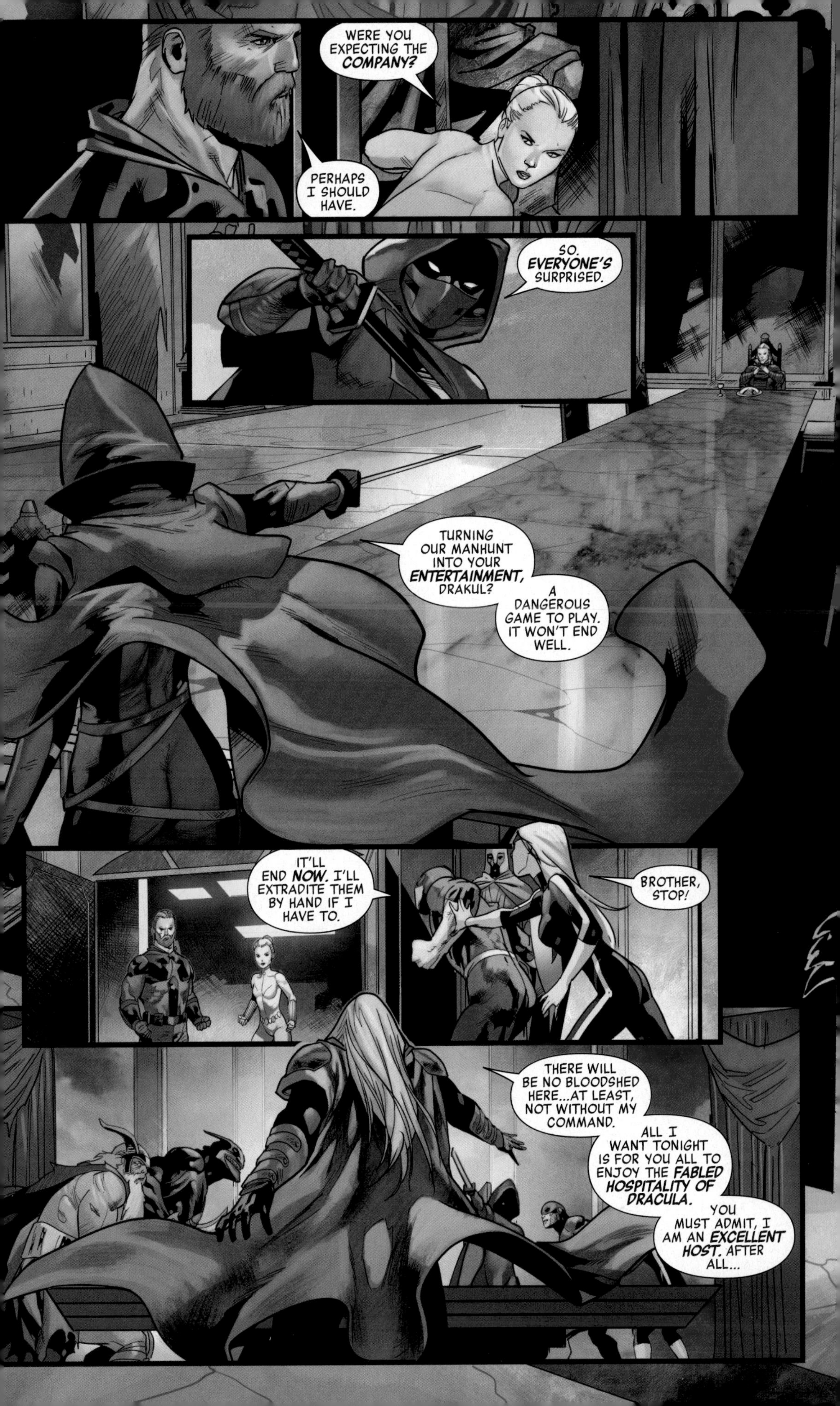

WERE YOU EXPECTING THE COMPANY?
PERHAPS I SHOULD HAVE.
SO. EVERYONE'S SURPRISED.
TURNING OUR MANHUNT INTO YOUR ENTERTAINMENT, DRAKUL?
A DANGEROUS GAME TO PLAY. IT WON'T END WELL.
IT'LL END NOW. I'LL EXTRADITE THEM BY HAND IF I HAVE TO.
BROTHER, STOP!
THERE WILL BE NO BLOODSHED HERE...AT LEAST, NOT WITHOUT MY COMMAND.
ALL I WANT TONIGHT IS FOR YOU ALL TO ENJOY THE FABLED HOSPITALITY OF DRACULA.
YOU MUST ADMIT, I AM AN EXCELLENT HOST. AFTER ALL...

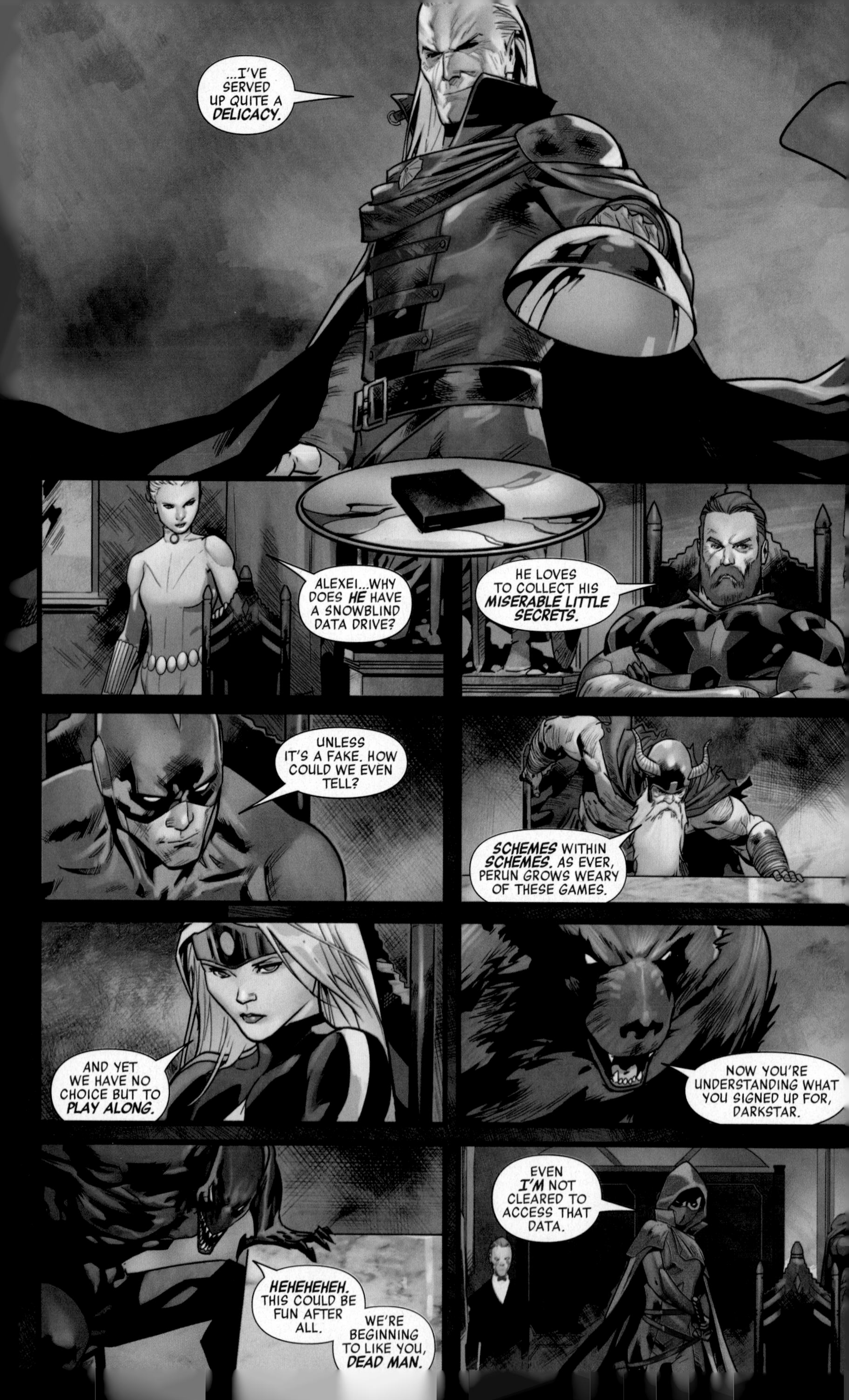
...I'VE SERVED UP QUITE A DELICACY.
ALEXEI...WHY DOES HE HAVE A SNOWBLIND DATA DRIVE?
HE LOVES TO COLLECT HIS MISERABLE LITTLE SECRETS.
UNLESS IT'S A FAKE. HOW COULD WE EVEN TELL?
SCHEMES WITHIN SCHEMES. AS EVER, PERUN GROWS WEARY OF THESE GAMES.
AND YET WE HAVE NO CHOICE BUT TO PLAY ALONG.
NOW YOU'RE UNDERSTANDING WHAT YOU SIGNED UP FOR, DARKSTAR.
HEHEHEHEH. THIS COULD BE FUN AFTER ALL.
WE'RE BEGINNING TO LIKE YOU, DEAD MAN.
EVEN I'M NOT CLEARED TO ACCESS THAT DATA.

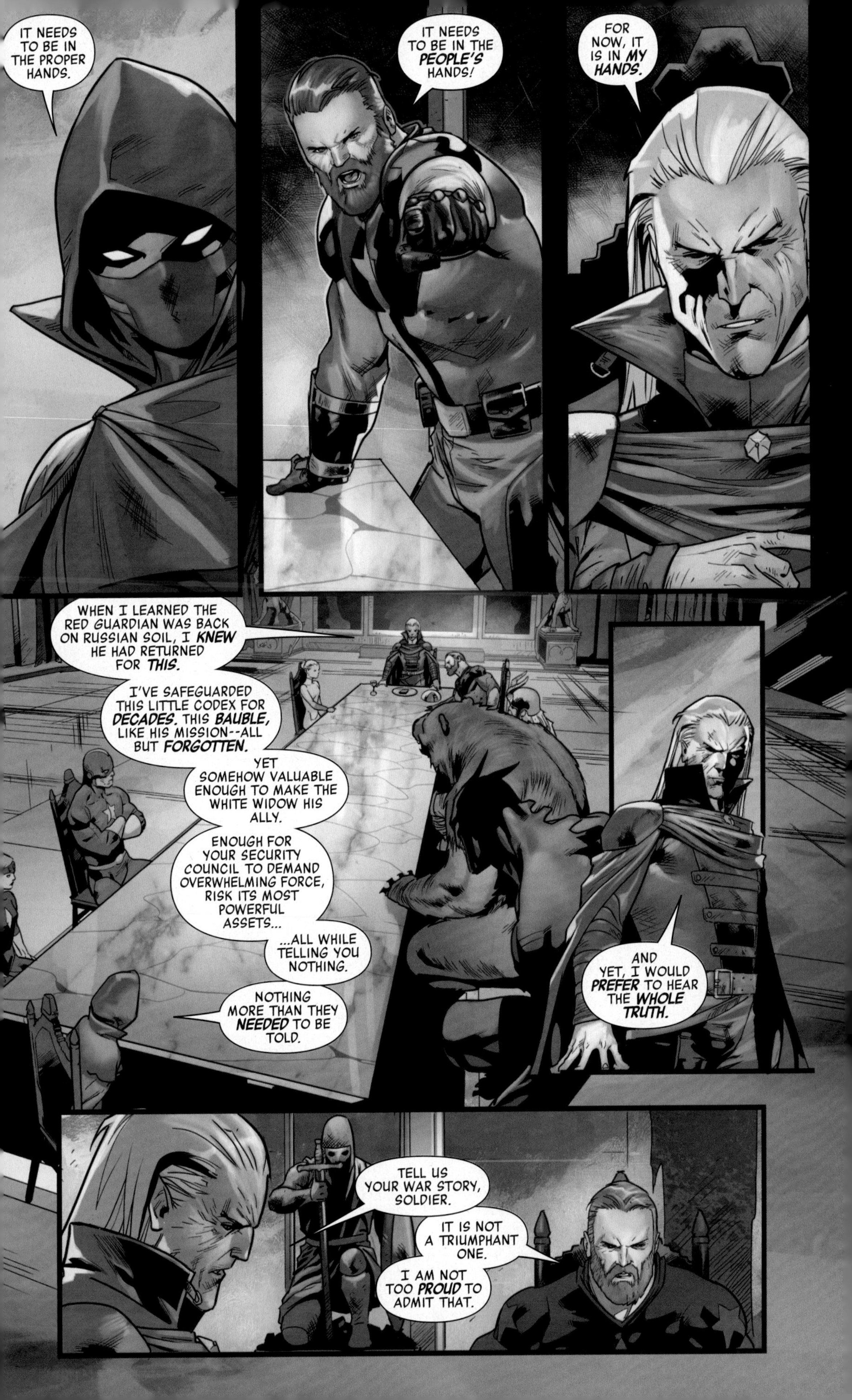
IT NEEDS TO BE IN THE PROPER HANDS.
IT NEEDS TO BE IN THE PEOPLE'S HANDS!
FOR NOW, IT IS IN MY HANDS.
WHEN I LEARNED THE RED GUARDIAN WAS BACK ON RUSSIAN SOIL, I KNEW HE HAD RETURNED FOR THIS.
I'VE SAFEGUARDED THIS LITTLE CODEX FOR DECADES. THIS BAUBLE, LIKE HIS MISSION--ALL BUT FORGOTTEN.
YET SOMEHOW VALUABLE ENOUGH TO MAKE THE WHITE WIDOW HIS ALLY.
ENOUGH FOR YOUR SECURITY COUNCIL TO DEMAND OVERWHELMING FORCE, RISK ITS MOST POWERFUL ASSETS...
...ALL WHILE TELLING YOU NOTHING.
NOTHING MORE THAN THEY NEEDED TO BE TOLD.
AND YET, I WOULD PREFER TO HEAR THE WHOLE TRUTH.
TELL US YOUR WAR STORY, SOLDIER.
IT IS NOT A TRIUMPHANT ONE.
I AM NOT TOO PROUD TO ADMIT THAT.

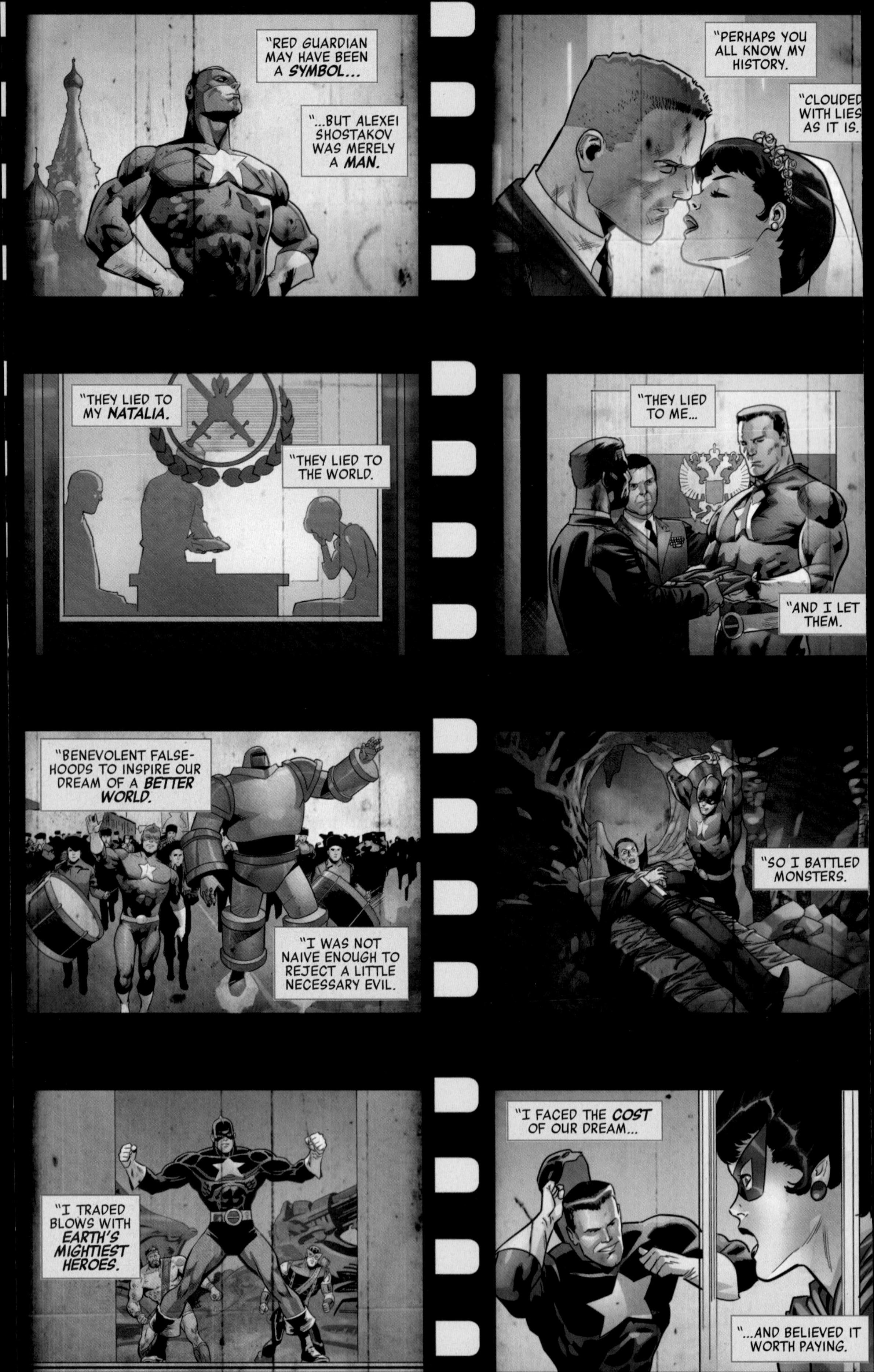
"RED GUARDIAN MAY HAVE BEEN A SYMBOL...
"...BUT ALEXEI SHOSTAKOV WAS MERELY A MAN.
"PERHAPS YOU ALL KNOW MY HISTORY.
"CLOUDED WITH LIES AS IT IS.
"THEY LIED TO MY NATALIA.
"THEY LIED TO THE WORLD.
"THEY LIED TO ME...
"AND I LET THEM.
"BENEVOLENT FALSE-HOODS TO INSPIRE OUR DREAM OF A BETTER WORLD.
"I WAS NOT NAIVE ENOUGH TO REJECT A LITTLE NECESSARY EVIL.
"SO I BATTLED MONSTERS.
"I TRADED BLOWS WITH EARTH'S MIGHTIEST HEROES.
"I FACED THE COST OF OUR DREAM...
"...AND BELIEVED IT WORTH PAYING.

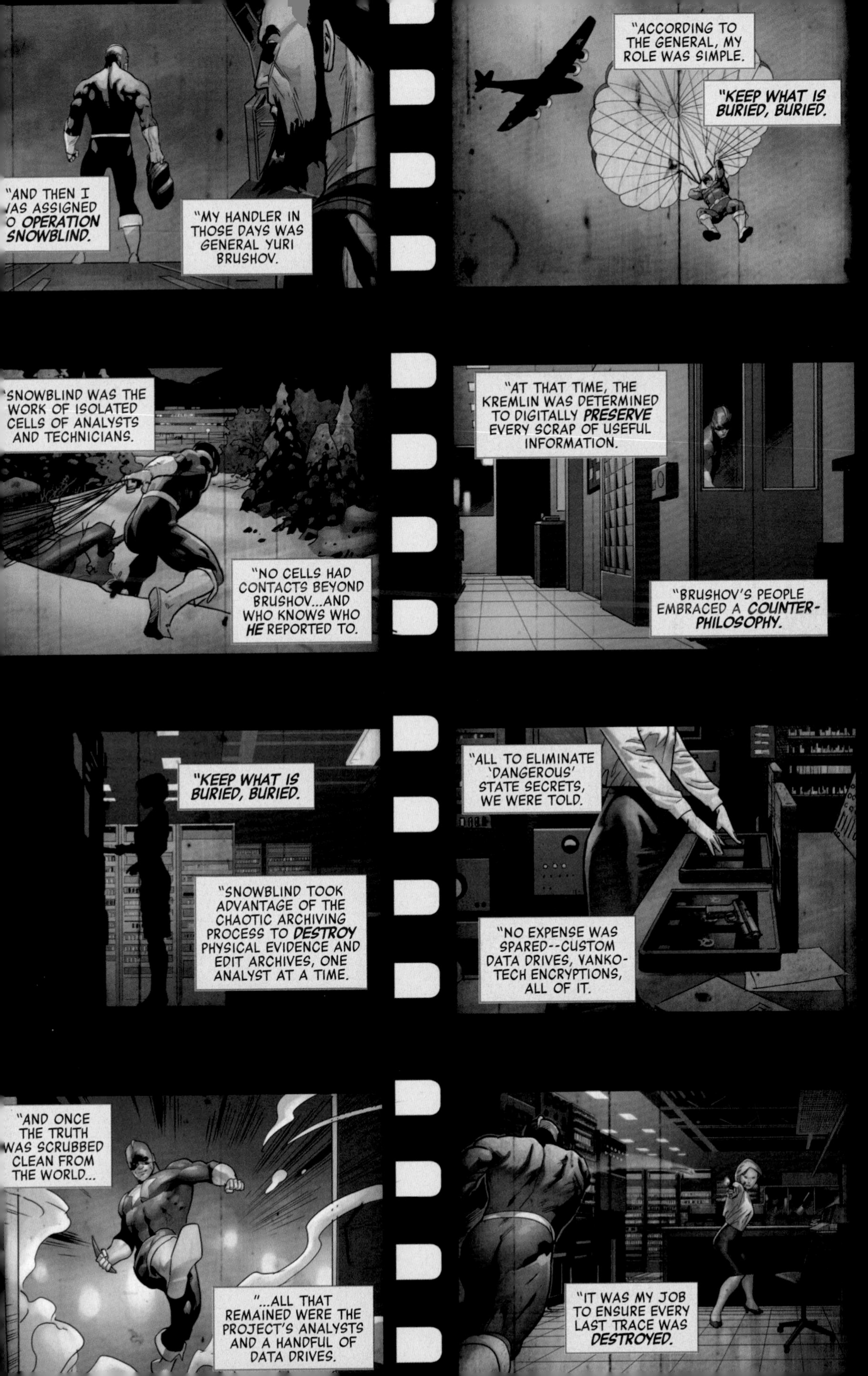
"AND THEN I
/AS ASSIGNED
O OPERATION
SNOWBLIND.
"MY HANDLER IN THOSE DAYS WAS GENERAL YURI BRUSHOV.
"ACCORDING TO THE GENERAL, MY ROLE WAS SIMPLE.
"KEEP WHAT IS BURIED, BURIED.
'SNOWBLIND WAS THE WORK OF ISOLATED CELLS OF ANALYSTS AND TECHNICIANS.
"NO CELLS HAD CONTACTS BEYOND BRUSHOV...AND WHO KNOWS WHO HE REPORTED TO.
"AT THAT TIME, THE KREMLIN WAS DETERMINED TO DIGITALLY PRESERVE EVERY SCRAP OF USEFUL INFORMATION.
"BRUSHOV'S PEOPLE EMBRACED A COUNTER-PHILOSOPHY.
"KEEP WHAT IS BURIED, BURIED.
"SNOWBLIND TOOK ADVANTAGE OF THE CHAOTIC ARCHIVING PROCESS TO DESTROY PHYSICAL EVIDENCE AND EDIT ARCHIVES, ONE ANALYST AT A TIME.
"ALL TO ELIMINATE 'DANGEROUS' STATE SECRETS, WE WERE TOLD.
"NO EXPENSE WAS SPARED--CUSTOM DATA DRIVES, VANKO-TECH ENCRYPTIONS, ALL OF IT.
"AND ONCE THE TRUTH WAS SCRUBBED CLEAN FROM THE WORLD...
"...ALL THAT REMAINED WERE THE PROJECT'S ANALYSTS AND A HANDFUL OF DATA DRIVES.
"IT WAS MY JOB TO ENSURE EVERY LAST TRACE WAS DESTROYED.

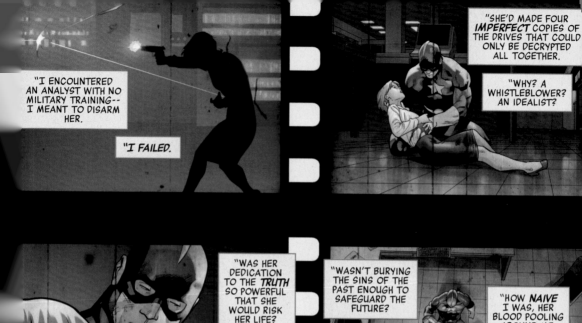

"I ENCOUNTERED AN ANALYST WITH NO MILITARY TRAINING-- I MEANT TO DISARM HER.

"I FAILED.

"SHE'D MADE FOUR *IMPERFECT* COPIES OF THE DRIVES THAT COULD ONLY BE DECRYPTED ALL TOGETHER.

"WHY? A WHISTLEBLOWER? AN IDEALIST?

"WAS HER DEDICATION TO THE *TRUTH* SO POWERFUL THAT SHE WOULD RISK HER LIFE?

"RISK THE PROSPEROUS FUTURE WE DREAMED OF BUILDING--IN PURSUIT OF IT?

"WASN'T BURYING THE SINS OF THE PAST ENOUGH TO SAFEGUARD THE FUTURE?

"HOW *NAIVE* I WAS, HER BLOOD POOLING AROUND ME.

"I FELT THAT I OWED HER, SO...I BROKE PROTOCOL.

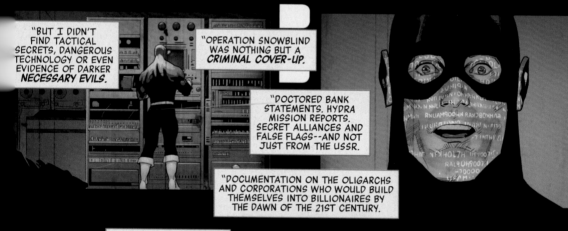

"BUT I DIDN'T FIND TACTICAL SECRETS, DANGEROUS TECHNOLOGY OR EVEN EVIDENCE OF DARKER *NECESSARY EVILS.*

"OPERATION SNOWBLIND WAS NOTHING BUT A *CRIMINAL COVER-UP.*

"DOCTORED BANK STATEMENTS. HYDRA MISSION REPORTS. SECRET ALLIANCES AND FALSE FLAGS--AND NOT JUST FROM THE USSR.

"DOCUMENTATION ON THE OLIGARCHS AND CORPORATIONS WHO WOULD BUILD THEMSELVES INTO BILLIONAIRES BY THE DAWN OF THE 21ST CENTURY.

"IF THIS WAS LEAKED, *MY DREAM* FOR RUSSIA'S FUTURE WAS *DEAD.*

"BUT WHAT ASSURANCE DID I HAVE THAT IT WOULD EVER ARRIVE?

"SO I TURNED OVER *DECOYS* TO BRUSHOV INSTEAD.

"I DON'T THINK HE EVER DOUBTED ME.

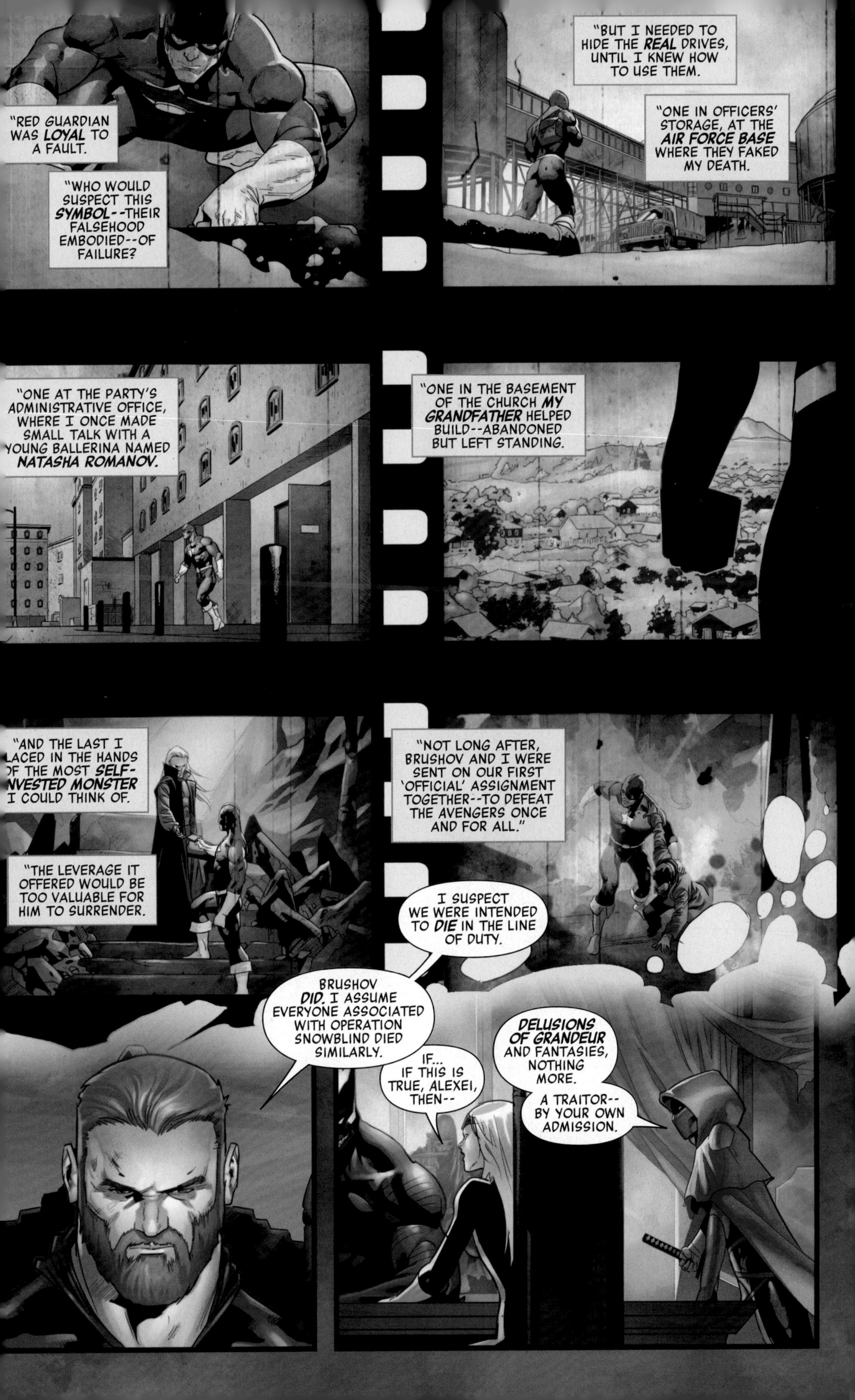

"RED GUARDIAN WAS LOYAL TO A FAULT.
"WHO WOULD SUSPECT THIS SYMBOL--THEIR FALSEHOOD EMBODIED--OF FAILURE?
"BUT I NEEDED TO HIDE THE REAL DRIVES, UNTIL I KNEW HOW TO USE THEM.
"ONE IN OFFICERS' STORAGE, AT THE AIR FORCE BASE WHERE THEY FAKED MY DEATH.
"ONE AT THE PARTY'S ADMINISTRATIVE OFFICE, WHERE I ONCE MADE SMALL TALK WITH A YOUNG BALLERINA NAMED NATASHA ROMANOV.
"ONE IN THE BASEMENT OF THE CHURCH MY GRANDFATHER HELPED BUILD--ABANDONED BUT LEFT STANDING.
"AND THE LAST I LACED IN THE HANDS OF THE MOST SELF-NVESTED MONSTER I COULD THINK OF.
"THE LEVERAGE IT OFFERED WOULD BE TOO VALUABLE FOR HIM TO SURRENDER.
"NOT LONG AFTER, BRUSHOV AND I WERE SENT ON OUR FIRST 'OFFICIAL' ASSIGNMENT TOGETHER--TO DEFEAT THE AVENGERS ONCE AND FOR ALL."
I SUSPECT WE WERE INTENDED TO DIE IN THE LINE OF DUTY.
BRUSHOV DID. I ASSUME EVERYONE ASSOCIATED WITH OPERATION SNOWBLIND DIED SIMILARLY.
IF... IF THIS IS TRUE, ALEXEI, THEN--
DELUSIONS OF GRANDEUR AND FANTASIES, NOTHING MORE.
A TRAITOR-- BY YOUR OWN ADMISSION.

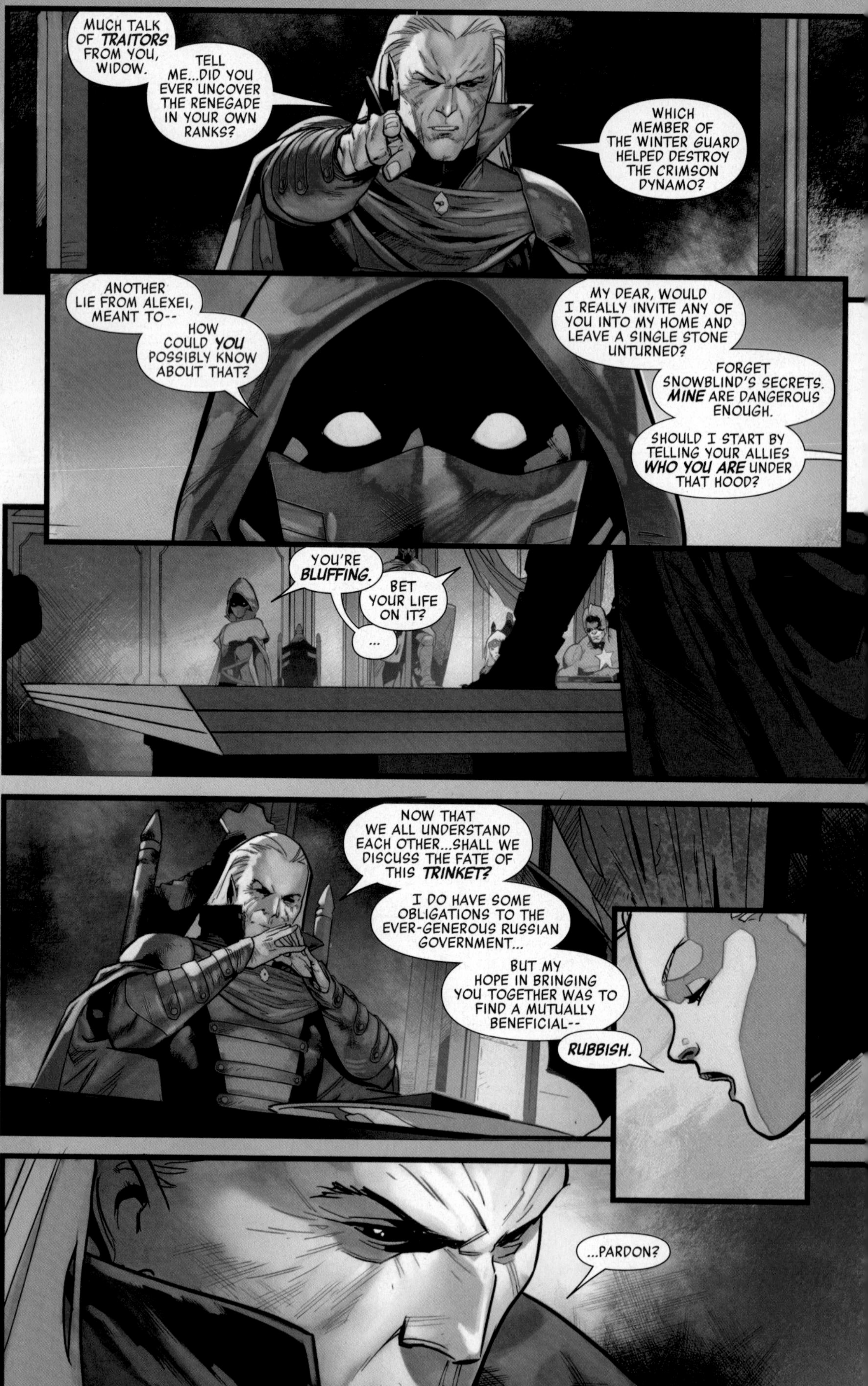
MUCH TALK OF TRAITORS FROM YOU, WIDOW.
TELL ME...DID YOU EVER UNCOVER THE RENEGADE IN YOUR OWN RANKS?
WHICH MEMBER OF THE WINTER GUARD HELPED DESTROY THE CRIMSON DYNAMO?
ANOTHER LIE FROM ALEXEI, MEANT TO--
HOW COULD YOU POSSIBLY KNOW ABOUT THAT?
MY DEAR, WOULD I REALLY INVITE ANY OF YOU INTO MY HOME AND LEAVE A SINGLE STONE UNTURNED?
FORGET SNOWBLIND'S SECRETS. MINE ARE DANGEROUS ENOUGH.
SHOULD I START BY TELLING YOUR ALLIES WHO YOU ARE UNDER THAT HOOD?
YOU'RE BLUFFING.
BET YOUR LIFE ON IT?
...
NOW THAT WE ALL UNDERSTAND EACH OTHER...SHALL WE DISCUSS THE FATE OF THIS TRINKET?
I DO HAVE SOME OBLIGATIONS TO THE EVER-GENEROUS RUSSIAN GOVERNMENT...
BUT MY HOPE IN BRINGING YOU TOGETHER WAS TO FIND A MUTUALLY BENEFICIAL--
RUBBISH.
...PARDON?

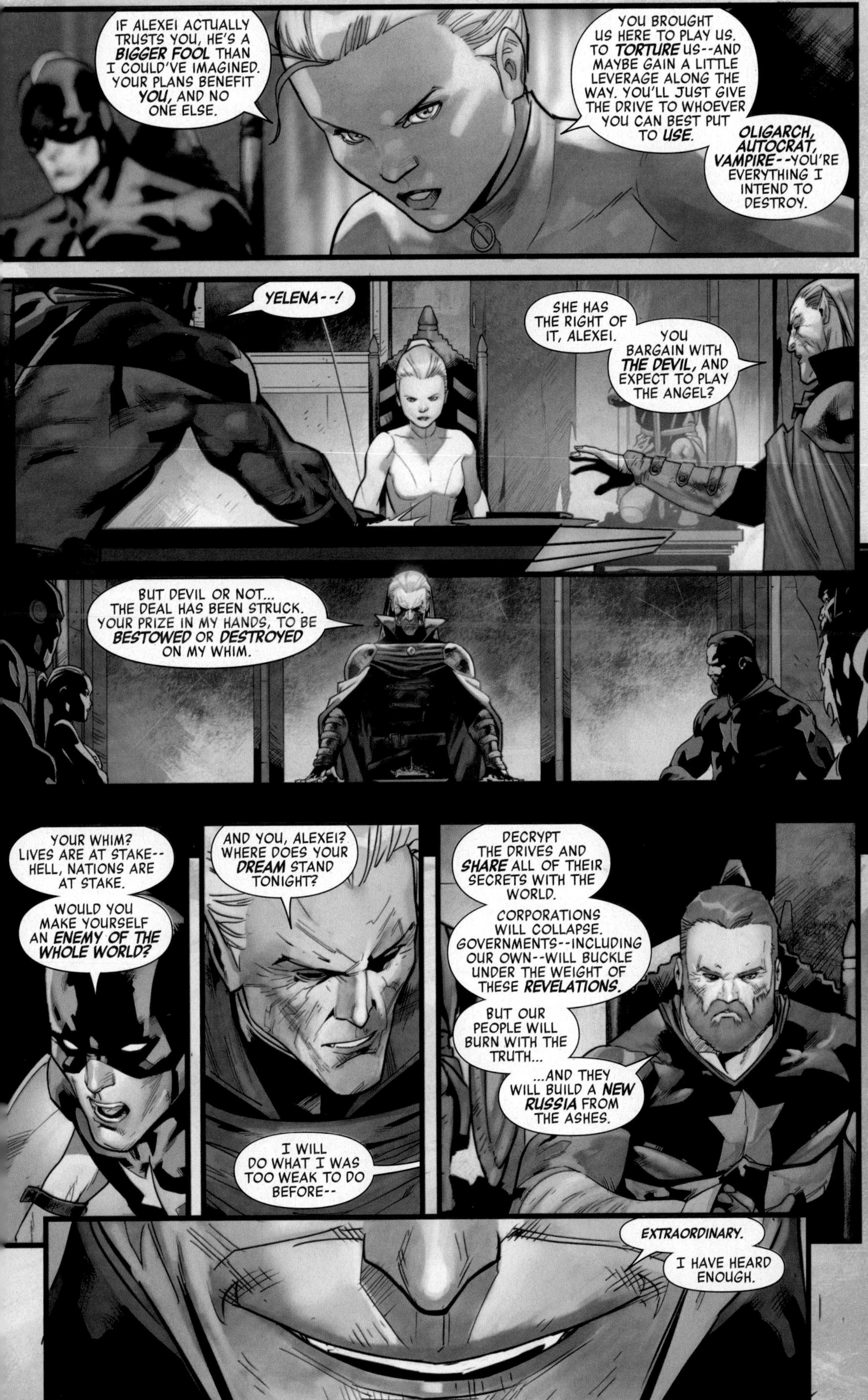

IF ALEXEI ACTUALLY TRUSTS YOU, HE'S A **BIGGER FOOL** THAN I COULD'VE IMAGINED. YOUR PLANS BENEFIT **YOU,** AND NO ONE ELSE.
YOU BROUGHT US HERE TO PLAY US. TO **TORTURE** US--AND MAYBE GAIN A LITTLE LEVERAGE ALONG THE WAY. YOU'LL JUST GIVE THE DRIVE TO WHOEVER YOU CAN BEST PUT TO **USE.**
OLIGARCH, AUTOCRAT, VAMPIRE--YOU'RE EVERYTHING I INTEND TO DESTROY.
YELENA--!
SHE HAS THE RIGHT OF IT, ALEXEI.
YOU BARGAIN WITH **THE DEVIL,** AND EXPECT TO PLAY THE ANGEL?
BUT DEVIL OR NOT... THE DEAL HAS BEEN STRUCK. YOUR PRIZE IN MY HANDS, TO BE **BESTOWED** OR **DESTROYED** ON MY WHIM.
YOUR WHIM? LIVES ARE AT STAKE--HELL, NATIONS ARE AT STAKE.
WOULD YOU MAKE YOURSELF AN **ENEMY OF THE WHOLE WORLD?**
AND YOU, ALEXEI? WHERE DOES YOUR **DREAM** STAND TONIGHT?
I WILL DO WHAT I WAS TOO WEAK TO DO BEFORE--
DECRYPT THE DRIVES AND **SHARE** ALL OF THEIR SECRETS WITH THE WORLD.
CORPORATIONS WILL COLLAPSE. GOVERNMENTS--INCLUDING OUR OWN--WILL BUCKLE UNDER THE WEIGHT OF THESE **REVELATIONS.**
BUT OUR PEOPLE WILL BURN WITH THE TRUTH...
...AND THEY WILL BUILD A **NEW RUSSIA** FROM THE ASHES.
EXTRAORDINARY.
I HAVE HEARD ENOUGH.

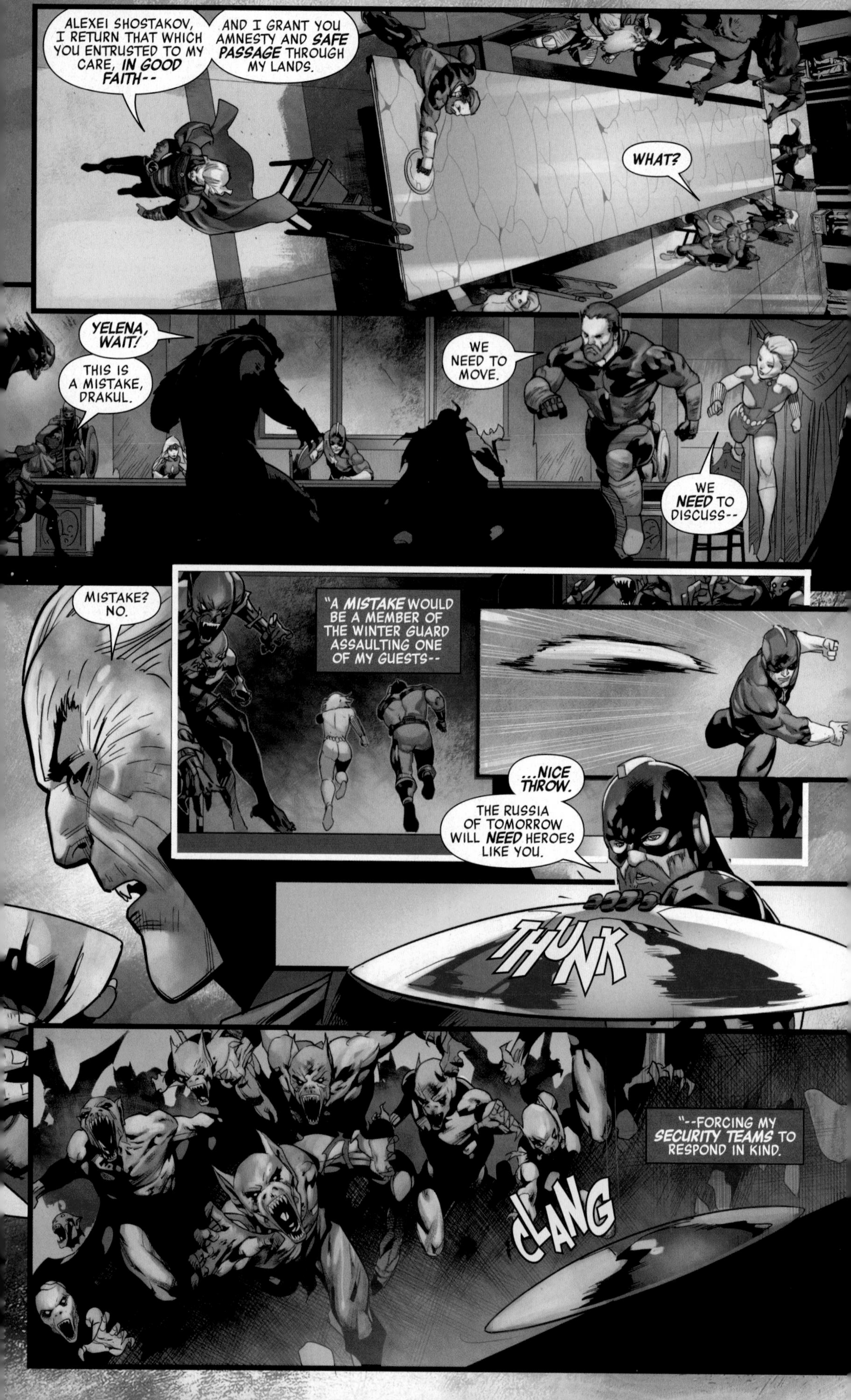

ALEXEI SHOSTAKOV, I RETURN THAT WHICH YOU ENTRUSTED TO MY CARE, *IN GOOD FAITH*--
AND I GRANT YOU AMNESTY AND *SAFE PASSAGE* THROUGH MY LANDS.
WHAT?
YELENA, WAIT!
THIS IS A MISTAKE, DRAKUL.
WE NEED TO MOVE.
WE *NEED* TO DISCUSS--
MISTAKE? NO.
"A *MISTAKE* WOULD BE A MEMBER OF THE WINTER GUARD ASSAULTING ONE OF MY GUESTS--
...NICE THROW.
THE RUSSIA OF TOMORROW WILL *NEED* HEROES LIKE YOU.
THUNK
"--FORCING MY *SECURITY TEAMS* TO RESPOND IN KIND.
CLANG

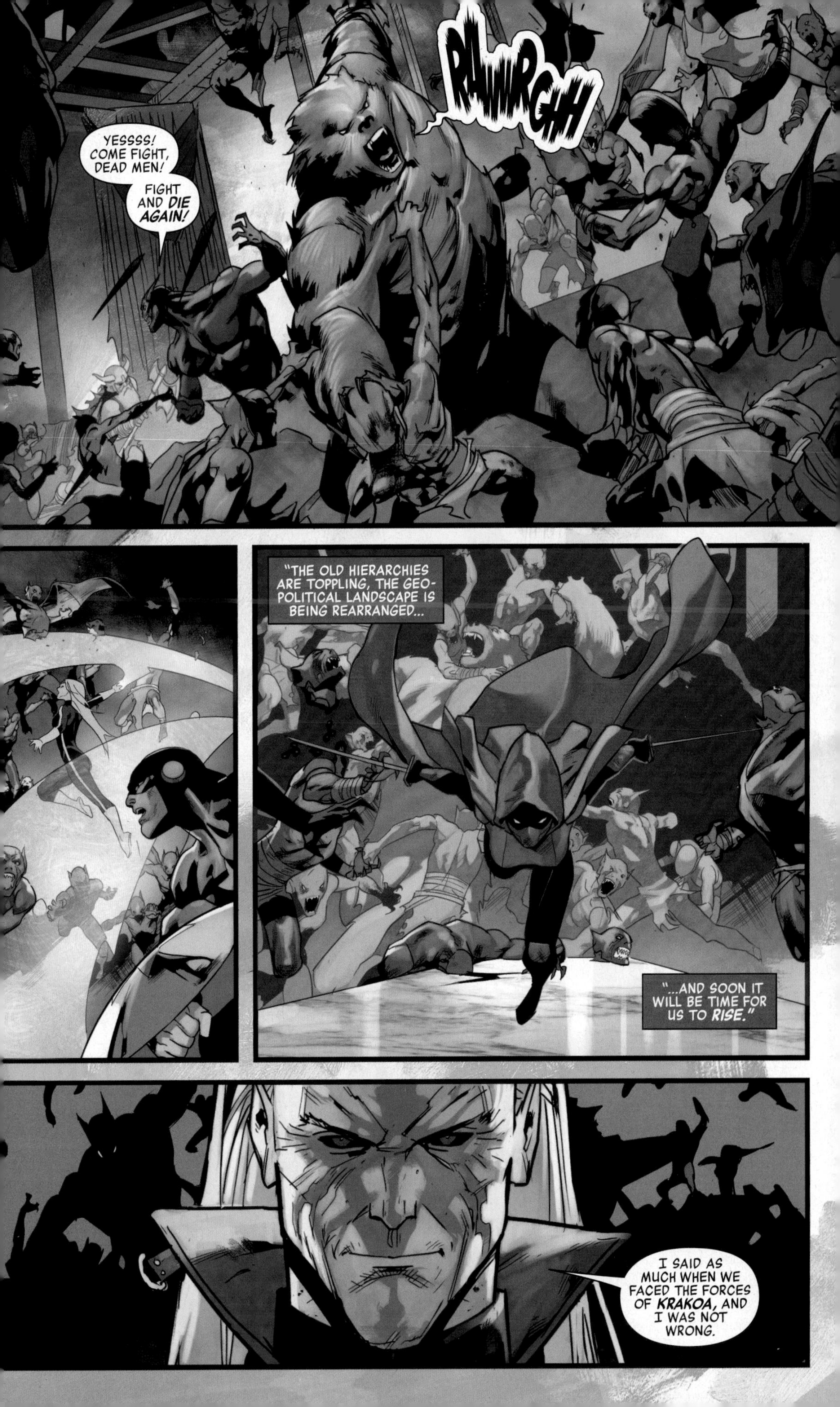
RAWWRGHH
YESSSS! COME FIGHT, DEAD MEN!
FIGHT AND DIE AGAIN!
"THE OLD HIERARCHIES ARE TOPPLING, THE GEO-POLITICAL LANDSCAPE IS BEING REARRANGED...
"...AND SOON IT WILL BE TIME FOR US TO RISE."
I SAID AS MUCH WHEN WE FACED THE FORCES OF KRAKOA, AND I WAS NOT WRONG.

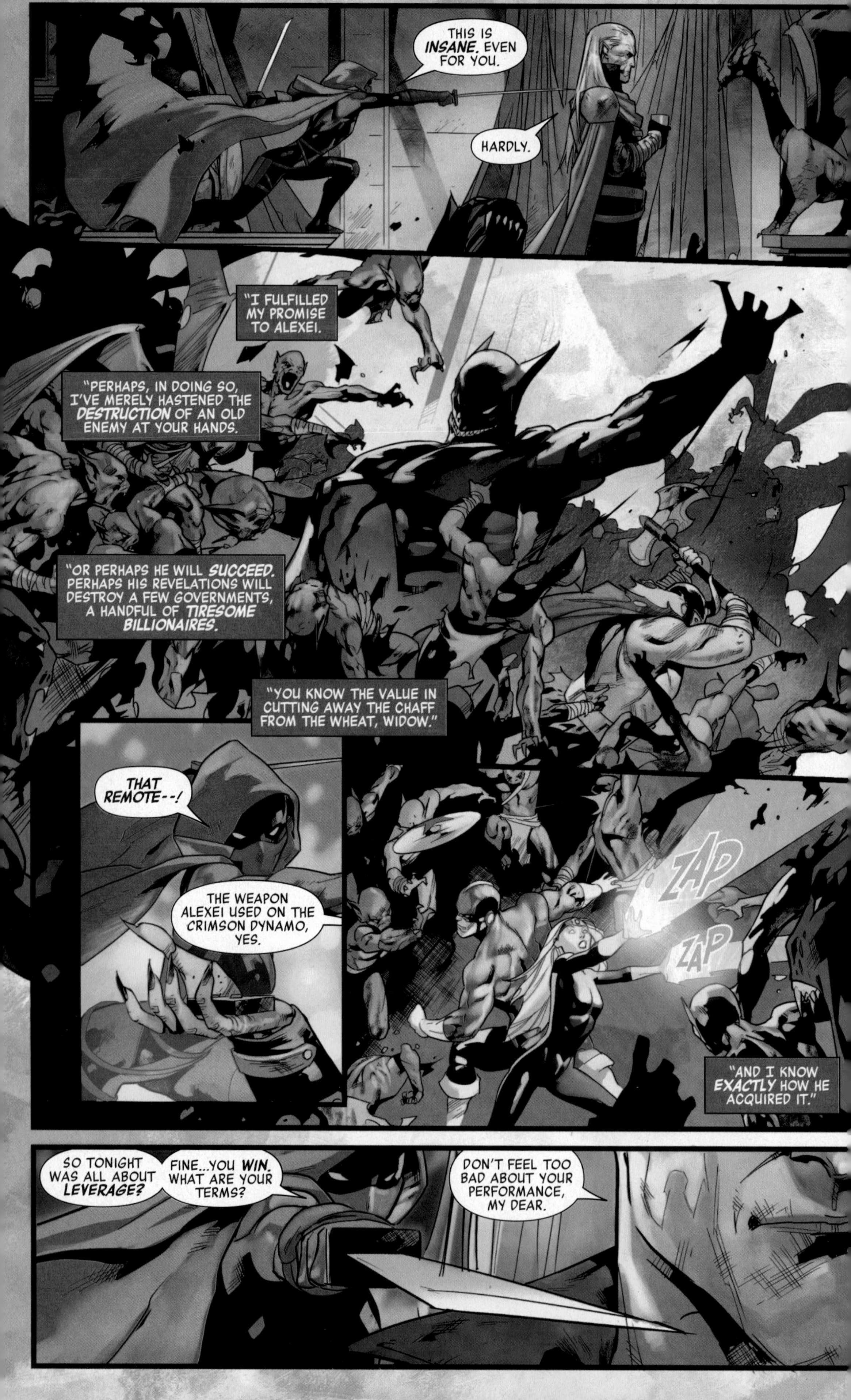

THIS IS INSANE. EVEN FOR YOU.
HARDLY.
"I FULFILLED MY PROMISE TO ALEXEI.
"PERHAPS, IN DOING SO, I'VE MERELY HASTENED THE DESTRUCTION OF AN OLD ENEMY AT YOUR HANDS.
"OR PERHAPS HE WILL SUCCEED. PERHAPS HIS REVELATIONS WILL DESTROY A FEW GOVERNMENTS, A HANDFUL OF TIRESOME BILLIONAIRES.
"YOU KNOW THE VALUE IN CUTTING AWAY THE CHAFF FROM THE WHEAT, WIDOW."
THAT REMOTE--!
THE WEAPON ALEXEI USED ON THE CRIMSON DYNAMO, YES.
ZAP
ZAP
"AND I KNOW EXACTLY HOW HE ACQUIRED IT."
SO TONIGHT WAS ALL ABOUT LEVERAGE?
FINE...YOU WIN. WHAT ARE YOUR TERMS?
DON'T FEEL TOO BAD ABOUT YOUR PERFORMANCE, MY DEAR.

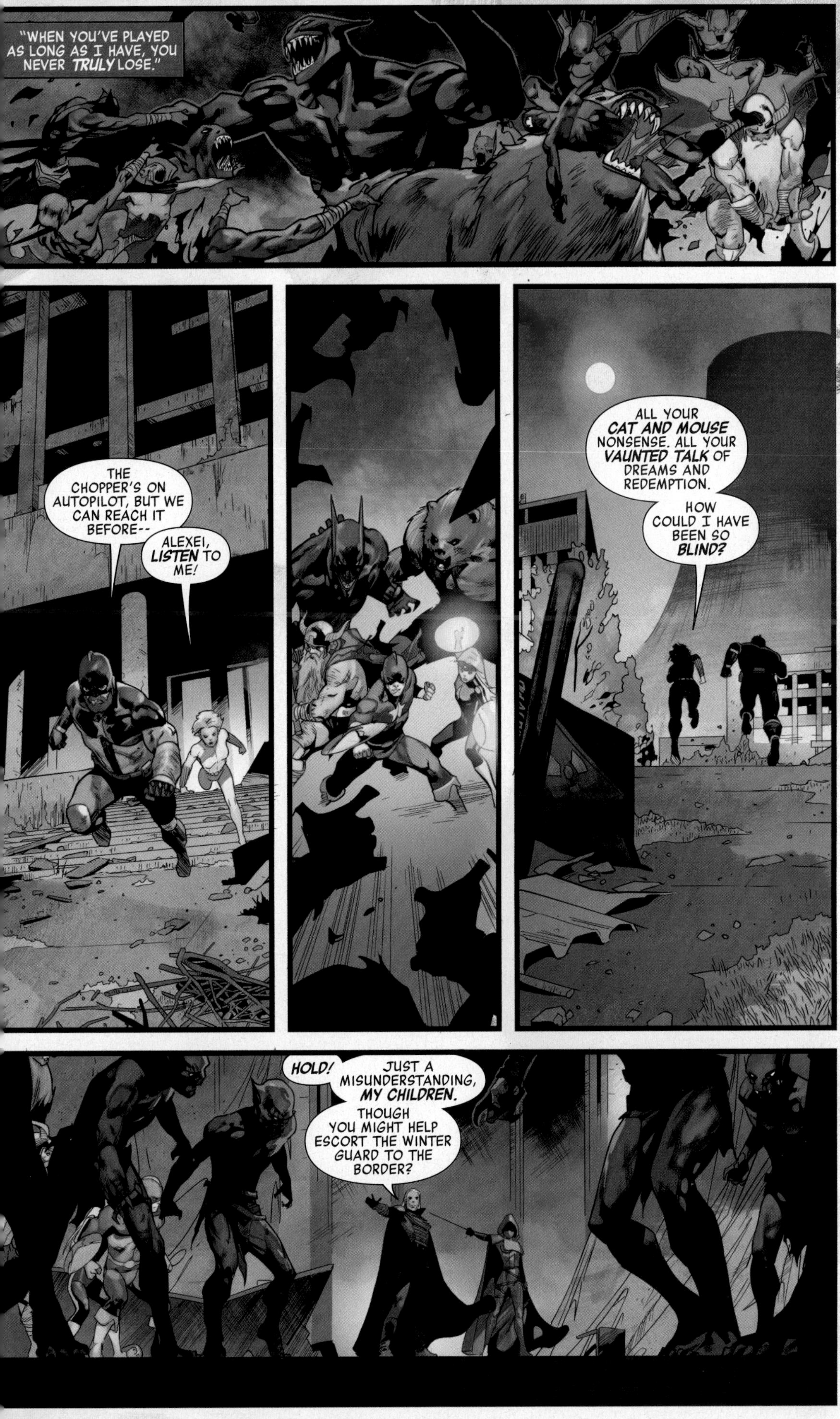
"WHEN YOU'VE PLAYED AS LONG AS I HAVE, YOU NEVER TRULY LOSE."
THE CHOPPER'S ON AUTOPILOT, BUT WE CAN REACH IT BEFORE--
ALEXEI, LISTEN TO ME!
ALL YOUR CAT AND MOUSE NONSENSE. ALL YOUR VAUNTED TALK OF DREAMS AND REDEMPTION.
HOW COULD I HAVE BEEN SO BLIND?
HOLD!
JUST A MISUNDERSTANDING, MY CHILDREN.
THOUGH YOU MIGHT HELP ESCORT THE WINTER GUARD TO THE BORDER?

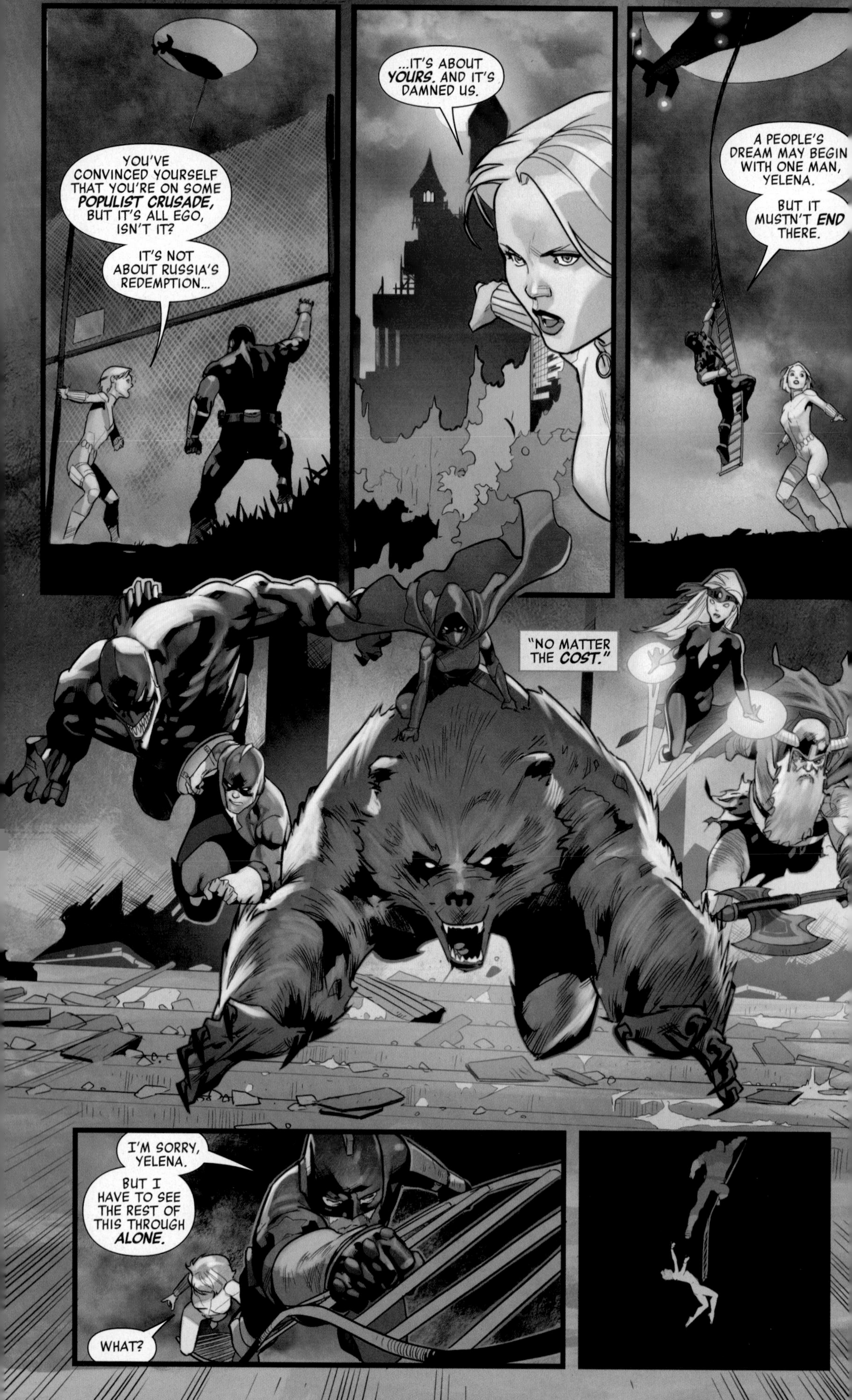
YOU'VE CONVINCED YOURSELF THAT YOU'RE ON SOME POPULIST CRUSADE, BUT IT'S ALL EGO, ISN'T IT?
IT'S NOT ABOUT RUSSIA'S REDEMPTION...
...IT'S ABOUT YOURS. AND IT'S DAMNED US.
A PEOPLE'S DREAM MAY BEGIN WITH ONE MAN, YELENA.
BUT IT MUSTN'T END THERE.
"NO MATTER THE COST."
I'M SORRY, YELENA.
BUT I HAVE TO SEE THE REST OF THIS THROUGH ALONE.
WHAT?

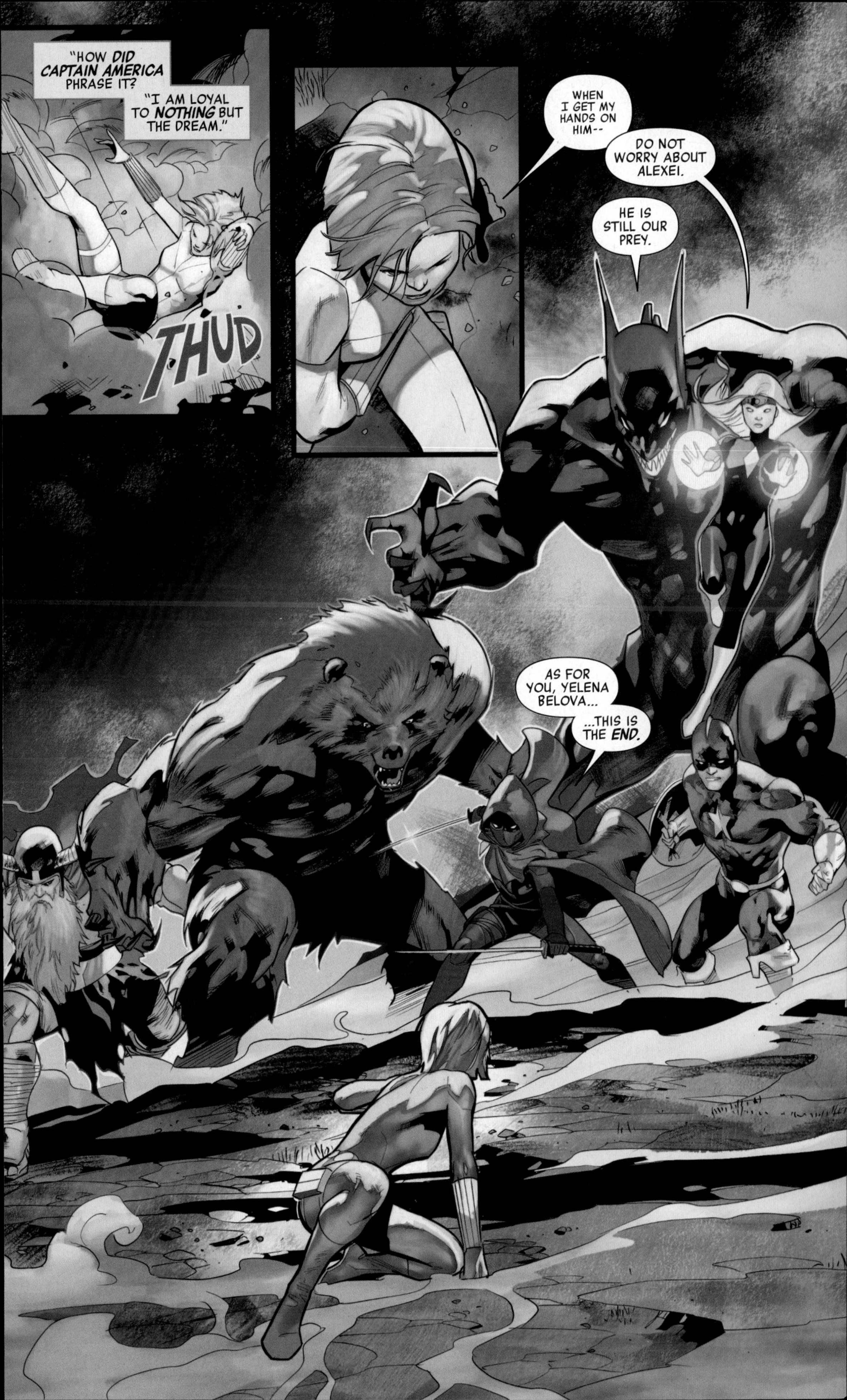

"HOW DID CAPTAIN AMERICA PHRASE IT?
"I AM LOYAL TO NOTHING BUT THE DREAM."
THUD
WHEN I GET MY HANDS ON HIM--
DO NOT WORRY ABOUT ALEXEI.
HE IS STILL OUR PREY.
AS FOR YOU, YELENA BELOVA...
...THIS IS THE END.

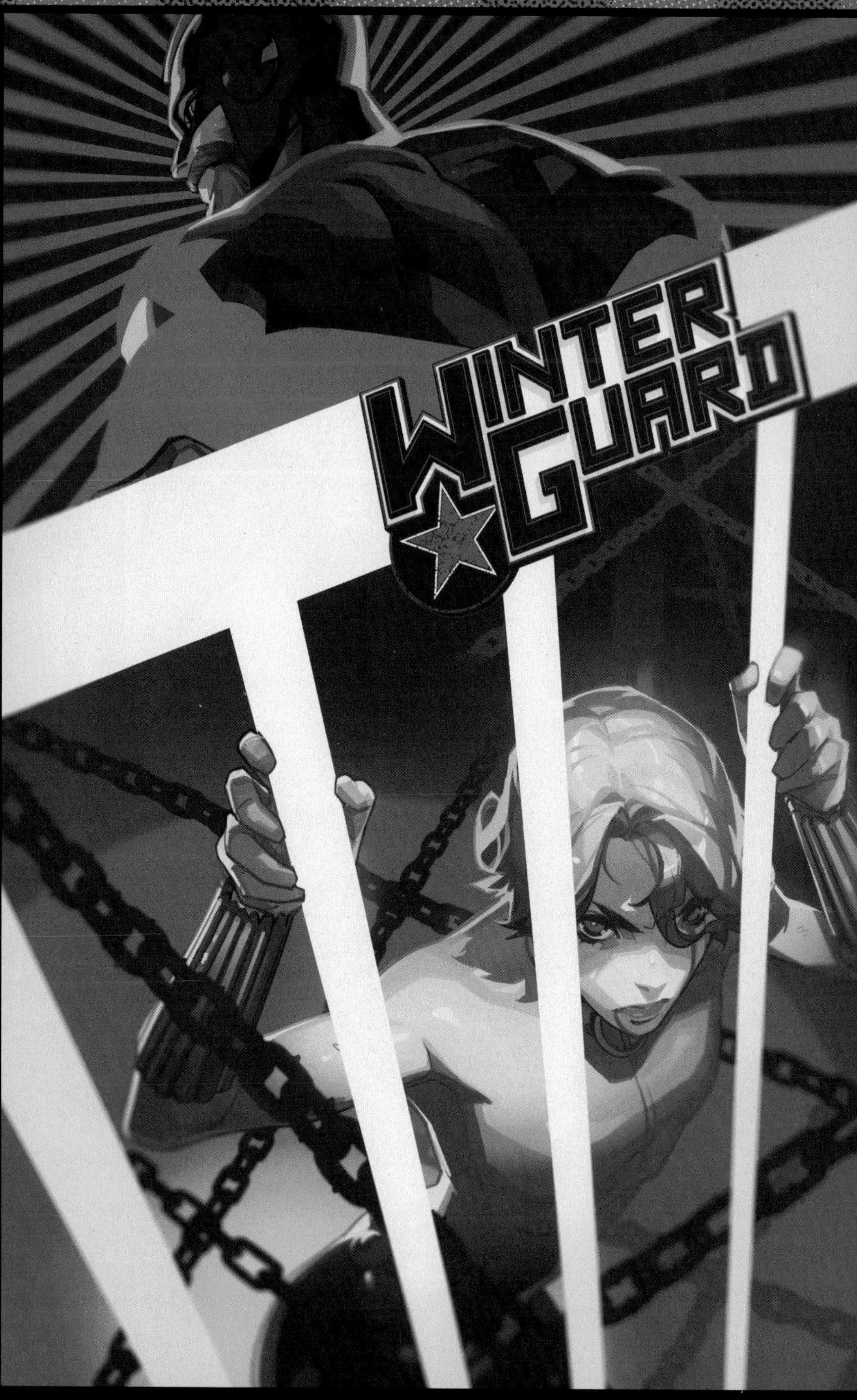
WINTER
GUARD

4

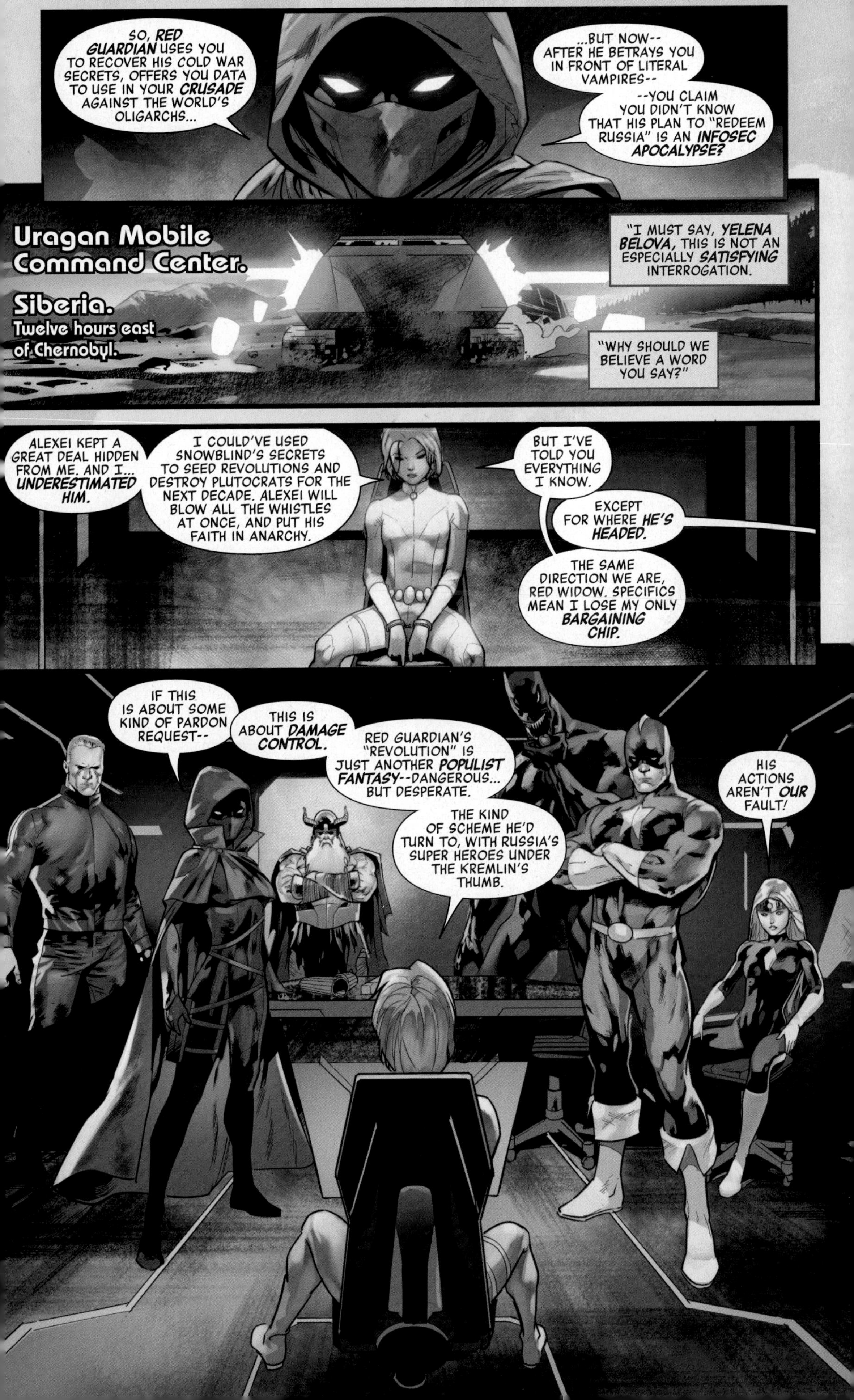
SO, RED GUARDIAN USES YOU TO RECOVER HIS COLD WAR SECRETS, OFFERS YOU DATA TO USE IN YOUR CRUSADE AGAINST THE WORLD'S OLIGARCHS...
...BUT NOW-- AFTER HE BETRAYS YOU IN FRONT OF LITERAL VAMPIRES--
--YOU CLAIM YOU DIDN'T KNOW THAT HIS PLAN TO "REDEEM RUSSIA" IS AN INFOSEC APOCALYPSE?
Uragan Mobile Command Center.
Siberia. Twelve hours east of Chernobyl.
"I MUST SAY, YELENA BELOVA, THIS IS NOT AN ESPECIALLY SATISFYING INTERROGATION.
"WHY SHOULD WE BELIEVE A WORD YOU SAY?"
ALEXEI KEPT A GREAT DEAL HIDDEN FROM ME. AND I... UNDERESTIMATED HIM.
I COULD'VE USED SNOWBLIND'S SECRETS TO SEED REVOLUTIONS AND DESTROY PLUTOCRATS FOR THE NEXT DECADE. ALEXEI WILL BLOW ALL THE WHISTLES AT ONCE, AND PUT HIS FAITH IN ANARCHY.
BUT I'VE TOLD YOU EVERYTHING I KNOW.
EXCEPT FOR WHERE HE'S HEADED.
THE SAME DIRECTION WE ARE, RED WIDOW. SPECIFICS MEAN I LOSE MY ONLY BARGAINING CHIP.
IF THIS IS ABOUT SOME KIND OF PARDON REQUEST--
THIS IS ABOUT DAMAGE CONTROL.
RED GUARDIAN'S "REVOLUTION" IS JUST ANOTHER POPULIST FANTASY--DANGEROUS... BUT DESPERATE.
THE KIND OF SCHEME HE'D TURN TO, WITH RUSSIA'S SUPER HEROES UNDER THE KREMLIN'S THUMB.
HIS ACTIONS AREN'T OUR FAULT!

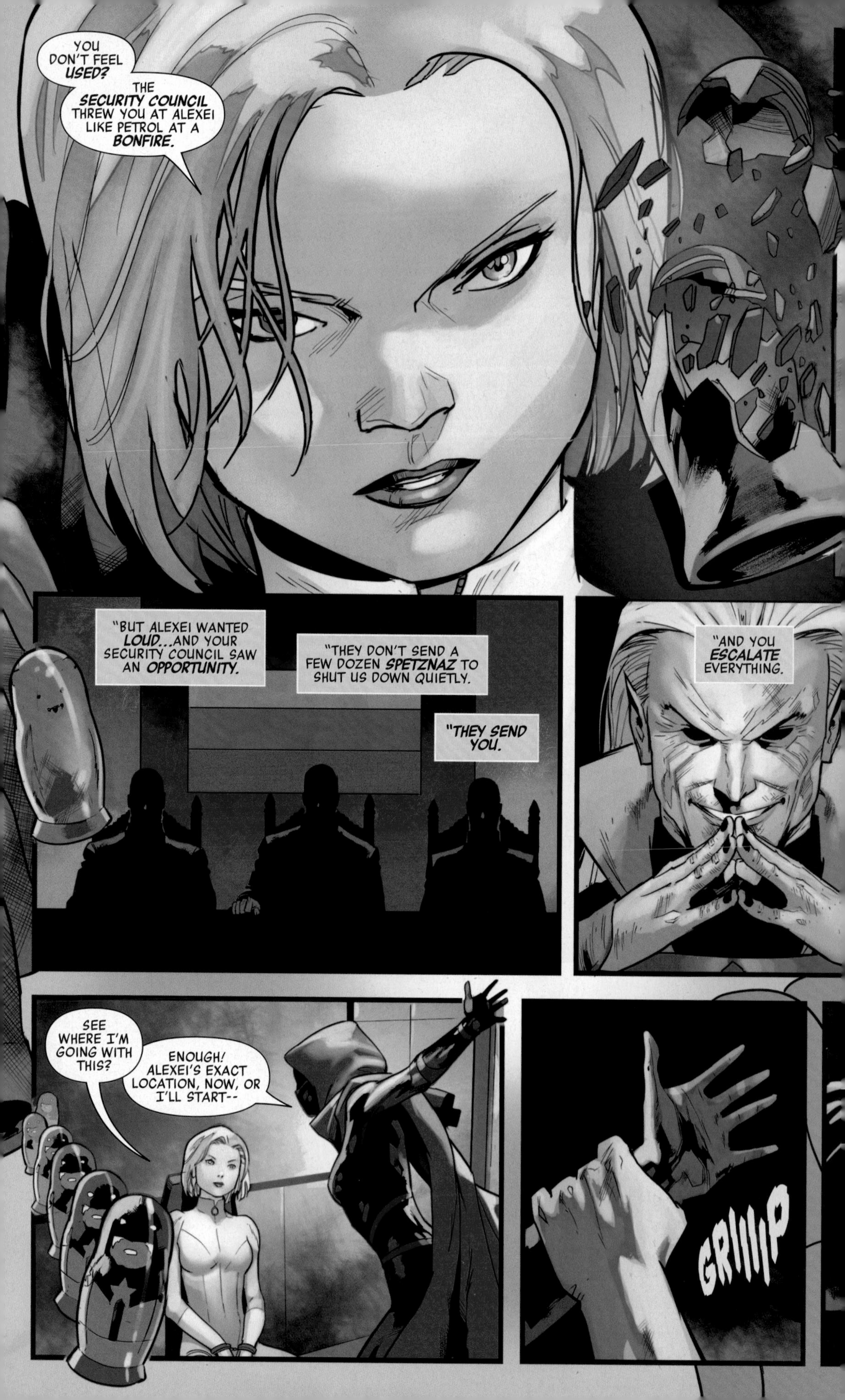
YOU DON'T FEEL USED?
THE SECURITY COUNCIL THREW YOU AT ALEXEI LIKE PETROL AT A BONFIRE.
"BUT ALEXEI WANTED LOUD...AND YOUR SECURITY COUNCIL SAW AN OPPORTUNITY.
"THEY DON'T SEND A FEW DOZEN SPETZNAZ TO SHUT US DOWN QUIETLY.
"THEY SEND YOU.
"AND YOU ESCALATE EVERYTHING.
SEE WHERE I'M GOING WITH THIS?
ENOUGH! ALEXEI'S EXACT LOCATION, NOW, OR I'LL START--
GRIIIIP

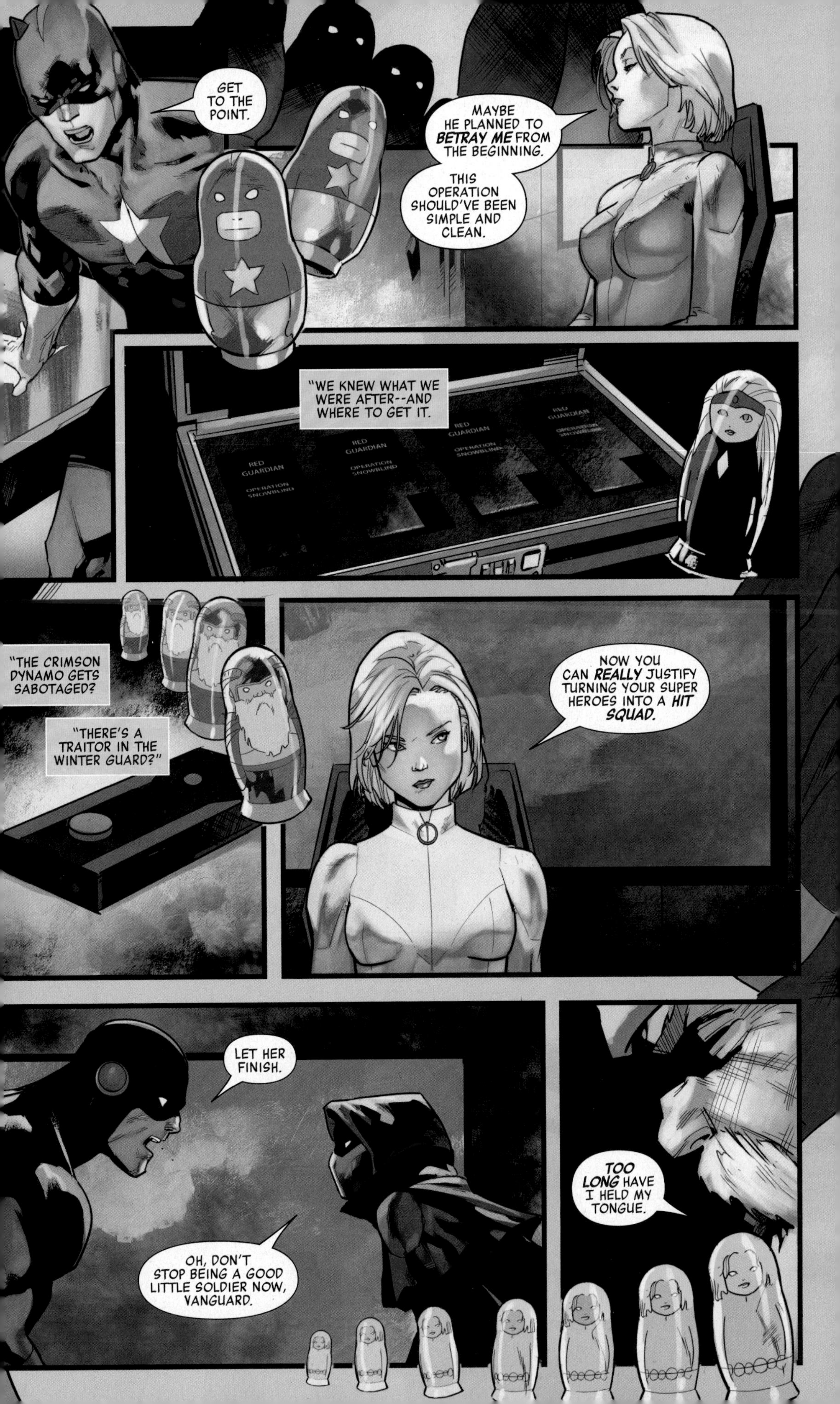

GET TO THE POINT.
MAYBE HE PLANNED TO **BETRAY ME** FROM THE BEGINNING.
THIS OPERATION SHOULD'VE BEEN SIMPLE AND CLEAN.
"WE KNEW WHAT WE WERE AFTER--AND WHERE TO GET IT.
RED GUARDIAN
OPERATION SNOWBLIND
"THE CRIMSON DYNAMO GETS SABOTAGED?
"THERE'S A TRAITOR IN THE WINTER GUARD?"
NOW YOU CAN **REALLY** JUSTIFY TURNING YOUR SUPER HEROES INTO A ***HIT SQUAD.***
LET HER FINISH.
OH, DON'T STOP BEING A GOOD LITTLE SOLDIER NOW, VANGUARD.
TOO LONG HAVE I HELD MY TONGUE.

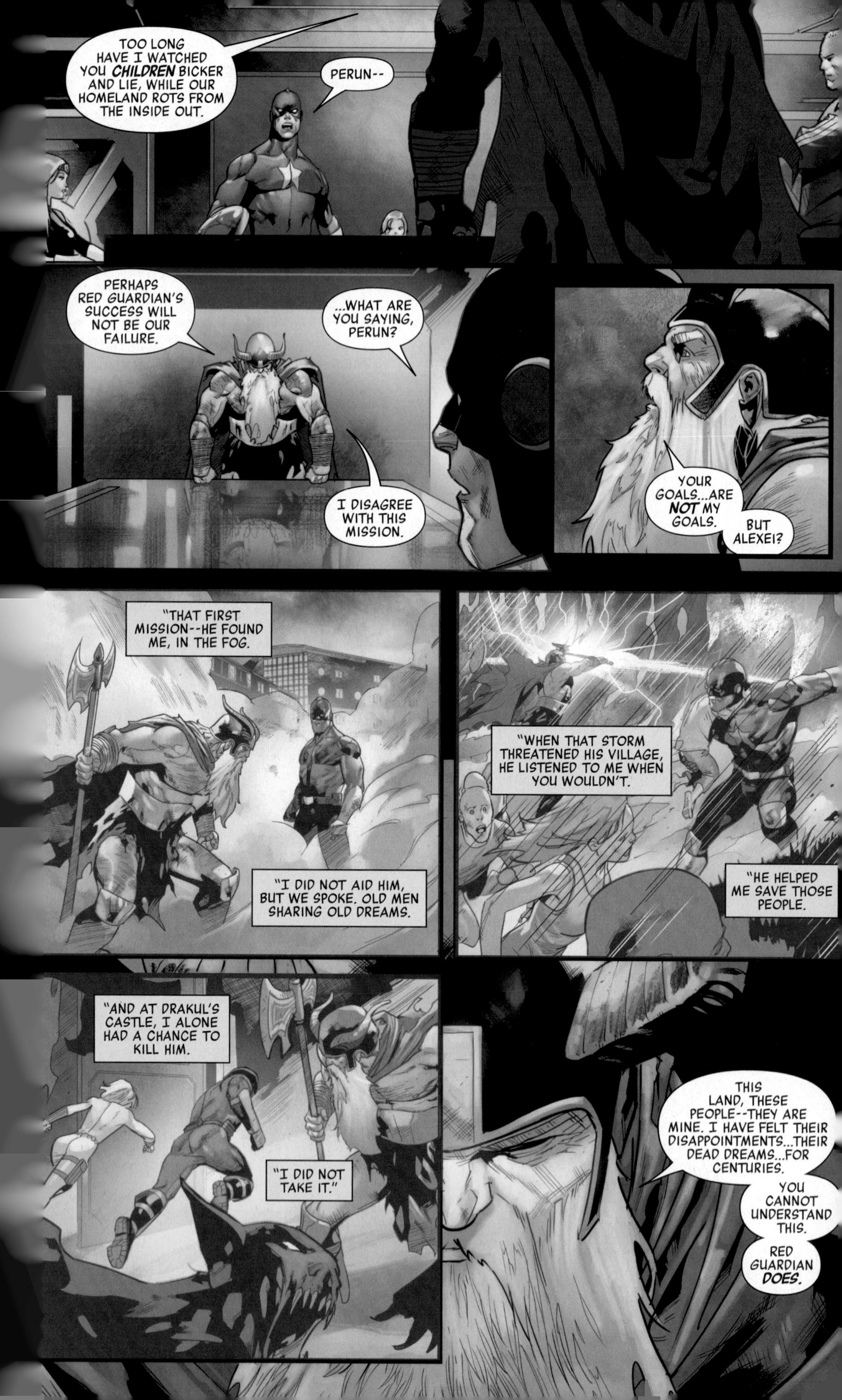

TOO LONG HAVE I WATCHED YOU CHILDREN BICKER AND LIE, WHILE OUR HOMELAND ROTS FROM THE INSIDE OUT.
PERUN--
PERHAPS RED GUARDIAN'S SUCCESS WILL NOT BE OUR FAILURE.
...WHAT ARE YOU SAYING, PERUN?
I DISAGREE WITH THIS MISSION.
YOUR GOALS...ARE NOT MY GOALS.
BUT ALEXEI?
"THAT FIRST MISSION--HE FOUND ME, IN THE FOG.
"I DID NOT AID HIM, BUT WE SPOKE. OLD MEN SHARING OLD DREAMS.
"WHEN THAT STORM THREATENED HIS VILLAGE, HE LISTENED TO ME WHEN YOU WOULDN'T.
"HE HELPED ME SAVE THOSE PEOPLE.
"AND AT DRAKUL'S CASTLE, I ALONE HAD A CHANCE TO KILL HIM.
"I DID NOT TAKE IT."
THIS LAND, THESE PEOPLE--THEY ARE MINE. I HAVE FELT THEIR DISAPPOINTMENTS...THEIR DEAD DREAMS...FOR CENTURIES.
YOU CANNOT UNDERSTAND THIS.
RED GUARDIAN DOES.

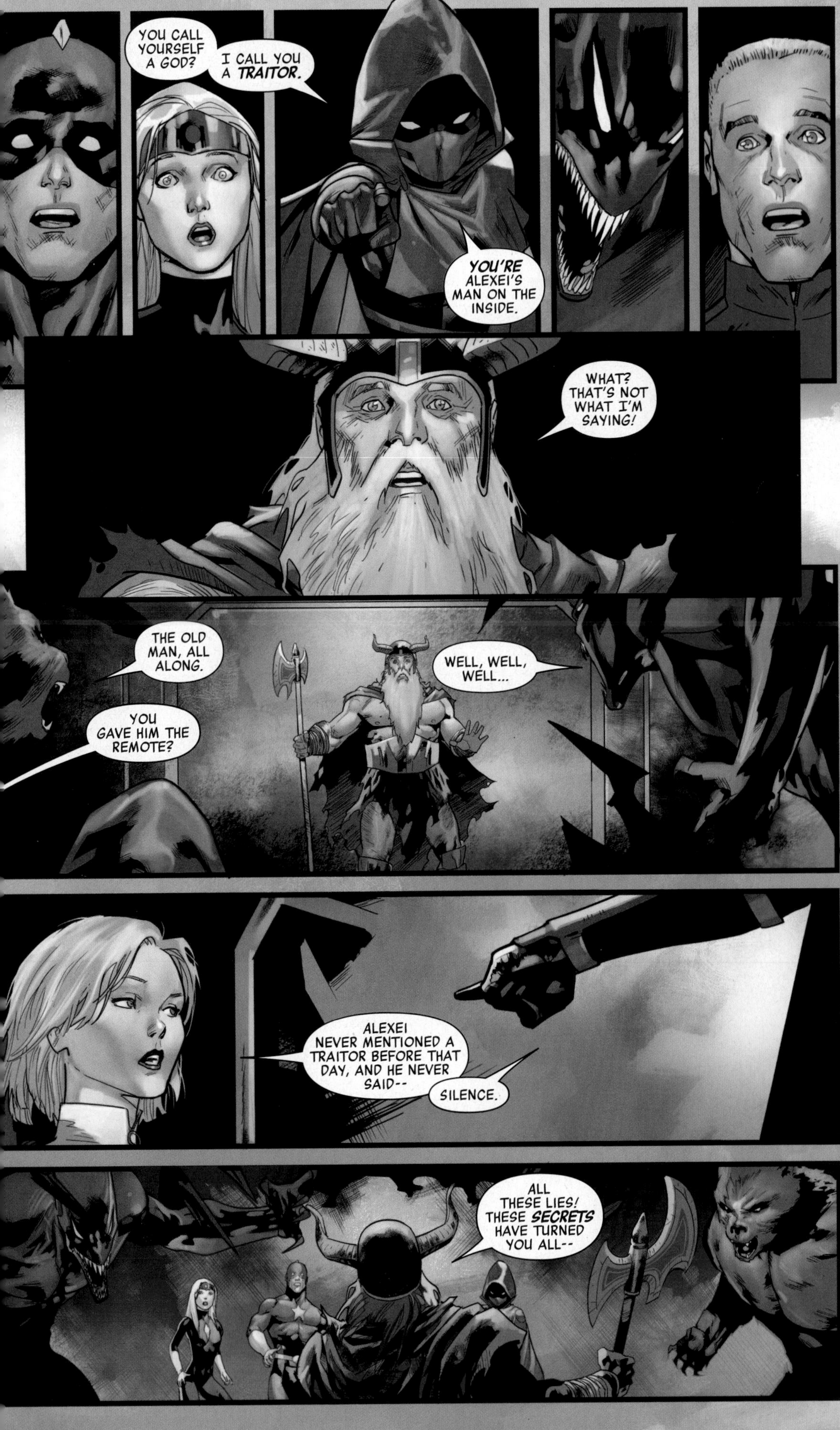

YOU CALL YOURSELF A GOD?
I CALL YOU A TRAITOR.
YOU'RE ALEXEI'S MAN ON THE INSIDE.
WHAT? THAT'S NOT WHAT I'M SAYING!
THE OLD MAN, ALL ALONG.
YOU GAVE HIM THE REMOTE?
WELL, WELL, WELL...
ALEXEI NEVER MENTIONED A TRAITOR BEFORE THAT DAY, AND HE NEVER SAID--
SILENCE.
ALL THESE LIES! THESE SECRETS HAVE TURNED YOU ALL--

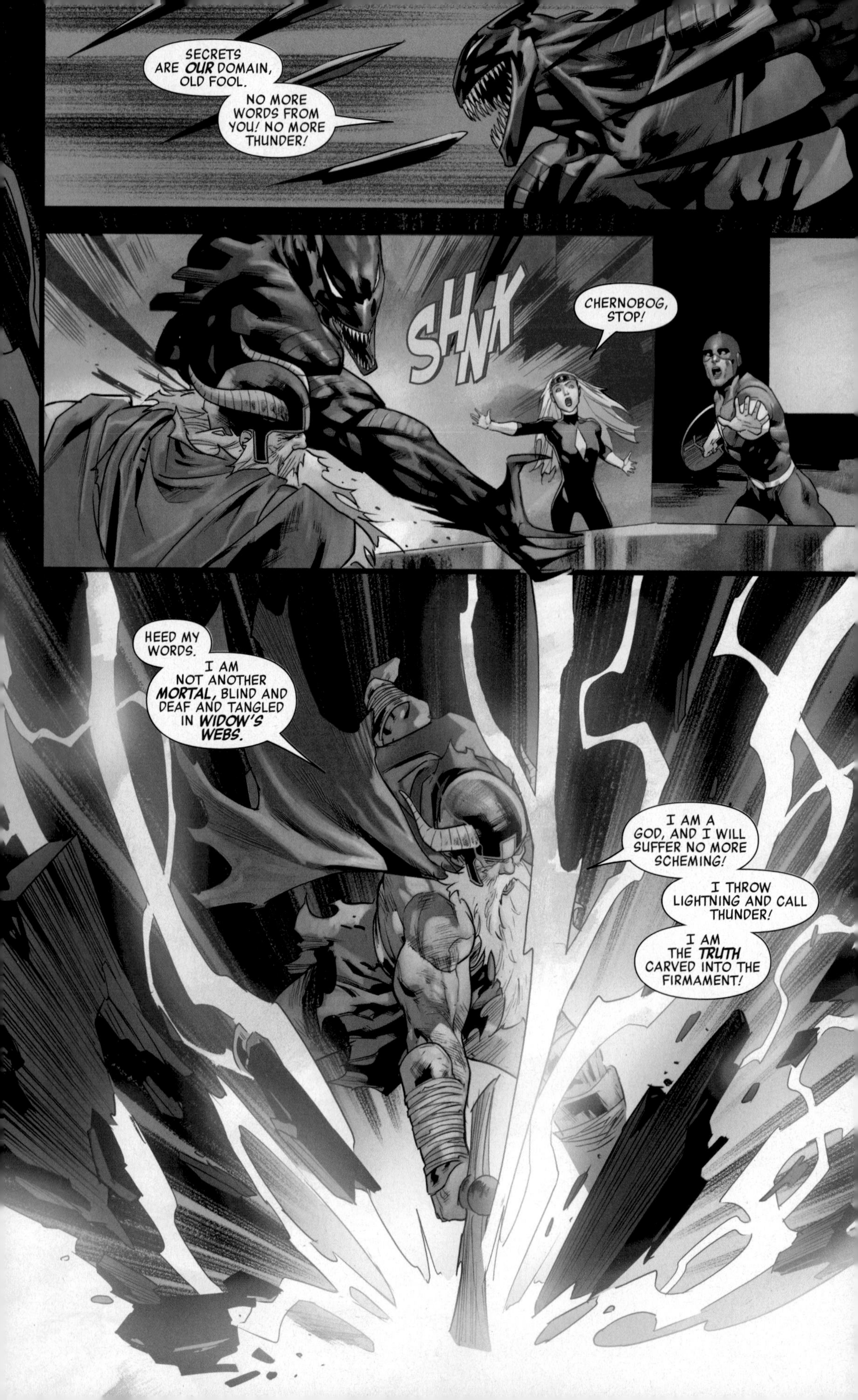

SECRETS ARE OUR DOMAIN, OLD FOOL.
NO MORE WORDS FROM YOU! NO MORE THUNDER!
SHNK
CHERNOBOG, STOP!
HEED MY WORDS.
I AM NOT ANOTHER MORTAL, BLIND AND DEAF AND TANGLED IN WIDOW'S WEBS.
I AM A GOD, AND I WILL SUFFER NO MORE SCHEMING!
I THROW LIGHTNING AND CALL THUNDER!
I AM THE TRUTH CARVED INTO THE FIRMAMENT!

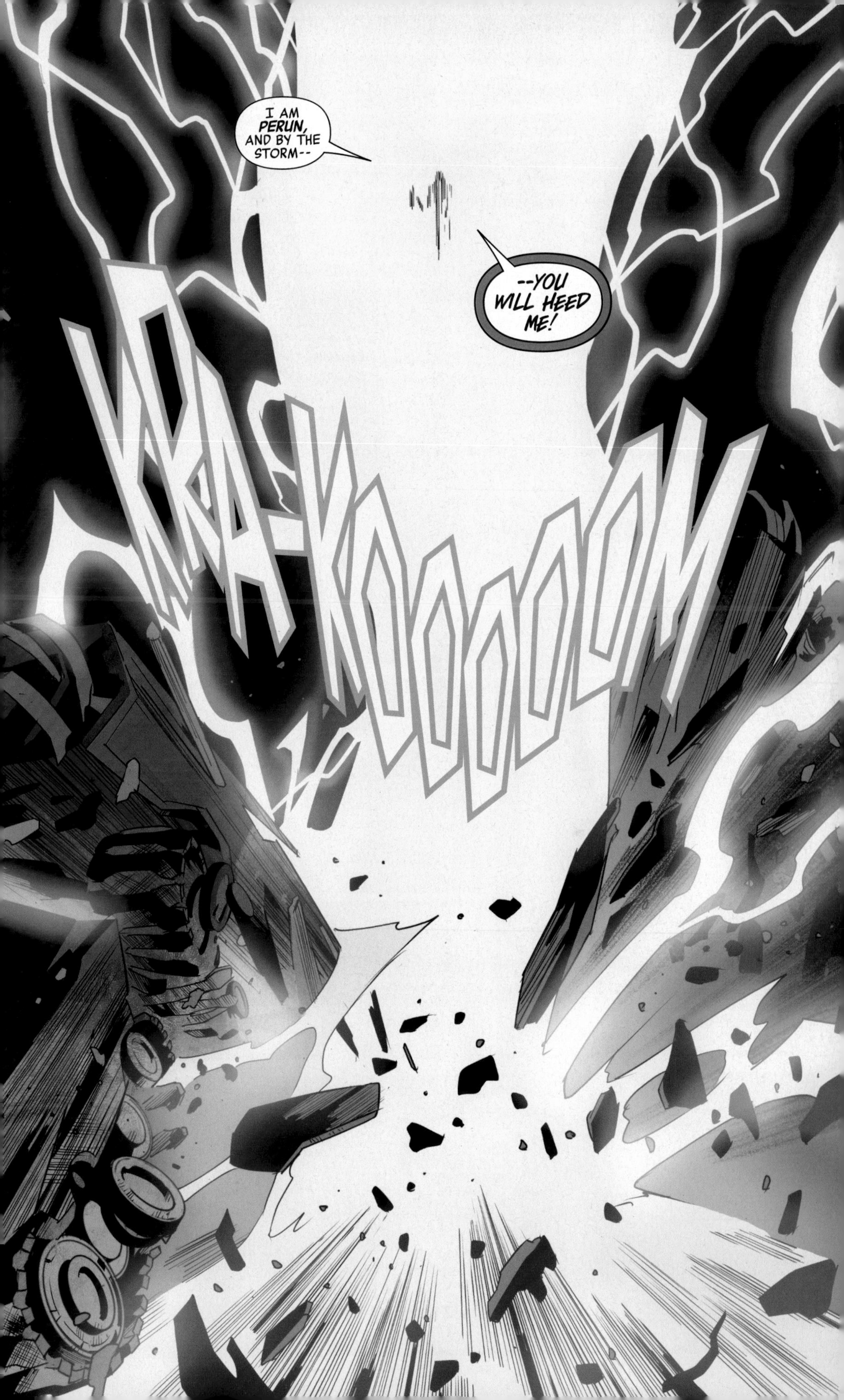

I AM PERUN, AND BY THE STORM--
--YOU WILL HEED ME!
KRA-KOOOOOOM

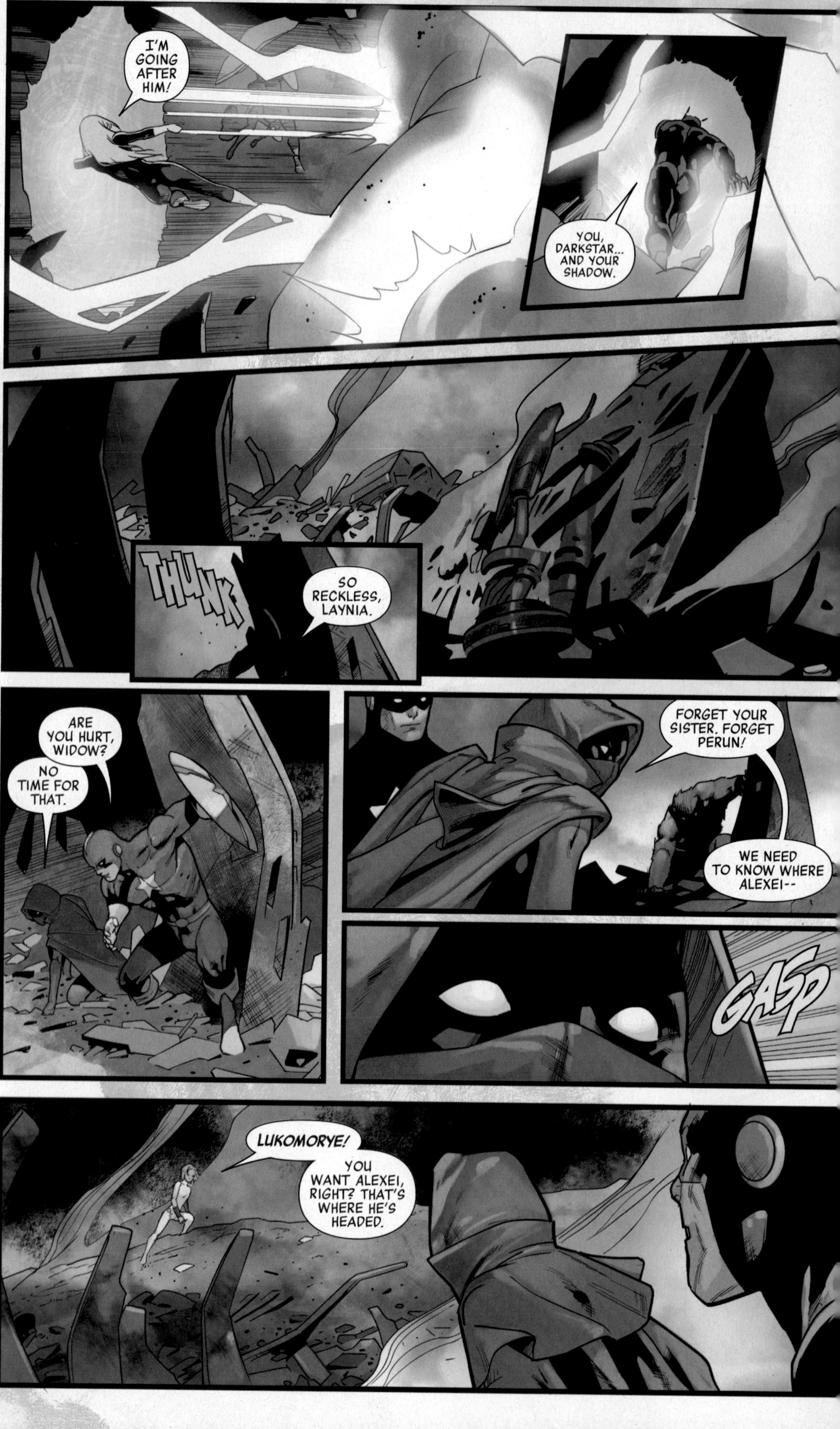
I'M GOING AFTER HIM!
YOU, DARKSTAR... AND YOUR SHADOW.
THUNK
SO RECKLESS, LAYNIA.
ARE YOU HURT, WIDOW?
NO TIME FOR THAT.
FORGET YOUR SISTER. FORGET PERUN!
WE NEED TO KNOW WHERE ALEXEI--
GASP
LUKOMORYE!
YOU WANT ALEXEI, RIGHT? THAT'S WHERE HE'S HEADED.

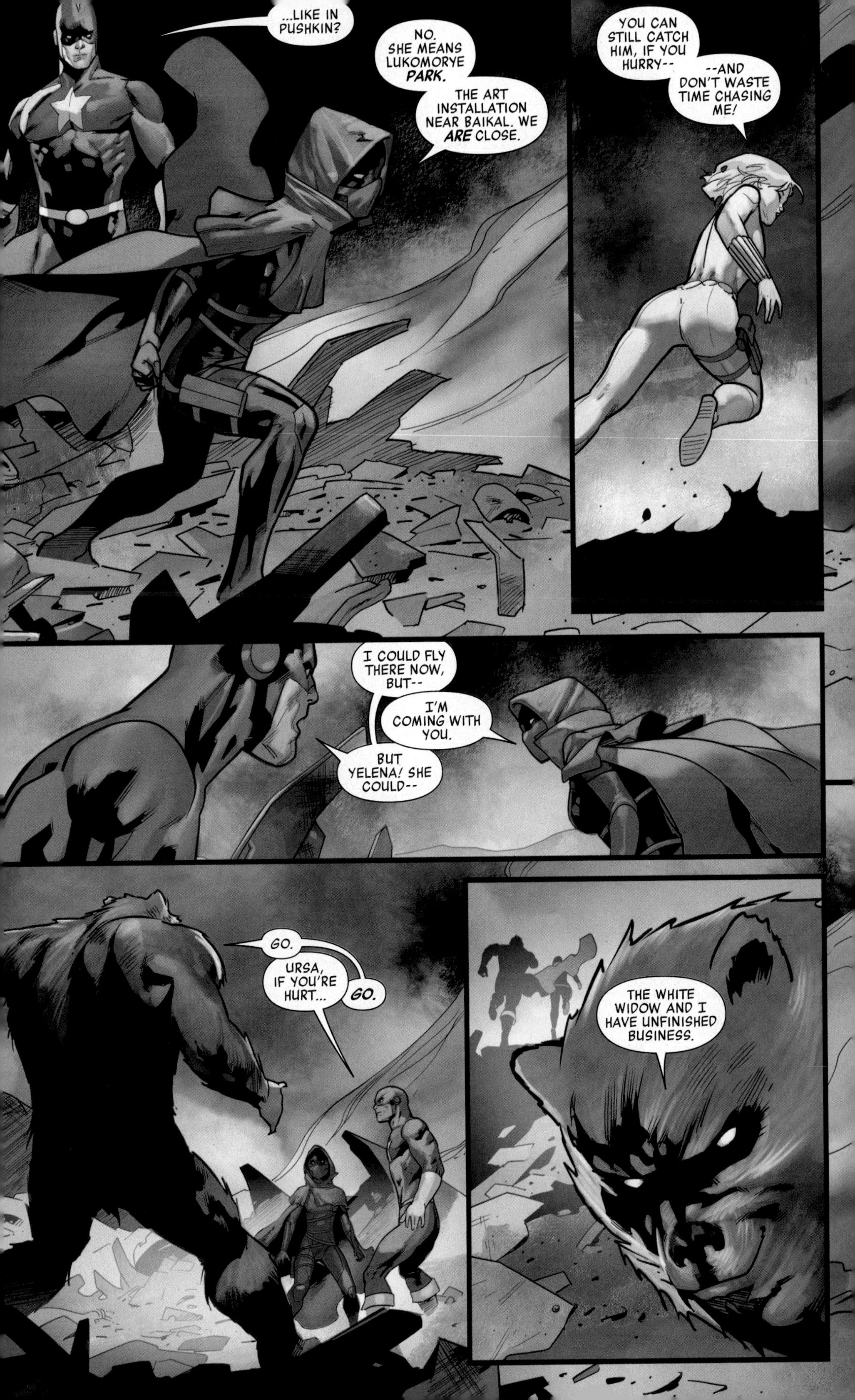
...LIKE IN PUSHKIN?
NO. SHE MEANS LUKOMORYE **PARK.**
THE ART INSTALLATION NEAR BAIKAL. WE **ARE** CLOSE.
YOU CAN STILL CATCH HIM, IF YOU HURRY--
--AND DON'T WASTE TIME CHASING ME!
I COULD FLY THERE NOW, BUT--
I'M COMING WITH YOU.
BUT YELENA! SHE COULD--
GO.
URSA, IF YOU'RE HURT...
GO.
THE WHITE WIDOW AND I HAVE UNFINISHED BUSINESS.

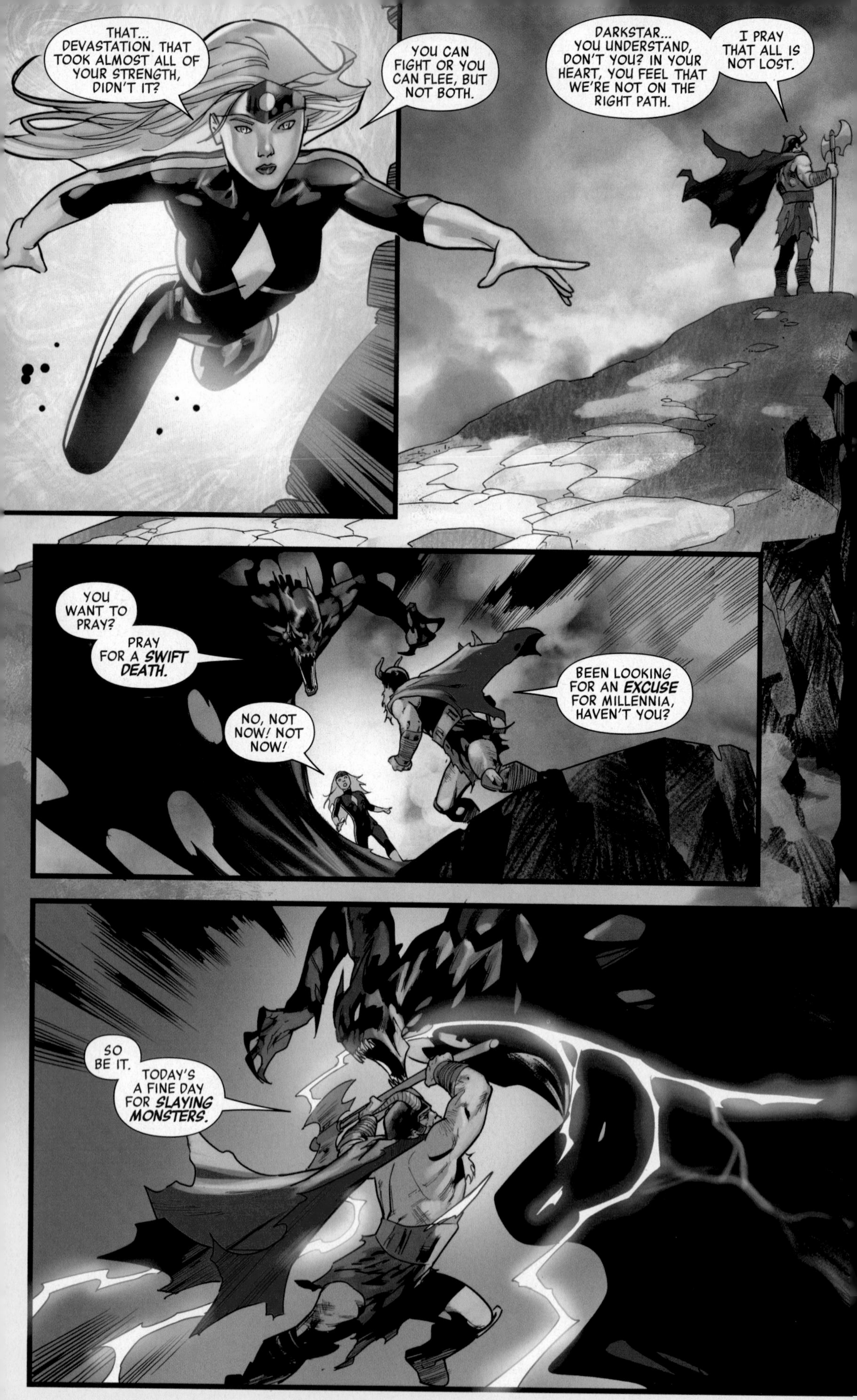

THAT... DEVASTATION. THAT TOOK ALMOST ALL OF YOUR STRENGTH, DIDN'T IT?
YOU CAN FIGHT OR YOU CAN FLEE, BUT NOT BOTH.
DARKSTAR... YOU UNDERSTAND, DON'T YOU? IN YOUR HEART, YOU FEEL THAT WE'RE NOT ON THE RIGHT PATH.
I PRAY THAT ALL IS NOT LOST.
YOU WANT TO PRAY?
PRAY FOR A *SWIFT DEATH.*
BEEN LOOKING FOR AN *EXCUSE* FOR MILLENNIA, HAVEN'T YOU?
NO, NOT NOW! NOT NOW!
SO BE IT.
TODAY'S A FINE DAY FOR *SLAYING MONSTERS*.

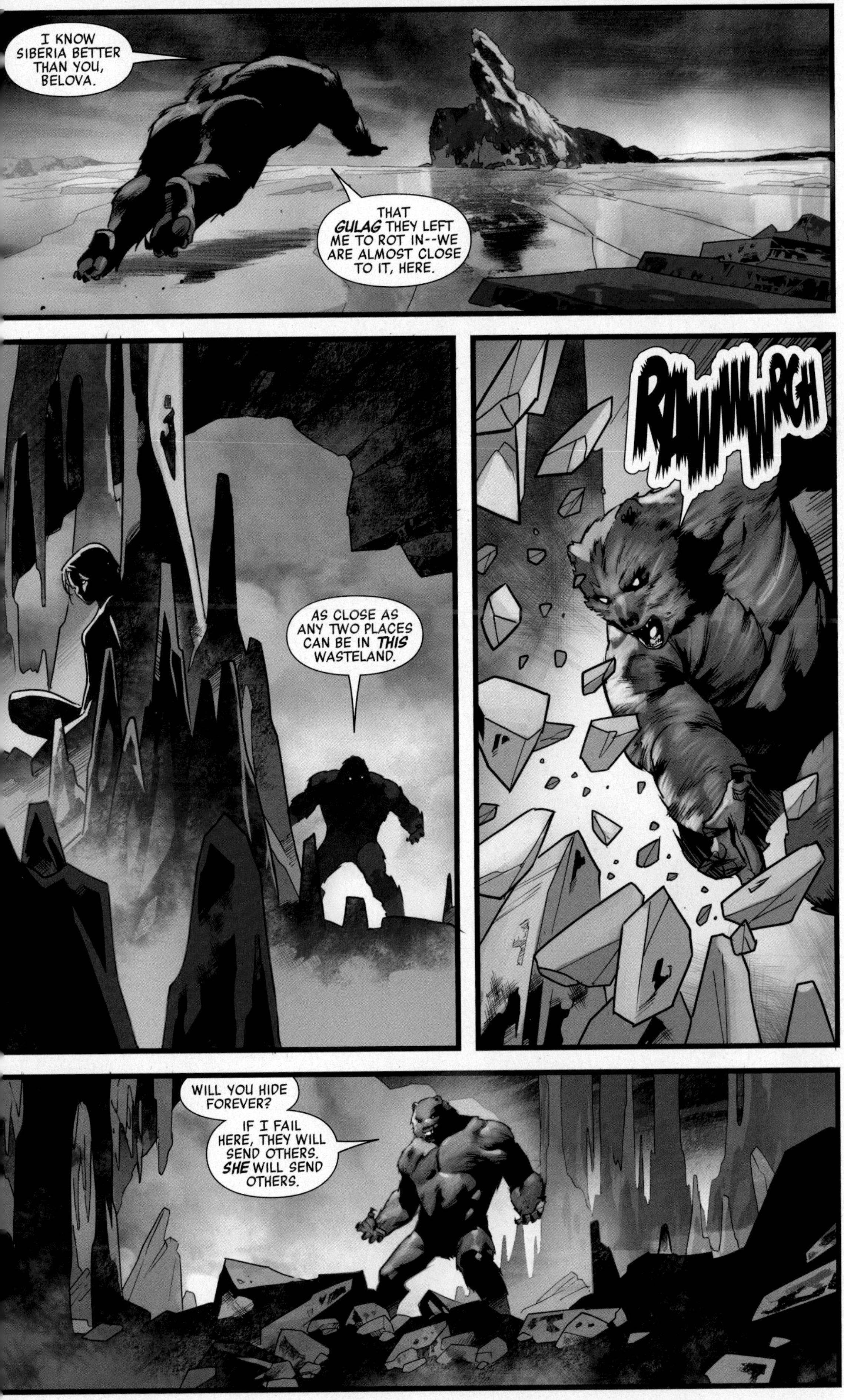
I KNOW SIBERIA BETTER THAN YOU, BELOVA.
THAT GULAG THEY LEFT ME TO ROT IN--WE ARE ALMOST CLOSE TO IT, HERE.
AS CLOSE AS ANY TWO PLACES CAN BE IN THIS WASTELAND.
RAWWWRGH
WILL YOU HIDE FOREVER?
IF I FAIL HERE, THEY WILL SEND OTHERS. SHE WILL SEND OTHERS.

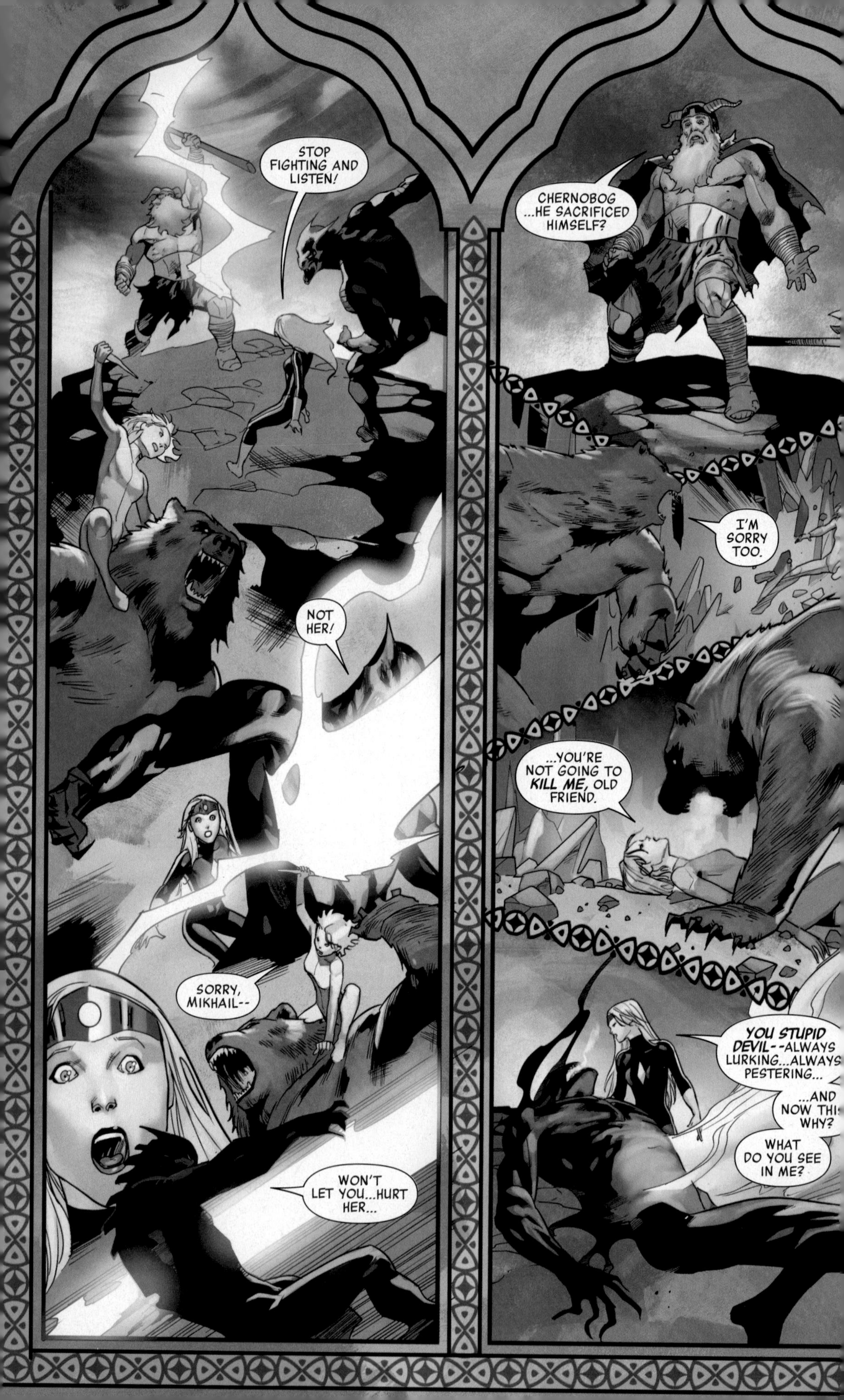
STOP FIGHTING AND LISTEN!
NOT HER!
SORRY, MIKHAIL--
WON'T LET YOU...HURT HER...
CHERNOBOG ...HE SACRIFICED HIMSELF?
I'M SORRY TOO.
...YOU'RE NOT GOING TO KILL ME, OLD FRIEND.
YOU STUPID DEVIL--ALWAYS LURKING...ALWAYS PESTERING...
...AND NOW THIS WHY?
WHAT DO YOU SEE IN ME?

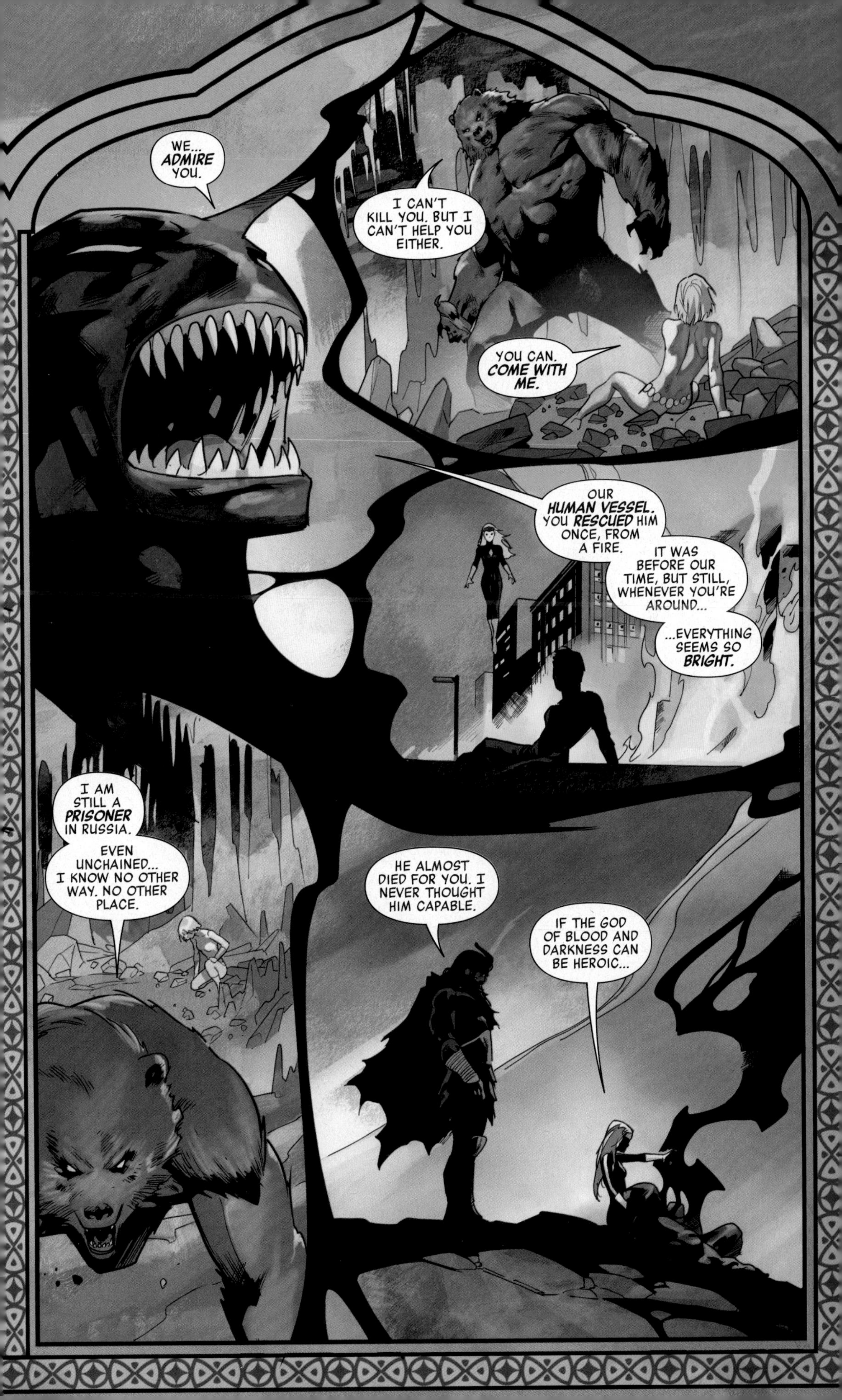
WE... ADMIRE YOU.
I CAN'T KILL YOU. BUT I CAN'T HELP YOU EITHER.
YOU CAN. COME WITH ME.
OUR HUMAN VESSEL. YOU RESCUED HIM ONCE, FROM A FIRE.
IT WAS BEFORE OUR TIME, BUT STILL, WHENEVER YOU'RE AROUND...
...EVERYTHING SEEMS SO BRIGHT.
I AM STILL A PRISONER IN RUSSIA.
EVEN UNCHAINED... I KNOW NO OTHER WAY. NO OTHER PLACE.
HE ALMOST DIED FOR YOU. I NEVER THOUGHT HIM CAPABLE.
IF THE GOD OF BLOOD AND DARKNESS CAN BE HEROIC...

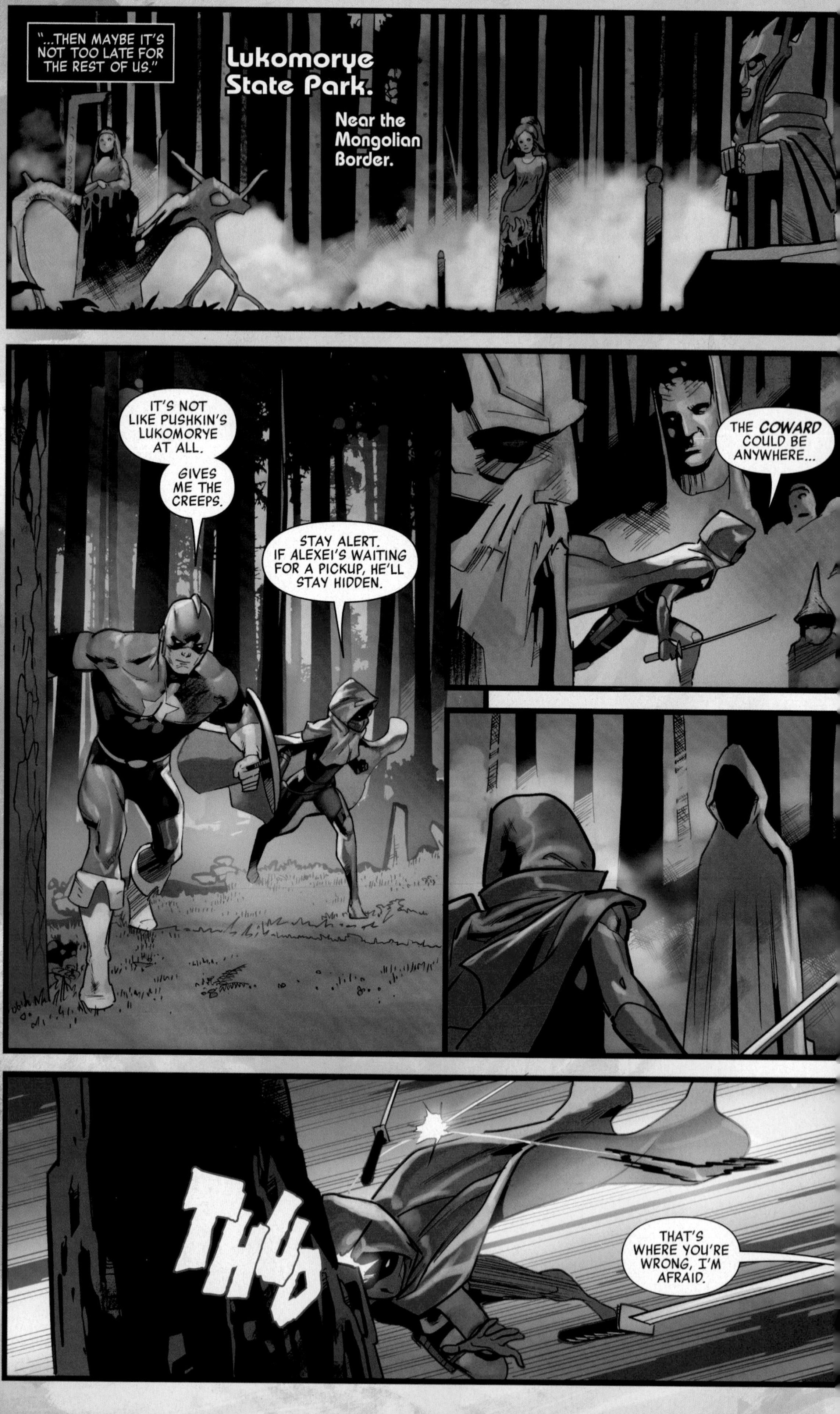
"...THEN MAYBE IT'S NOT TOO LATE FOR THE REST OF US."
Lukomorye State Park.
Near the Mongolian Border.
IT'S NOT LIKE PUSHKIN'S LUKOMORYE AT ALL.
GIVES ME THE CREEPS.
STAY ALERT. IF ALEXEI'S WAITING FOR A PICKUP, HE'LL STAY HIDDEN.
THE COWARD COULD BE ANYWHERE...
THUD
THAT'S WHERE YOU'RE WRONG, I'M AFRAID.

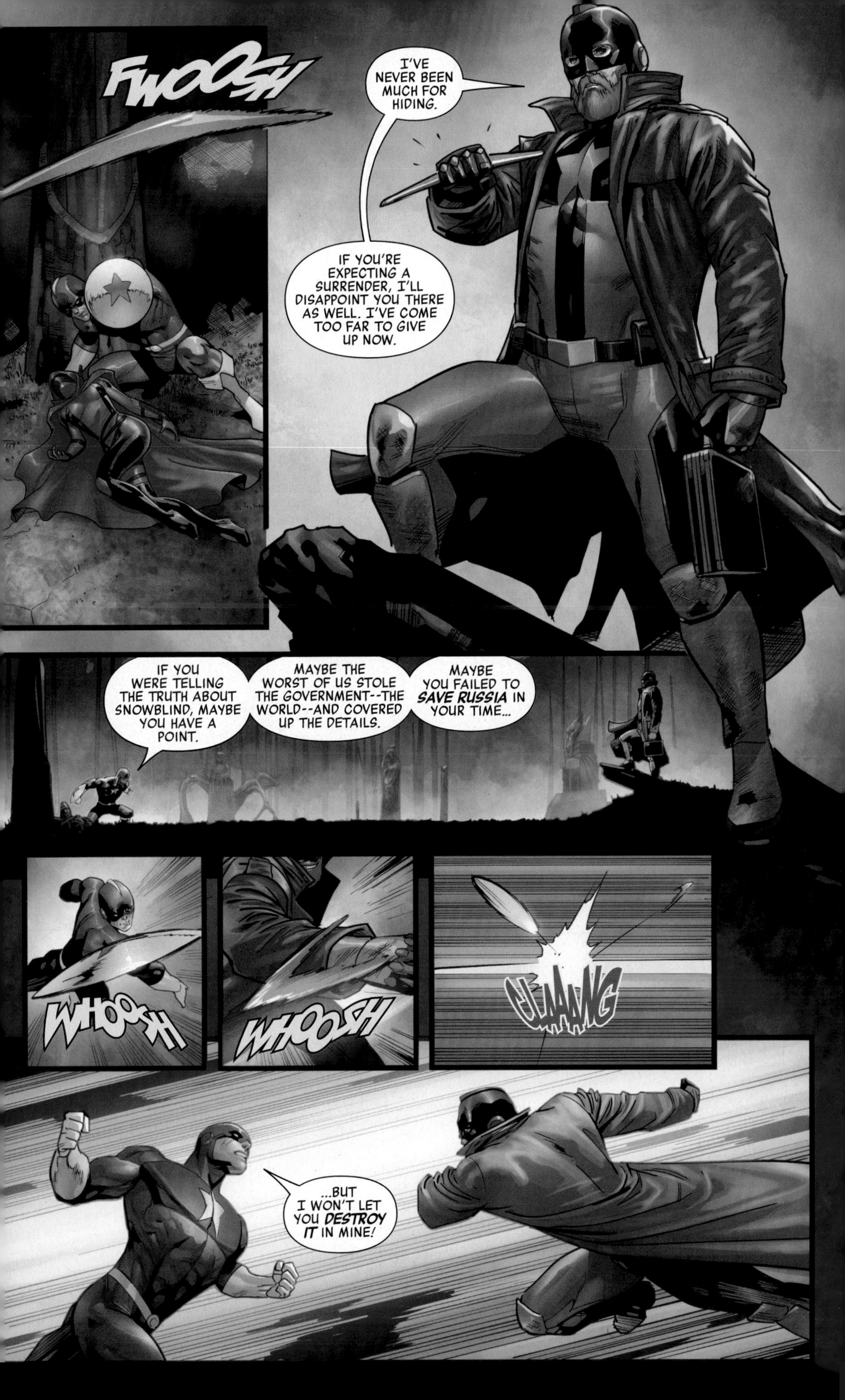
FWOOSH
I'VE NEVER BEEN MUCH FOR HIDING.
IF YOU'RE EXPECTING A SURRENDER, I'LL DISAPPOINT YOU THERE AS WELL. I'VE COME TOO FAR TO GIVE UP NOW.
IF YOU WERE TELLING THE TRUTH ABOUT SNOWBLIND, MAYBE YOU HAVE A POINT.
MAYBE THE WORST OF US STOLE THE GOVERNMENT--THE WORLD--AND COVERED UP THE DETAILS.
MAYBE YOU FAILED TO SAVE RUSSIA IN YOUR TIME...
WHOOSH
WHOOSH
CLAAANG
...BUT I WON'T LET YOU DESTROY IT IN MINE!

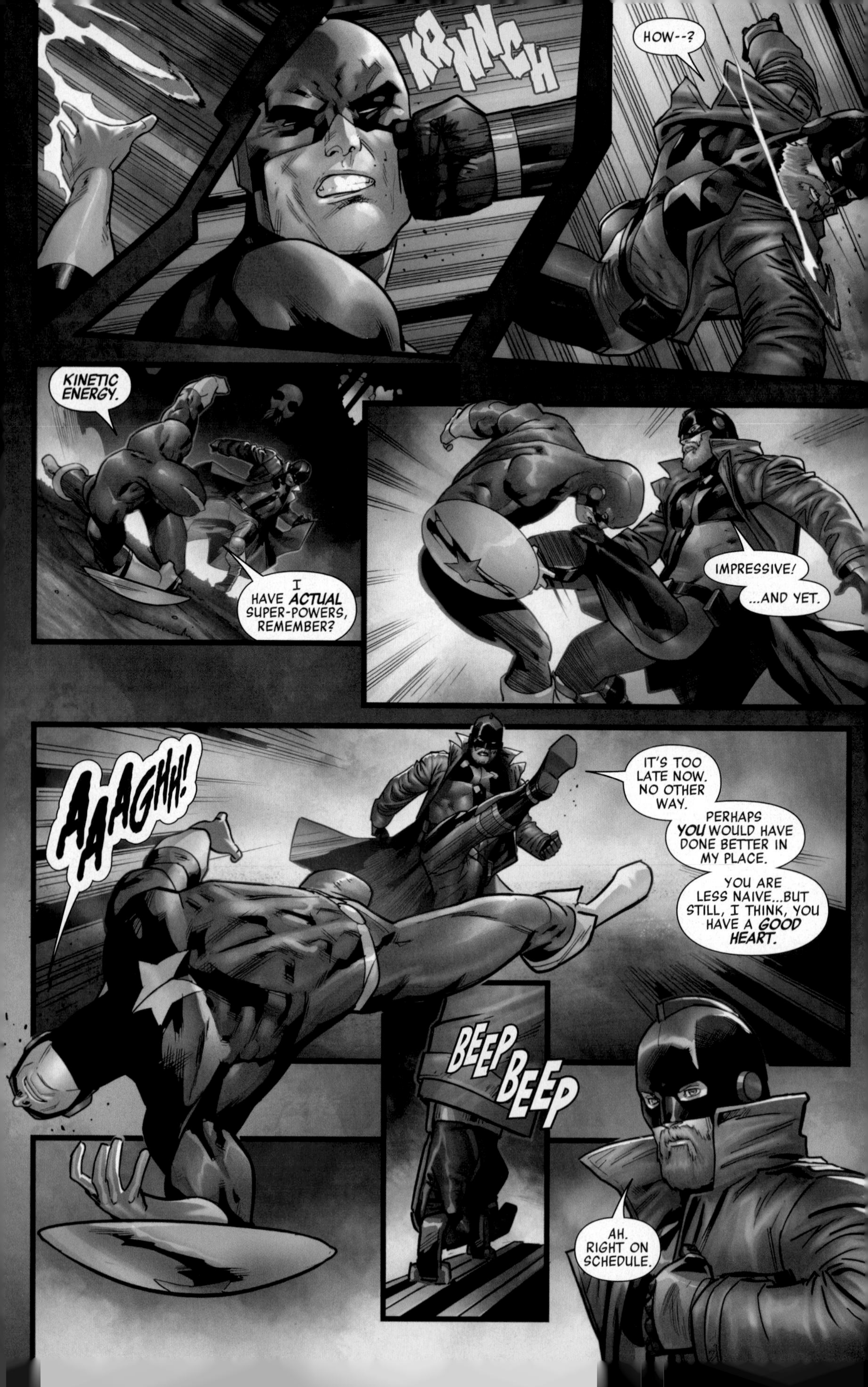
KRNNCH
HOW--?
KINETIC ENERGY.
I HAVE ACTUAL SUPER-POWERS, REMEMBER?
IMPRESSIVE!
...AND YET.
AAAGHH!
IT'S TOO LATE NOW. NO OTHER WAY.
PERHAPS YOU WOULD HAVE DONE BETTER IN MY PLACE.
YOU ARE LESS NAIVE...BUT STILL, I THINK, YOU HAVE A GOOD HEART.
BEEP BEEP
AH. RIGHT ON SCHEDULE.

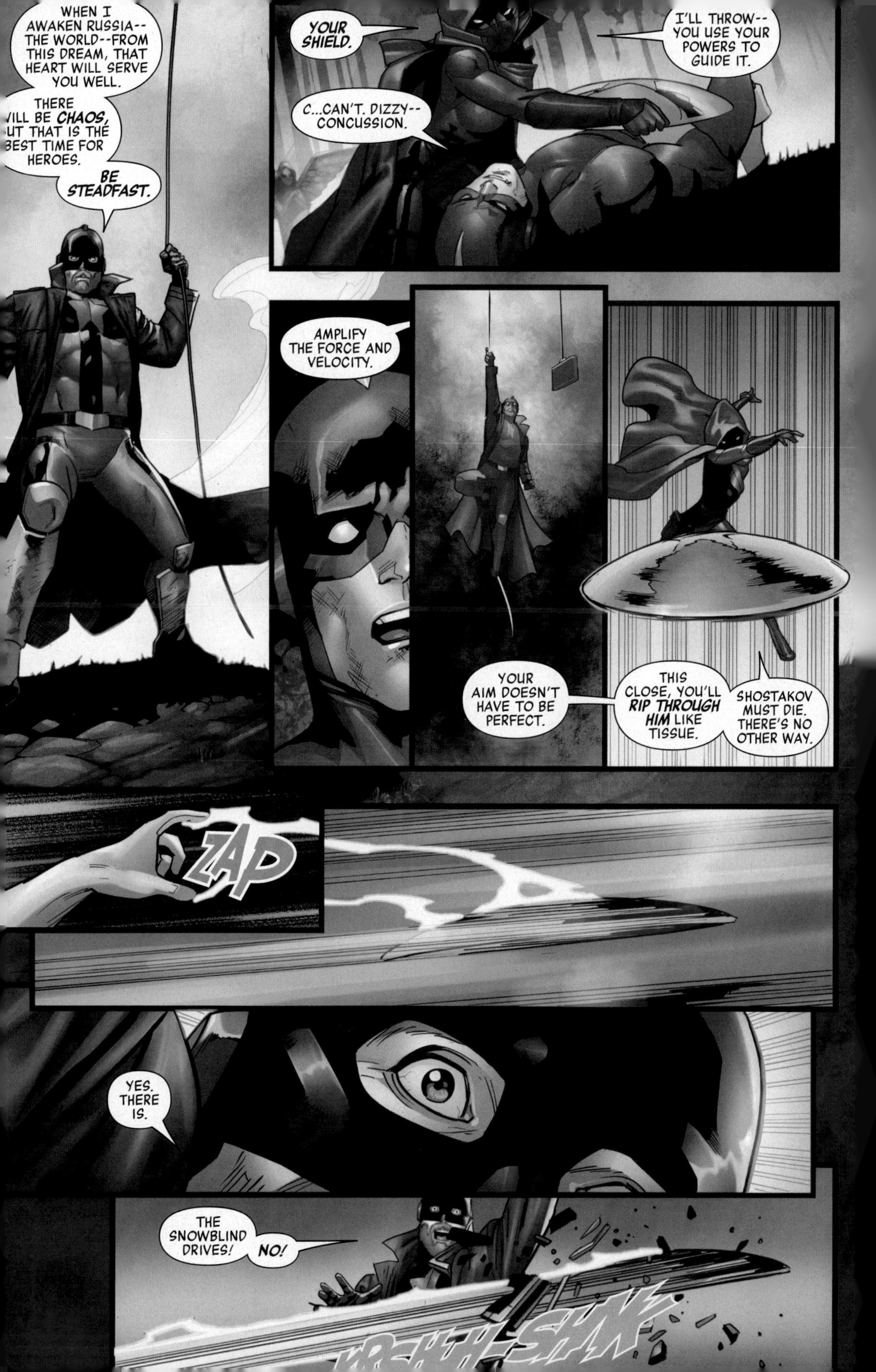
WHEN I AWAKEN RUSSIA--THE WORLD--FROM THIS DREAM, THAT HEART WILL SERVE YOU WELL.
THERE WILL BE CHAOS, BUT THAT IS THE BEST TIME FOR HEROES.
BE STEADFAST.
YOUR SHIELD.
I'LL THROW--YOU USE YOUR POWERS TO GUIDE IT.
C...CAN'T. DIZZY--CONCUSSION.
AMPLIFY THE FORCE AND VELOCITY.
YOUR AIM DOESN'T HAVE TO BE PERFECT.
THIS CLOSE, YOU'LL RIP THROUGH HIM LIKE TISSUE.
SHOSTAKOV MUST DIE. THERE'S NO OTHER WAY.
ZAP
YES. THERE IS.
THE SNOWBLIND DRIVES!
NO!

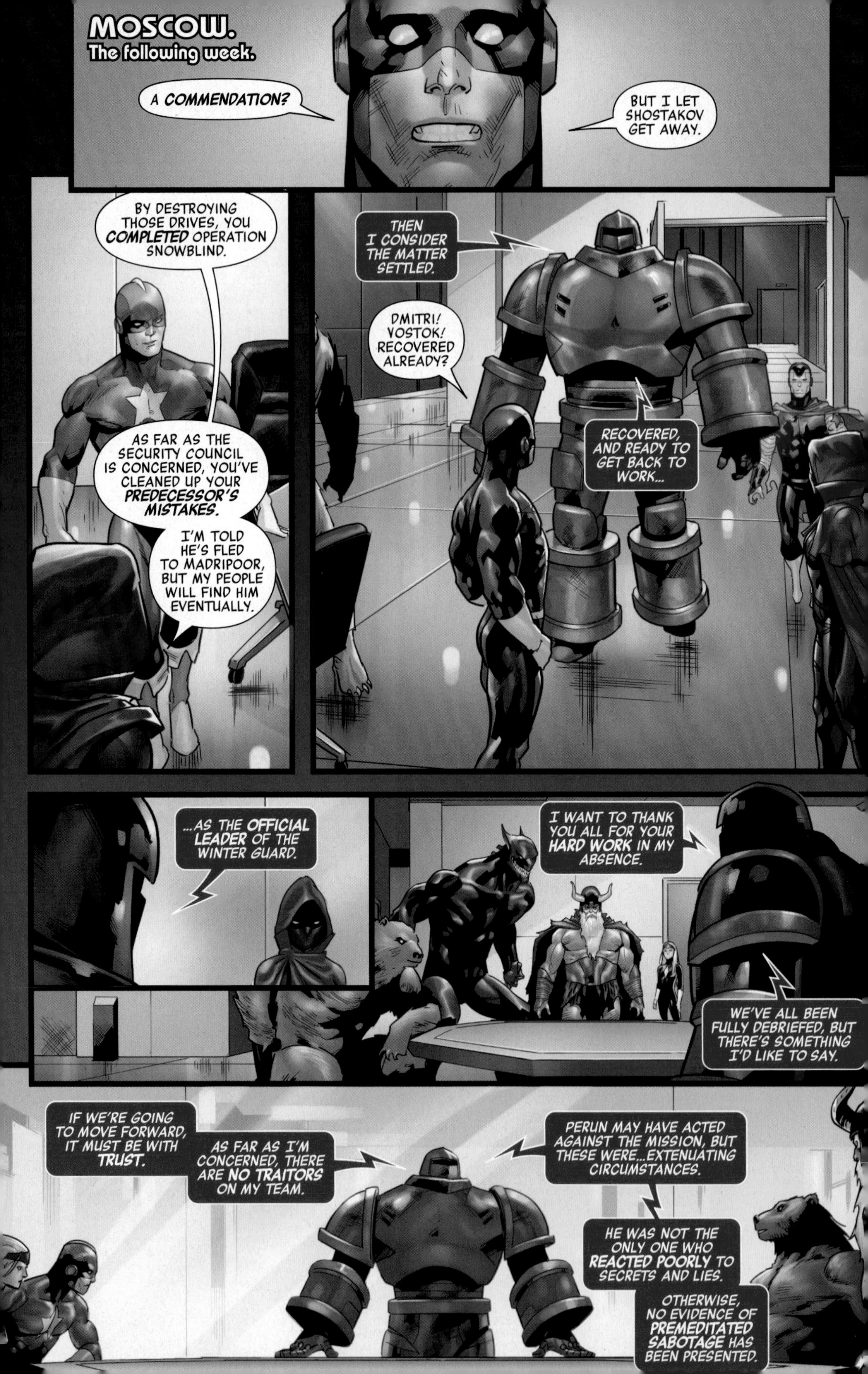
MOSCOW.
The following week.
A COMMENDATION?
BUT I LET SHOSTAKOV GET AWAY.
BY DESTROYING THOSE DRIVES, YOU COMPLETED OPERATION SNOWBLIND.
AS FAR AS THE SECURITY COUNCIL IS CONCERNED, YOU'VE CLEANED UP YOUR PREDECESSOR'S MISTAKES.
I'M TOLD HE'S FLED TO MADRIPOOR, BUT MY PEOPLE WILL FIND HIM EVENTUALLY.
THEN I CONSIDER THE MATTER SETTLED.
DMITRI! VOSTOK! RECOVERED ALREADY?
RECOVERED, AND READY TO GET BACK TO WORK...
...AS THE OFFICIAL LEADER OF THE WINTER GUARD.
I WANT TO THANK YOU ALL FOR YOUR HARD WORK IN MY ABSENCE.
WE'VE ALL BEEN FULLY DEBRIEFED, BUT THERE'S SOMETHING I'D LIKE TO SAY.
IF WE'RE GOING TO MOVE FORWARD, IT MUST BE WITH TRUST.
AS FAR AS I'M CONCERNED, THERE ARE NO TRAITORS ON MY TEAM.
PERUN MAY HAVE ACTED AGAINST THE MISSION, BUT THESE WERE...EXTENUATING CIRCUMSTANCES.
HE WAS NOT THE ONLY ONE WHO REACTED POORLY TO SECRETS AND LIES.
OTHERWISE, NO EVIDENCE OF PREMEDITATED SABOTAGE HAS BEEN PRESENTED.

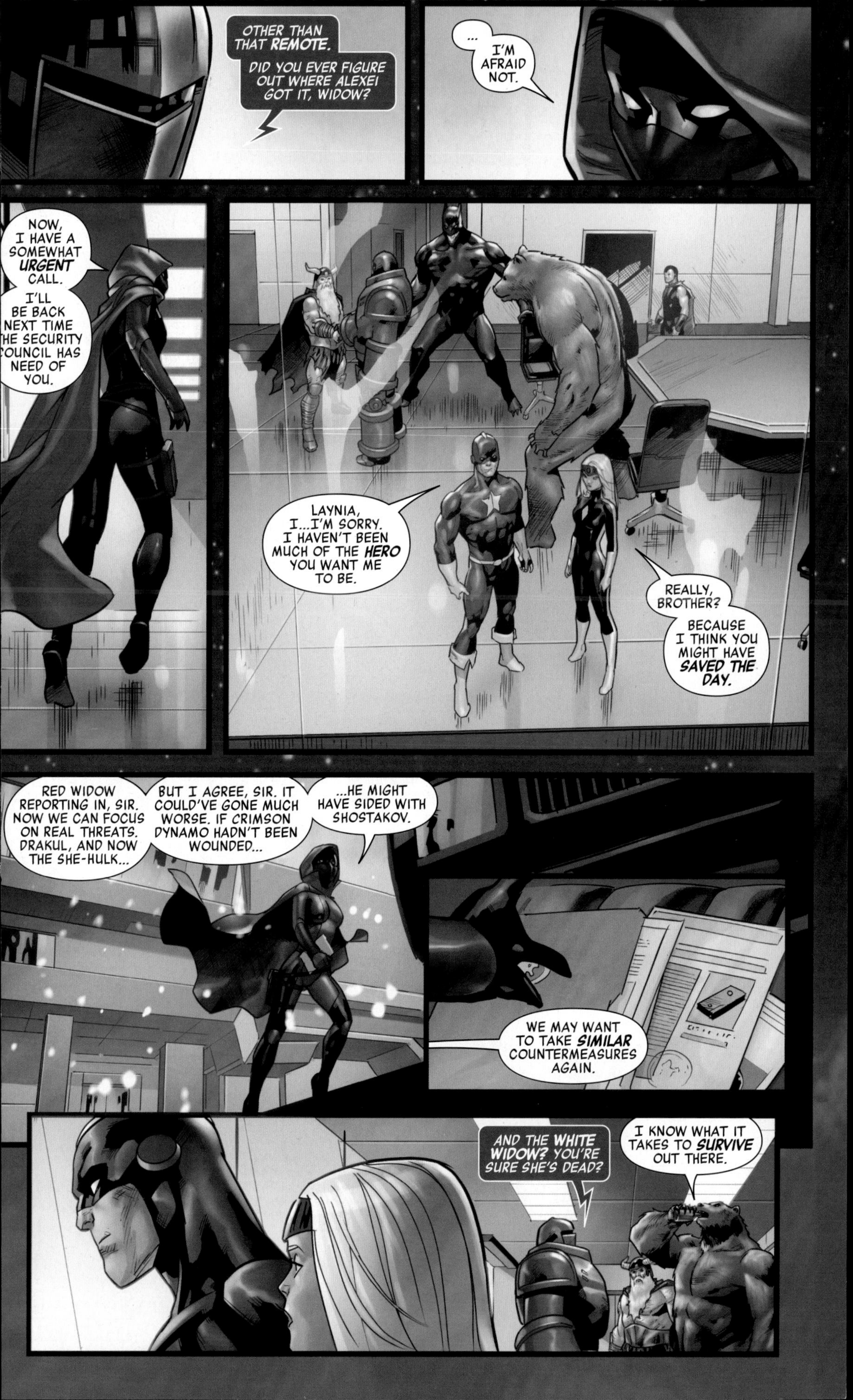
OTHER THAN THAT REMOTE.
DID YOU EVER FIGURE OUT WHERE ALEXEI GOT IT, WIDOW?
...
I'M AFRAID NOT.
NOW, I HAVE A SOMEWHAT URGENT CALL.
I'LL BE BACK NEXT TIME THE SECURITY COUNCIL HAS NEED OF YOU.
LAYNIA, I...I'M SORRY. I HAVEN'T BEEN MUCH OF THE HERO YOU WANT ME TO BE.
REALLY, BROTHER?
BECAUSE I THINK YOU MIGHT HAVE SAVED THE DAY.
RED WIDOW REPORTING IN, SIR. NOW WE CAN FOCUS ON REAL THREATS. DRAKUL, AND NOW THE SHE-HULK...
BUT I AGREE, SIR. IT COULD'VE GONE MUCH WORSE. IF CRIMSON DYNAMO HADN'T BEEN WOUNDED...
...HE MIGHT HAVE SIDED WITH SHOSTAKOV.
WE MAY WANT TO TAKE SIMILAR COUNTERMEASURES AGAIN.
AND THE WHITE WIDOW? YOU'RE SURE SHE'S DEAD?
I KNOW WHAT IT TAKES TO SURVIVE OUT THERE.

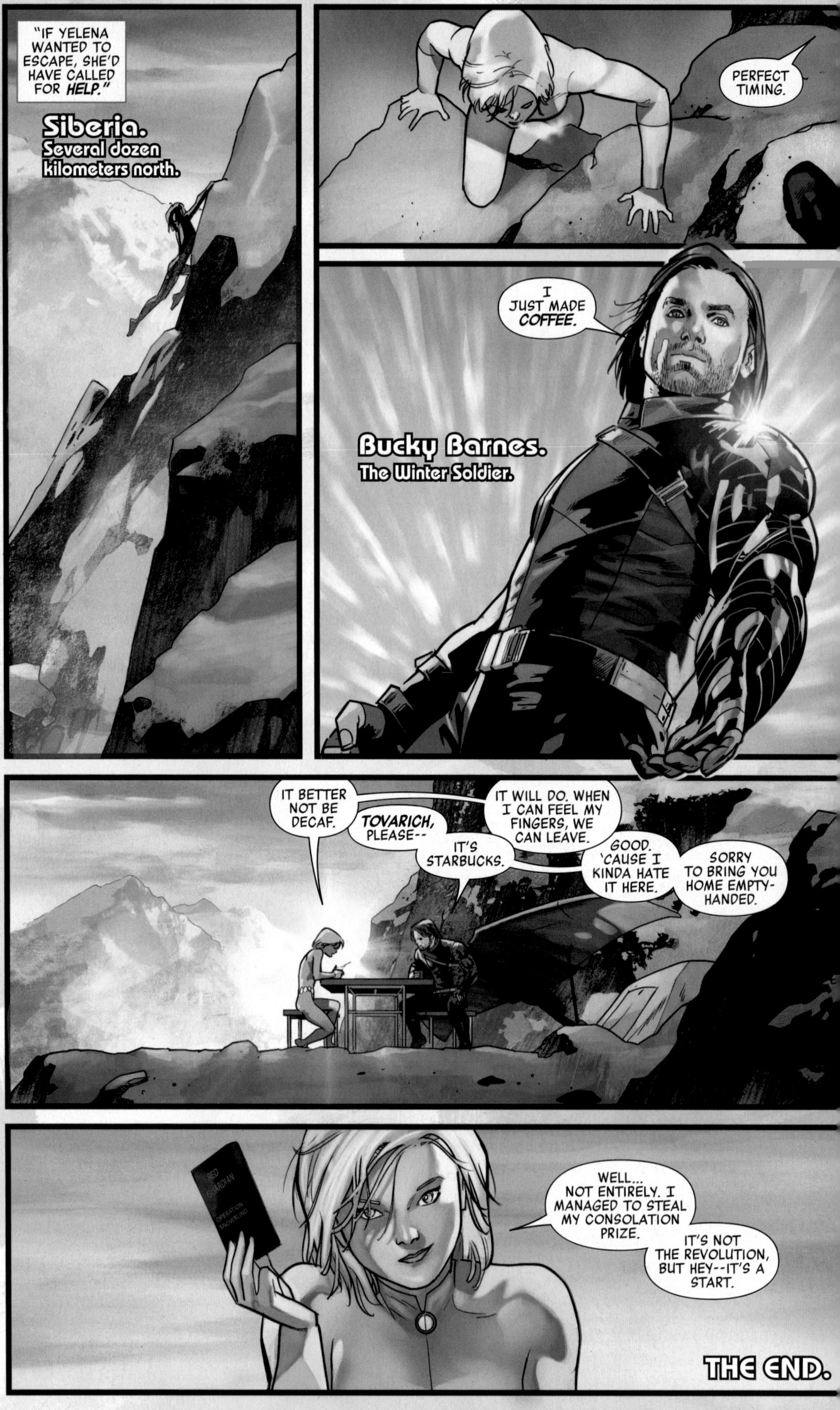

"IF YELENA WANTED TO ESCAPE, SHE'D HAVE CALLED FOR HELP."
Siberia. Several dozen kilometers north.
PERFECT TIMING.
I JUST MADE COFFEE.
Bucky Barnes. The Winter Soldier.
IT BETTER NOT BE DECAF.
IT WILL DO. WHEN I CAN FEEL MY FINGERS, WE CAN LEAVE.
TOVARICH, PLEASE--
IT'S STARBUCKS.
GOOD. 'CAUSE I KINDA HATE IT HERE.
SORRY TO BRING YOU HOME EMPTY-HANDED.
RED GUARDIAN
OPERATION SNOWBLIND
WELL... NOT ENTIRELY. I MANAGED TO STEAL MY CONSOLATION PRIZE.
IT'S NOT THE REVOLUTION, BUT HEY--IT'S A START.
THE END.

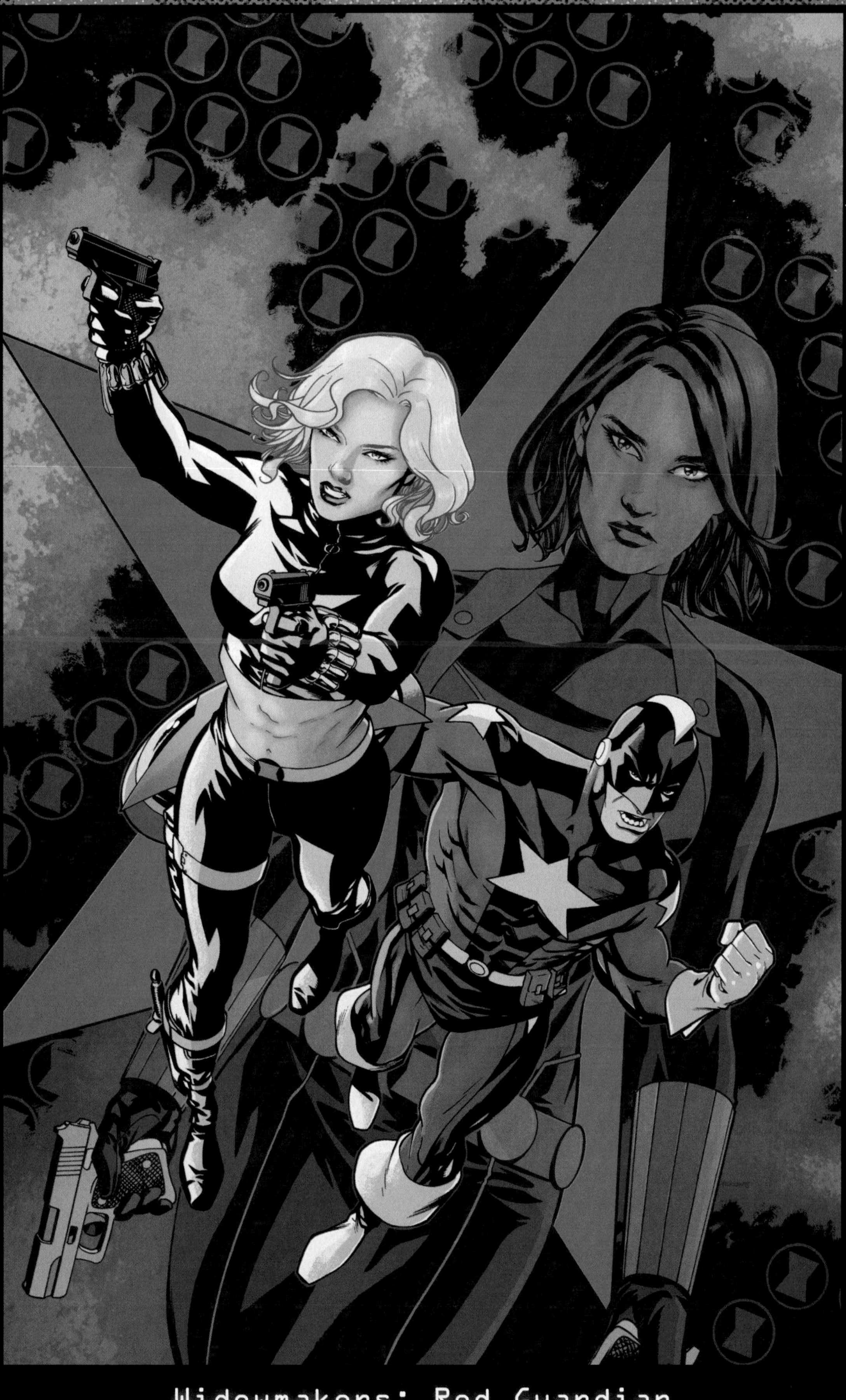

Widowmakers: Red Guardian and Yelena Belova

WIDOWMAKERS
RED GUARDIAN AND YELENA BELOVA

Alexei Shostakov – A.K.A. the Red Guardian
– is a former test pilot and intelligence agent of
the Soviet Union...and Natasha Romanoff's former
husband. After several faked deaths and other
painful intrigues, Alexei attempted a worldwide power
grab that brought him head-to-head with his ex-wife –
and the Black Widow won. He was arrested by S.H.I.E.L.D.
and placed in custody. But S.H.I.E.L.D. no longer exists...

Yelena Belova is a graduate of the Red Room who once
tried to replace Natasha Romanoff as Russia's premier spy.
She failed, but over the course of her journey, she realized
that Natasha was not her true enemy. She's fought both for
and against the Avengers and their many villains – most recently
helping Natasha take down the remnants of the Red Room – but
ultimately, Belova's only master is herself.

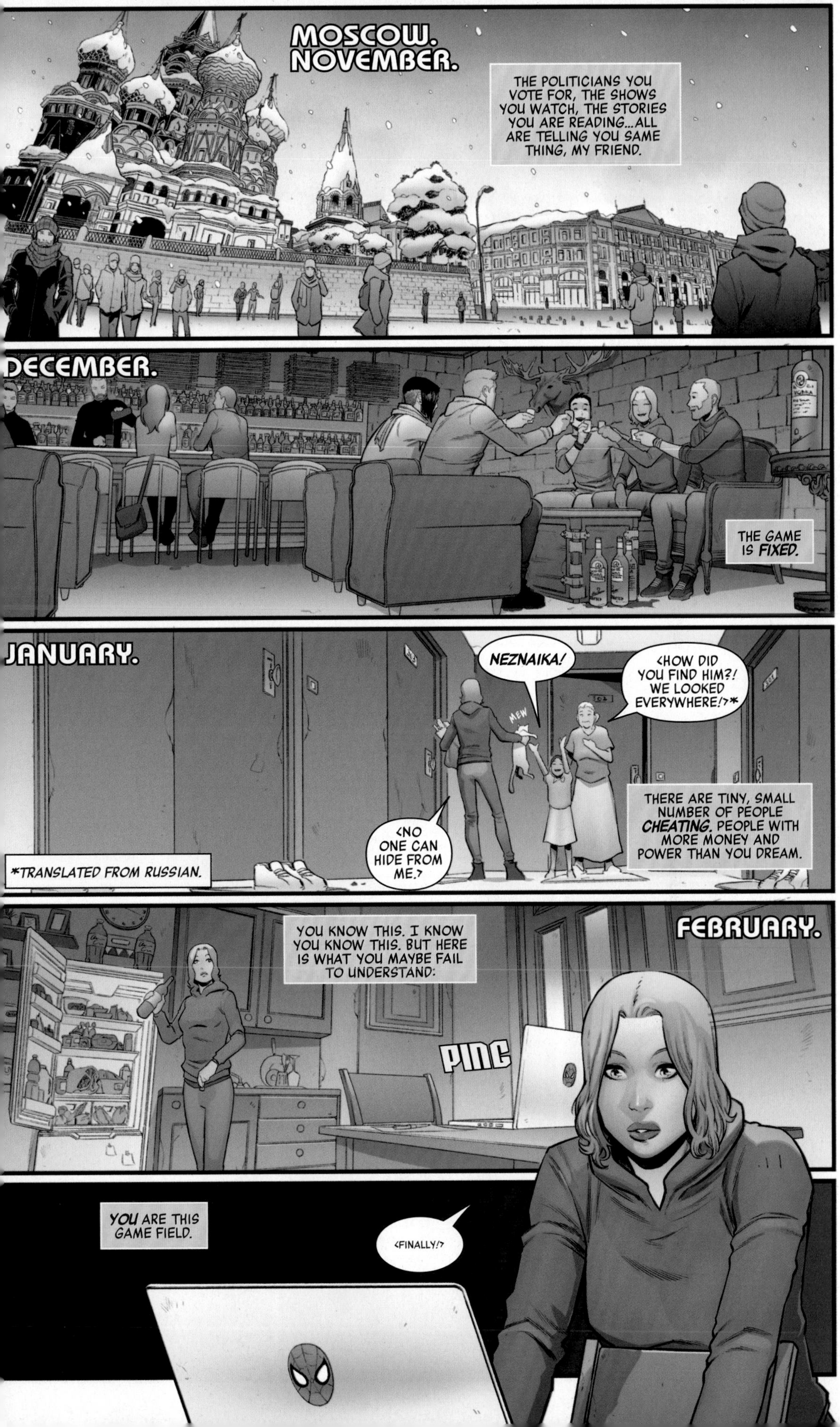
MOSCOW. NOVEMBER.
THE POLITICIANS YOU VOTE FOR, THE SHOWS YOU WATCH, THE STORIES YOU ARE READING...ALL ARE TELLING YOU SAME THING, MY FRIEND.
DECEMBER.
THE GAME IS FIXED.
JANUARY.
NEZNAIKA!
MEW
<HOW DID YOU FIND HIM?! WE LOOKED EVERYWHERE!>*
<NO ONE CAN HIDE FROM ME.>
THERE ARE TINY, SMALL NUMBER OF PEOPLE CHEATING. PEOPLE WITH MORE MONEY AND POWER THAN YOU DREAM.
*TRANSLATED FROM RUSSIAN.
YOU KNOW THIS. I KNOW YOU KNOW THIS. BUT HERE IS WHAT YOU MAYBE FAIL TO UNDERSTAND:
FEBRUARY.
PING
YOU ARE THIS GAME FIELD.
<FINALLY!>

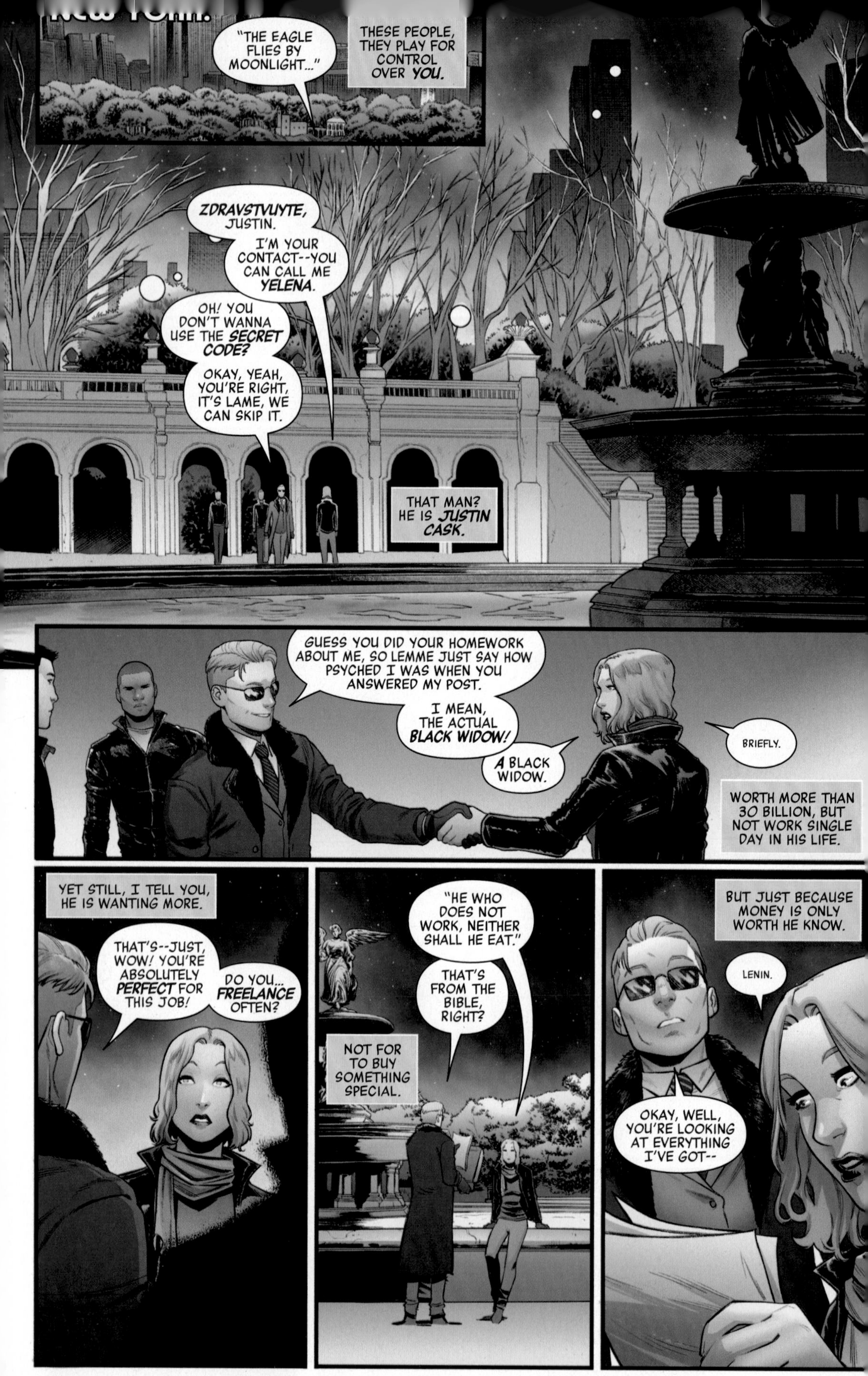

NEW YORK.
"THE EAGLE FLIES BY MOONLIGHT..."
THESE PEOPLE, THEY PLAY FOR CONTROL OVER YOU.
ZDRAVSTVUYTE, JUSTIN.
I'M YOUR CONTACT--YOU CAN CALL ME YELENA.
OH! YOU DON'T WANNA USE THE SECRET CODE?
OKAY, YEAH, YOU'RE RIGHT, IT'S LAME, WE CAN SKIP IT.
THAT MAN? HE IS JUSTIN CASK.
GUESS YOU DID YOUR HOMEWORK ABOUT ME, SO LEMME JUST SAY HOW PSYCHED I WAS WHEN YOU ANSWERED MY POST.
I MEAN, THE ACTUAL BLACK WIDOW!
A BLACK WIDOW.
BRIEFLY.
WORTH MORE THAN 30 BILLION, BUT NOT WORK SINGLE DAY IN HIS LIFE.
YET STILL, I TELL YOU, HE IS WANTING MORE.
THAT'S--JUST, WOW! YOU'RE ABSOLUTELY PERFECT FOR THIS JOB!
DO YOU... FREELANCE OFTEN?
"HE WHO DOES NOT WORK, NEITHER SHALL HE EAT."
THAT'S FROM THE BIBLE, RIGHT?
NOT FOR TO BUY SOMETHING SPECIAL.
BUT JUST BECAUSE MONEY IS ONLY WORTH HE KNOW.
LENIN.
OKAY, WELL, YOU'RE LOOKING AT EVERYTHING I'VE GOT--

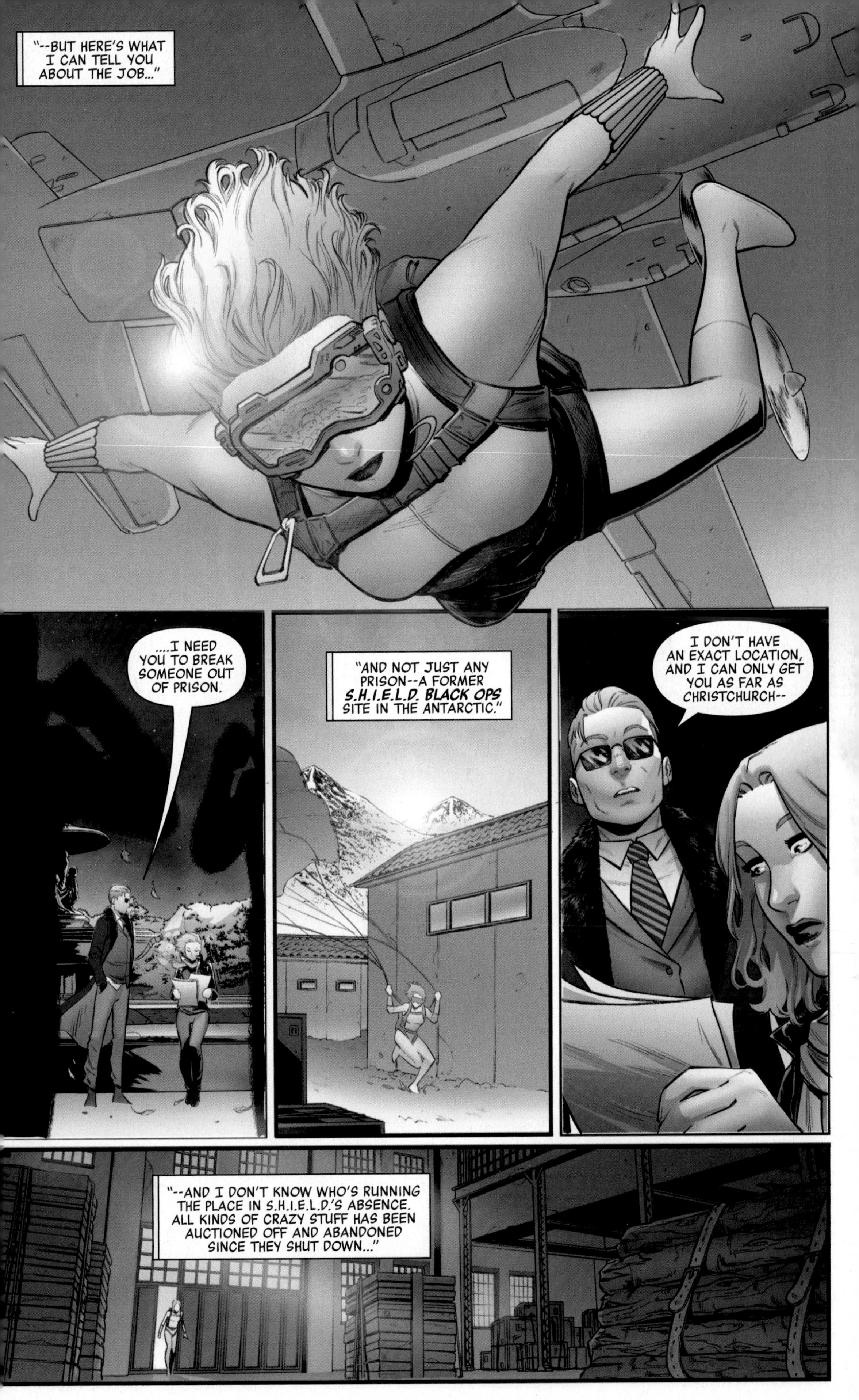
"--BUT HERE'S WHAT I CAN TELL YOU ABOUT THE JOB..."
....I NEED YOU TO BREAK SOMEONE OUT OF PRISON.
"AND NOT JUST ANY PRISON--A FORMER S.H.I.E.L.D. BLACK OPS SITE IN THE ANTARCTIC."
I DON'T HAVE AN EXACT LOCATION, AND I CAN ONLY GET YOU AS FAR AS CHRISTCHURCH--
"--AND I DON'T KNOW WHO'S RUNNING THE PLACE IN S.H.I.E.L.D.'S ABSENCE. ALL KINDS OF CRAZY STUFF HAS BEEN AUCTIONED OFF AND ABANDONED SINCE THEY SHUT DOWN..."

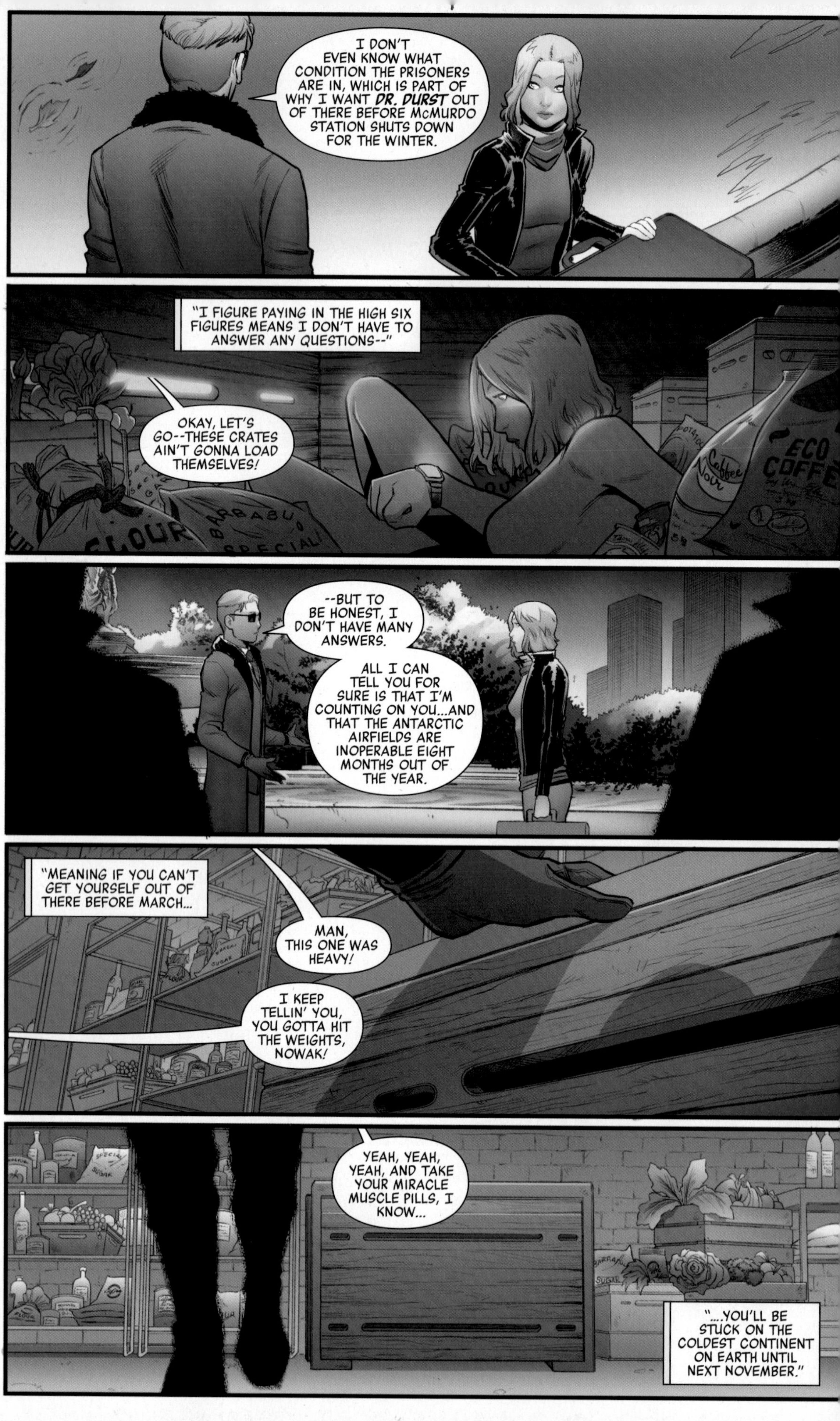
I DON'T EVEN KNOW WHAT CONDITION THE PRISONERS ARE IN, WHICH IS PART OF WHY I WANT DR. DURST OUT OF THERE BEFORE McMURDO STATION SHUTS DOWN FOR THE WINTER.
"I FIGURE PAYING IN THE HIGH SIX FIGURES MEANS I DON'T HAVE TO ANSWER ANY QUESTIONS--"
OKAY, LET'S GO--THESE CRATES AIN'T GONNA LOAD THEMSELVES!
FLOUR
BARBABU SPECIAL
ECO COFFEE
--BUT TO BE HONEST, I DON'T HAVE MANY ANSWERS.
ALL I CAN TELL YOU FOR SURE IS THAT I'M COUNTING ON YOU...AND THAT THE ANTARCTIC AIRFIELDS ARE INOPERABLE EIGHT MONTHS OUT OF THE YEAR.
"MEANING IF YOU CAN'T GET YOURSELF OUT OF THERE BEFORE MARCH...
MAN, THIS ONE WAS HEAVY!
I KEEP TELLIN' YOU, YOU GOTTA HIT THE WEIGHTS, NOWAK!
YEAH, YEAH, YEAH, AND TAKE YOUR MIRACLE MUSCLE PILLS, I KNOW...
"....YOU'LL BE STUCK ON THE COLDEST CONTINENT ON EARTH UNTIL NEXT NOVEMBER."

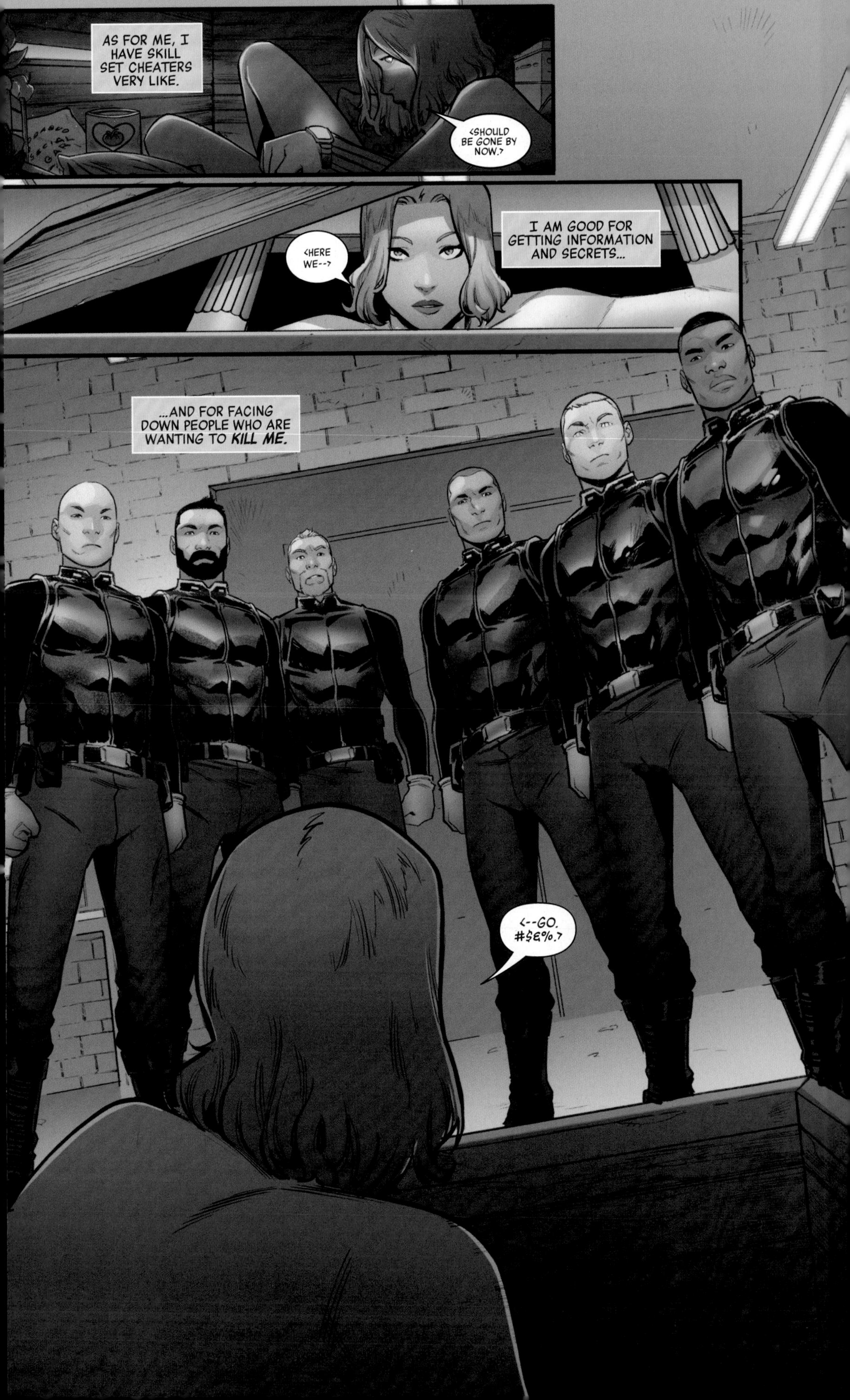

AS FOR ME, I HAVE SKILL SET CHEATERS VERY LIKE.
<SHOULD BE GONE BY NOW.>
<HERE WE-->
I AM GOOD FOR GETTING INFORMATION AND SECRETS...
...AND FOR FACING DOWN PEOPLE WHO ARE WANTING TO KILL ME.
<--GO. #$&%.>

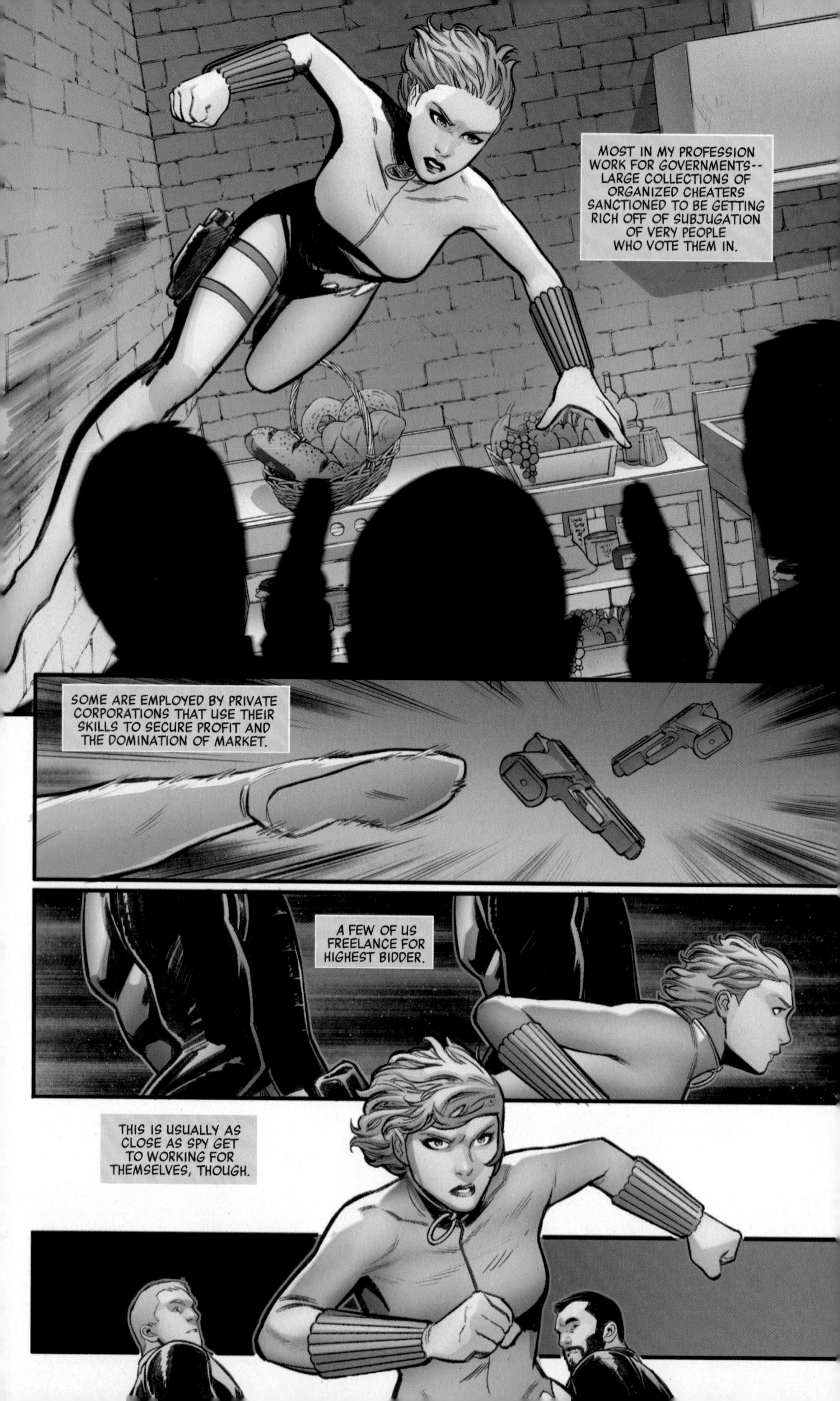

MOST IN MY PROFESSION WORK FOR GOVERNMENTS-- LARGE COLLECTIONS OF ORGANIZED CHEATERS SANCTIONED TO BE GETTING RICH OFF OF SUBJUGATION OF VERY PEOPLE WHO VOTE THEM IN.
SOME ARE EMPLOYED BY PRIVATE CORPORATIONS THAT USE THEIR SKILLS TO SECURE PROFIT AND THE DOMINATION OF MARKET.
A FEW OF US FREELANCE FOR HIGHEST BIDDER.
THIS IS USUALLY AS CLOSE AS SPY GET TO WORKING FOR THEMSELVES, THOUGH.

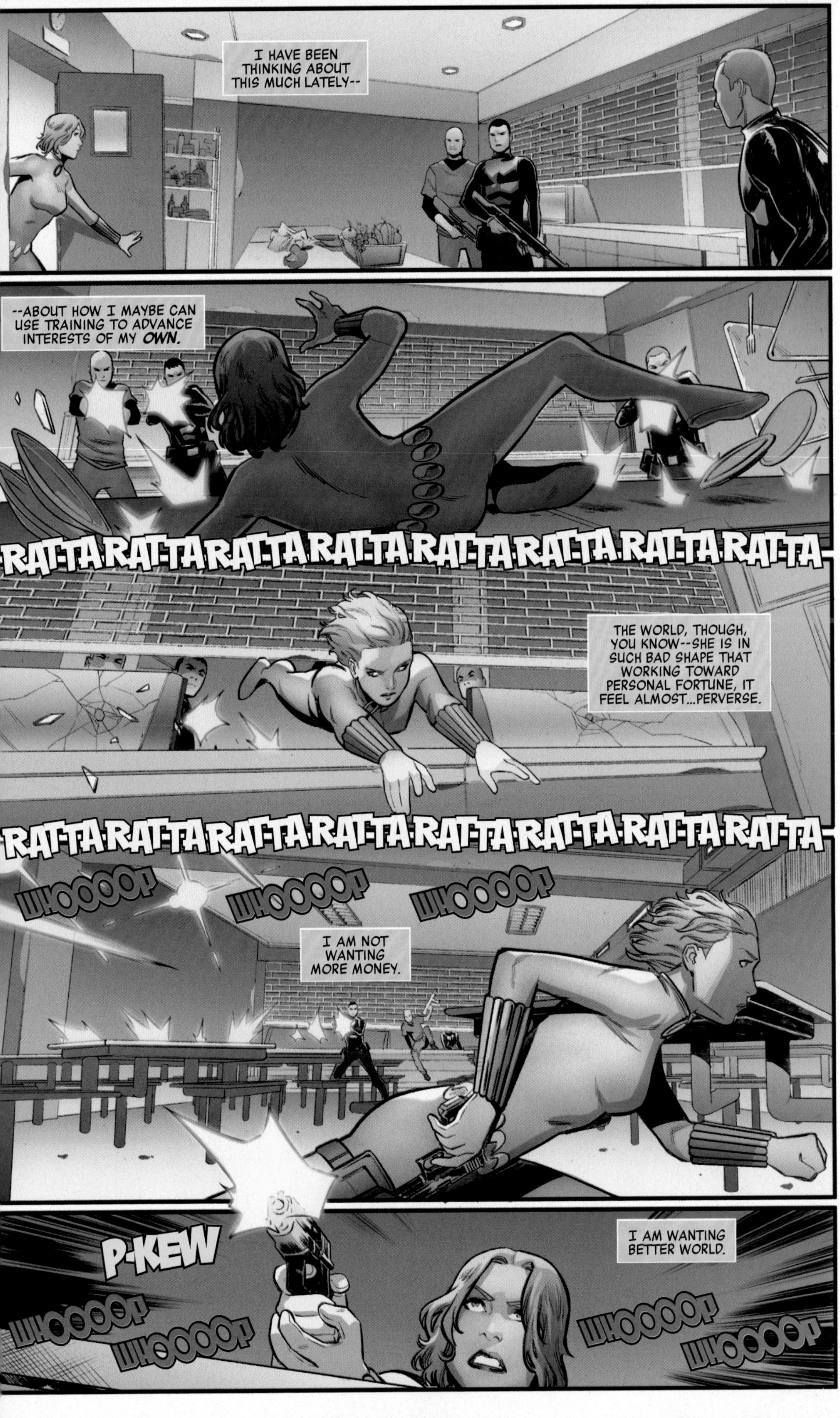
I HAVE BEEN THINKING ABOUT THIS MUCH LATELY--
--ABOUT HOW I MAYBE CAN USE TRAINING TO ADVANCE INTERESTS OF MY *OWN.*
RAT-TA RAT-TA RAT-TA RAT-TA RAT-TA RAT-TA RAT-TA RAT-TA
THE WORLD, THOUGH, YOU KNOW--SHE IS IN SUCH BAD SHAPE THAT WORKING TOWARD PERSONAL FORTUNE, IT FEEL ALMOST...PERVERSE.
RAT-TA RAT-TA RAT-TA RAT-TA RAT-TA RAT-TA RAT-TA RAT-TA
WHOOOOP WHOOOOP WHOOOOP
I AM NOT WANTING MORE MONEY.
P-KEW
I AM WANTING BETTER WORLD.
WHOOOOP WHOOOOP WHOOOOP WHOOOOP

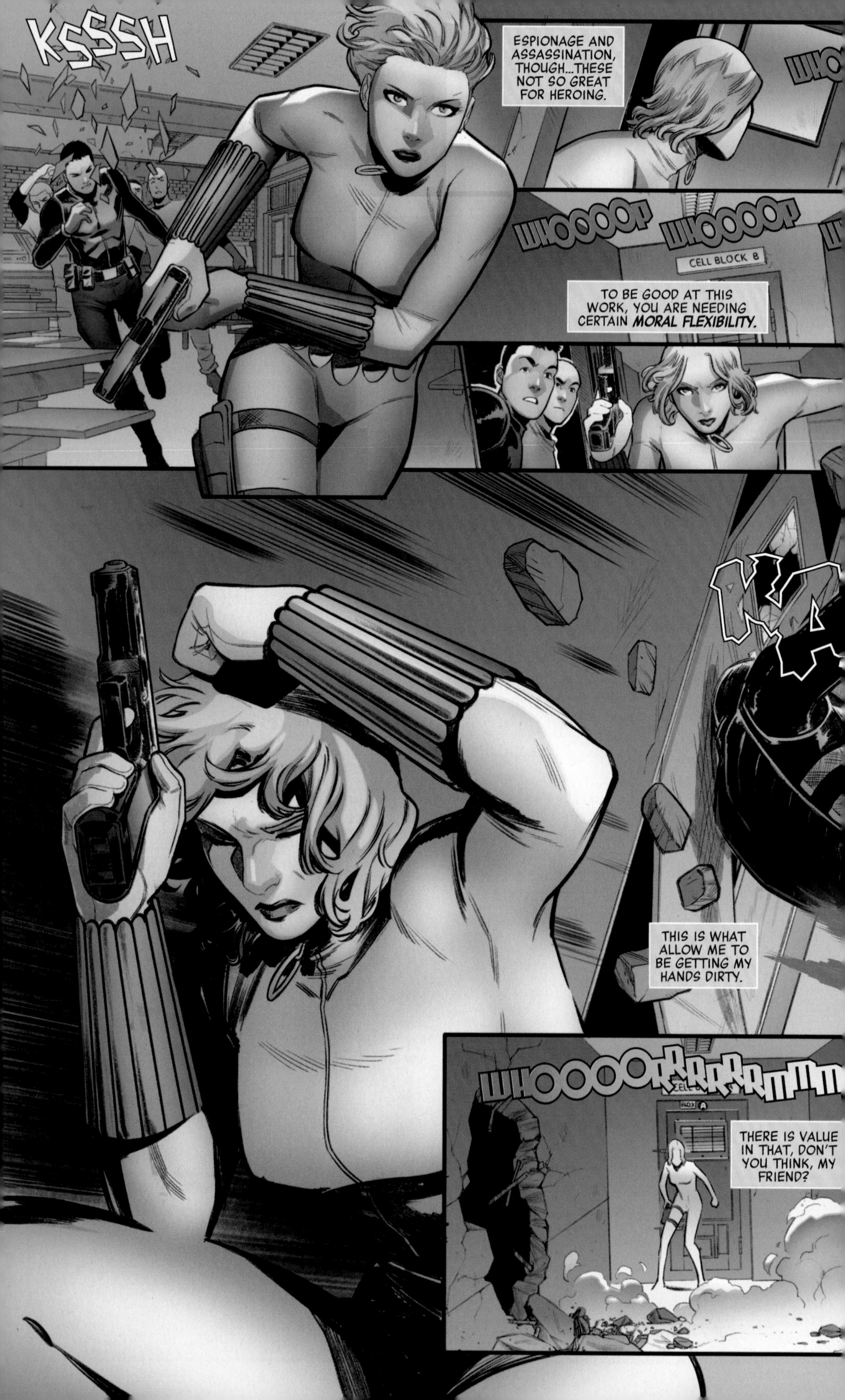
KSSSH
ESPIONAGE AND ASSASSINATION, THOUGH...THESE NOT SO GREAT FOR HEROING.
WHOOOOP
WHOOOOP
CELL BLOCK B
TO BE GOOD AT THIS WORK, YOU ARE NEEDING CERTAIN MORAL FLEXIBILITY.
THIS IS WHAT ALLOW ME TO BE GETTING MY HANDS DIRTY.
WHOOOORRRRRMMM
THERE IS VALUE IN THAT, DON'T YOU THINK, MY FRIEND?

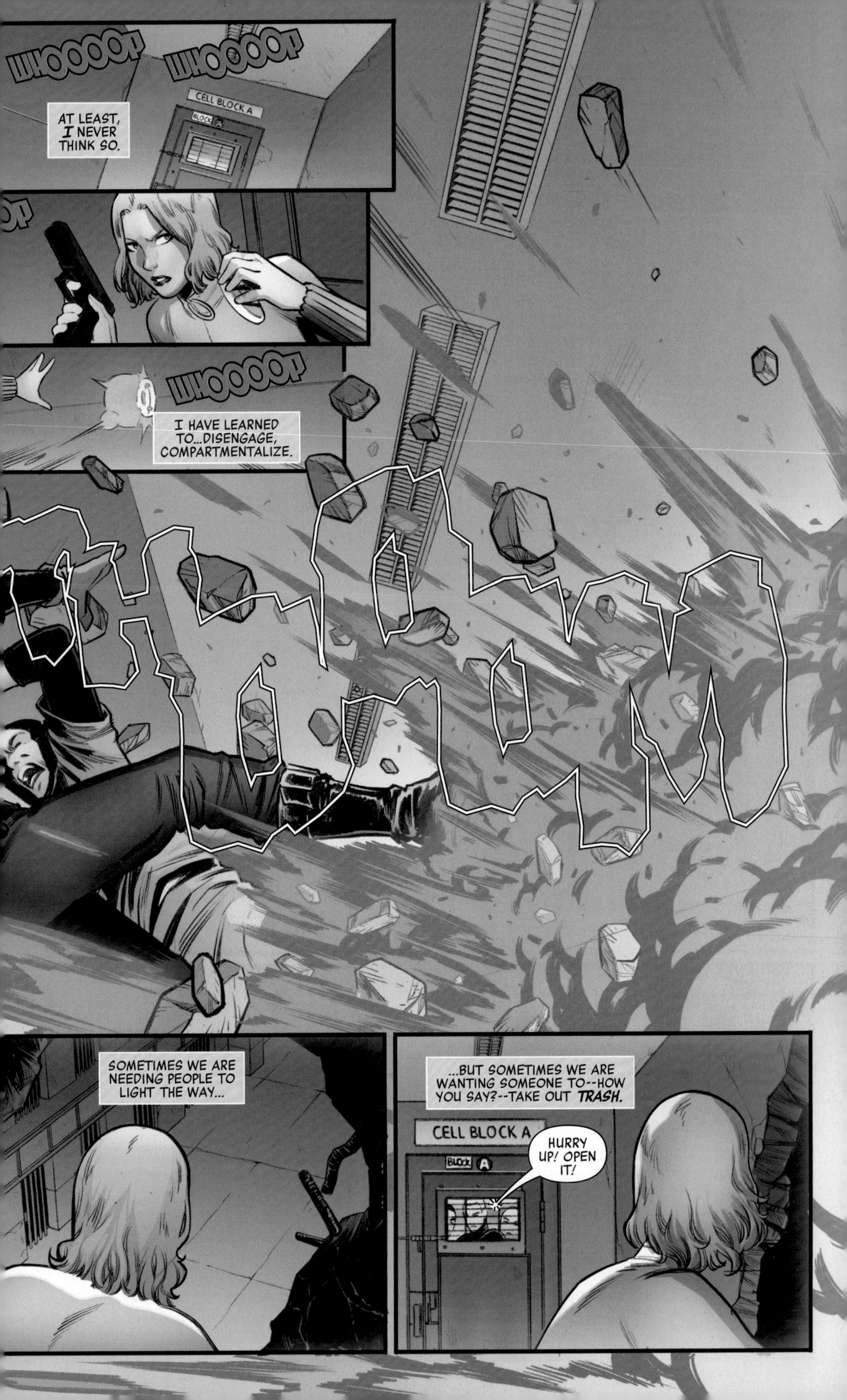
WHOOOOP
WHOOOOP
CELL BLOCK A
BLOCK
AT LEAST, *I* NEVER THINK SO.
WHOOOOP
I HAVE LEARNED TO...DISENGAGE, COMPARTMENTALIZE.
SOMETIMES WE ARE NEEDING PEOPLE TO LIGHT THE WAY...
...BUT SOMETIMES WE ARE WANTING SOMEONE TO--HOW YOU SAY?--TAKE OUT *TRASH.*
CELL BLOCK A
BLOCK A
HURRY UP! OPEN IT!

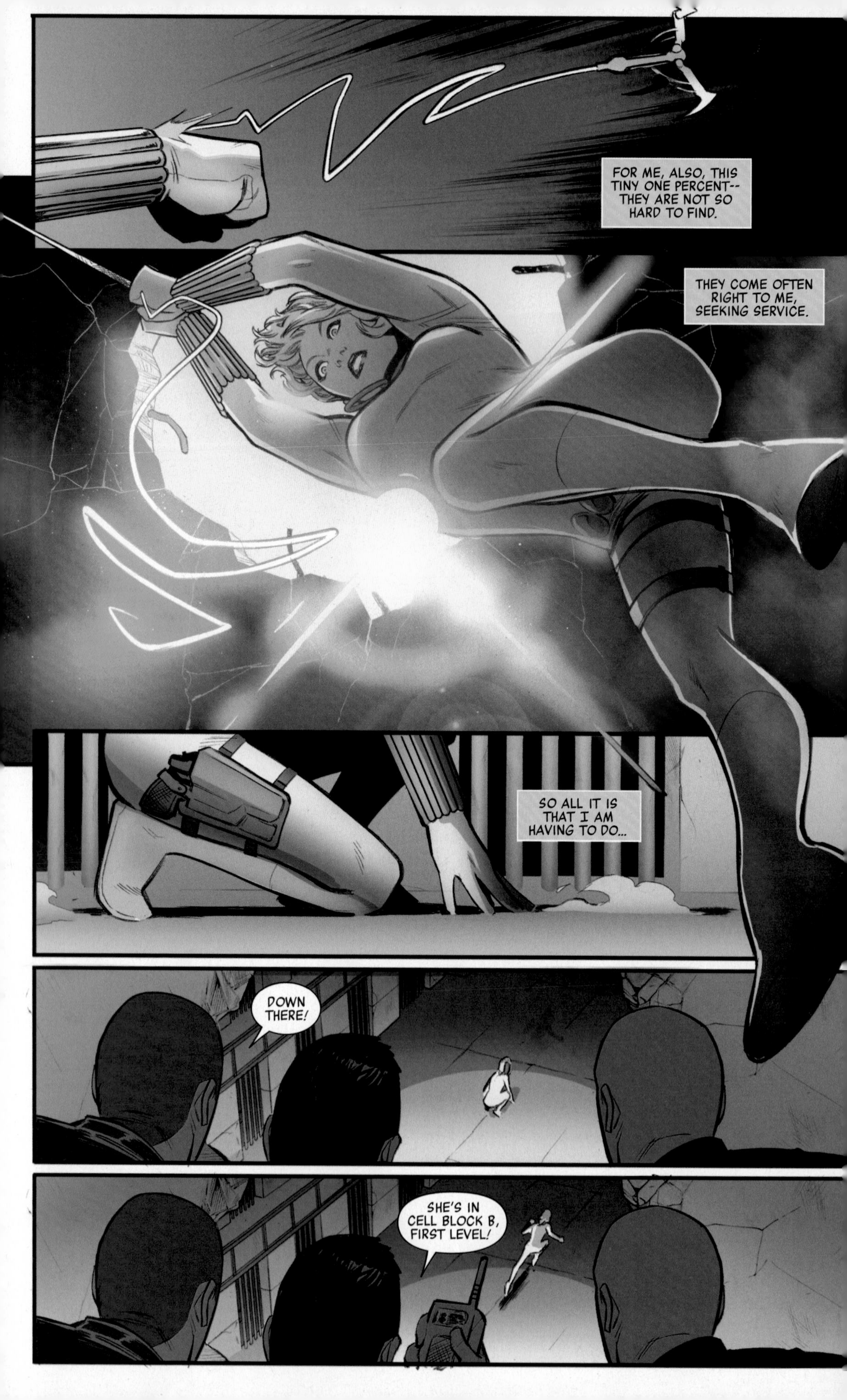
FOR ME, ALSO, THIS TINY ONE PERCENT-- THEY ARE NOT SO HARD TO FIND.
THEY COME OFTEN RIGHT TO ME, SEEKING SERVICE.
SO ALL IT IS THAT I AM HAVING TO DO...
DOWN THERE!
SHE'S IN CELL BLOCK B, FIRST LEVEL!

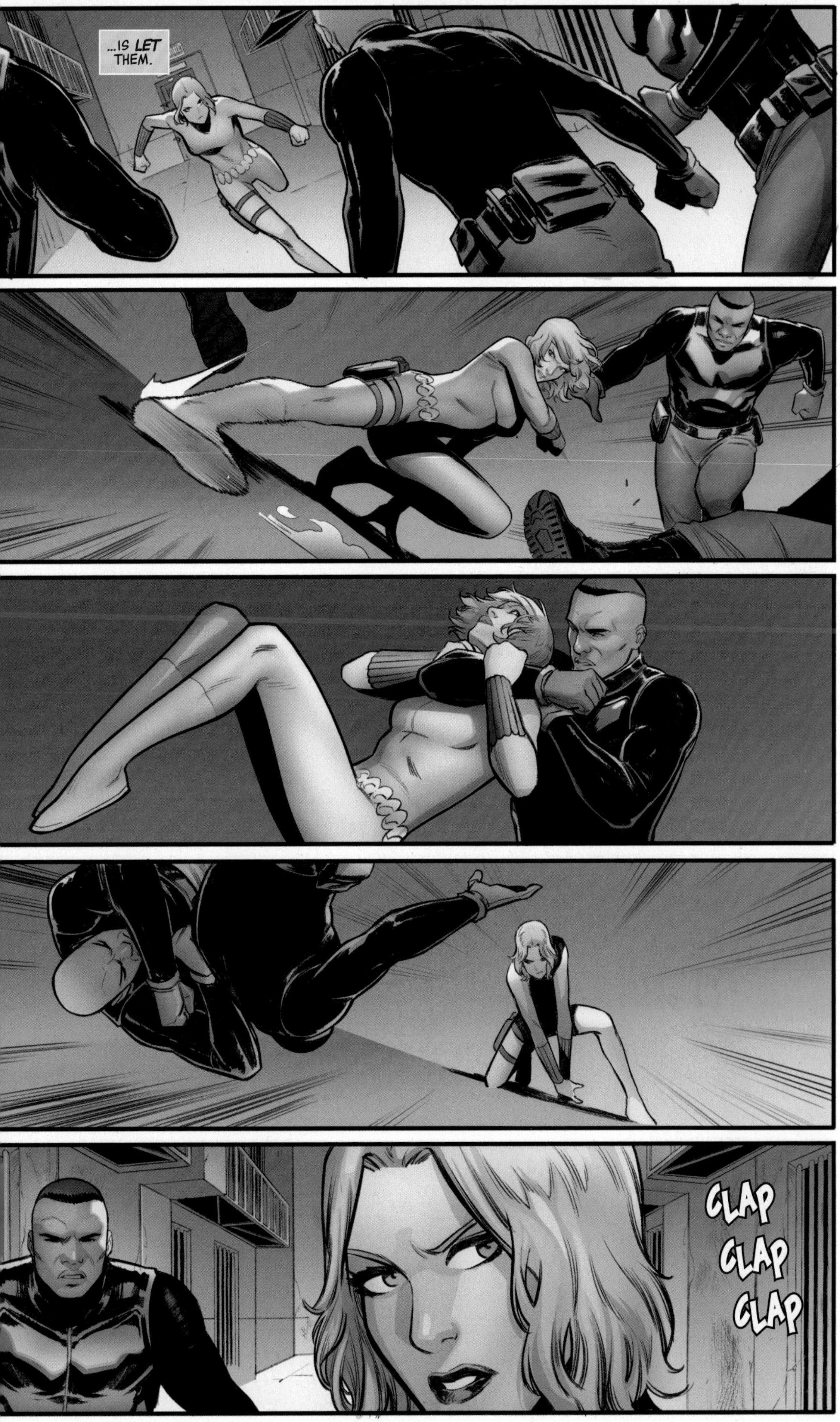

...IS LET THEM.
CLAP
CLAP
CLAP

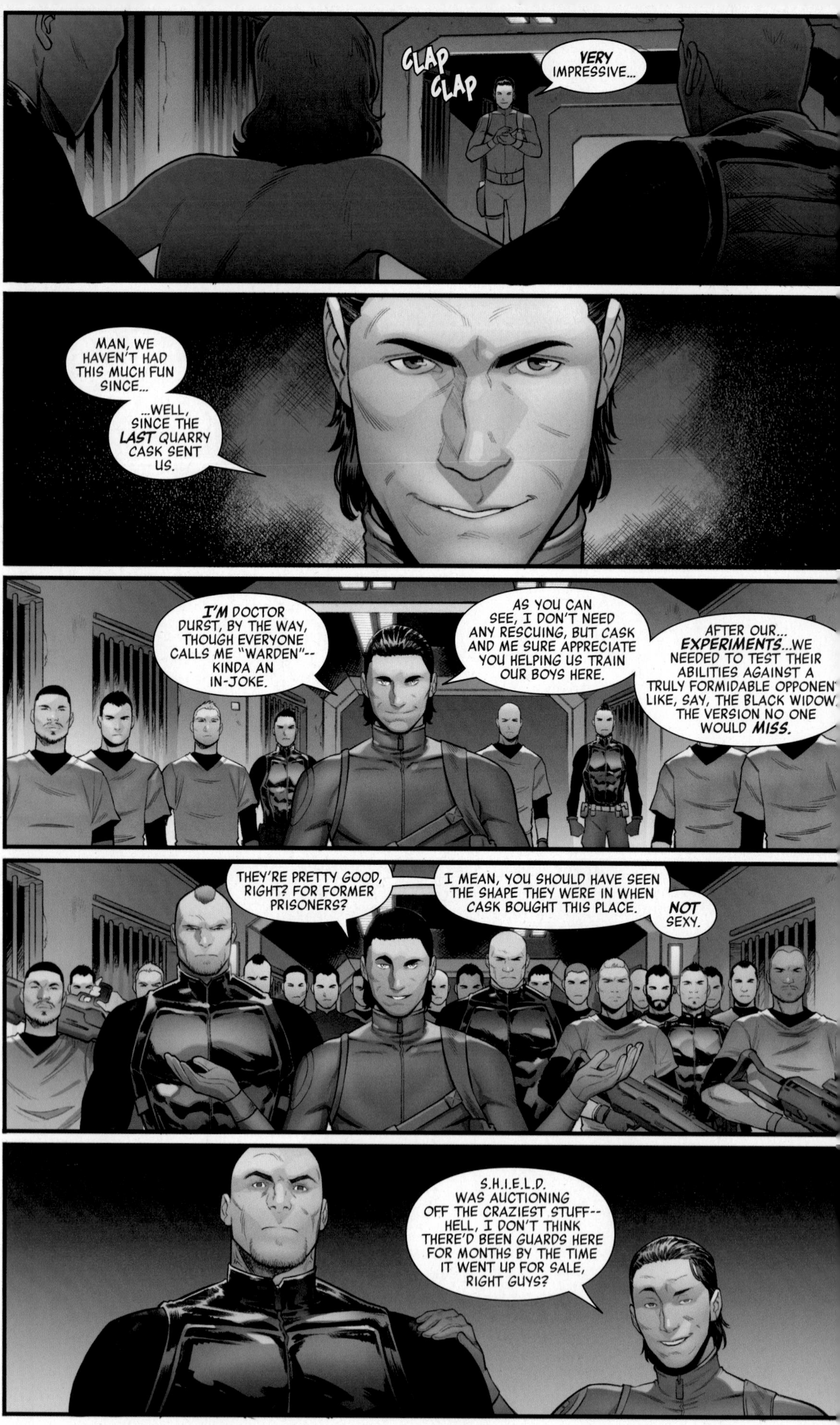

CLAP
CLAP
VERY IMPRESSIVE...
MAN, WE HAVEN'T HAD THIS MUCH FUN SINCE...
...WELL, SINCE THE LAST QUARRY CASK SENT US.
I'M DOCTOR DURST, BY THE WAY, THOUGH EVERYONE CALLS ME "WARDEN"-- KINDA AN IN-JOKE.
AS YOU CAN SEE, I DON'T NEED ANY RESCUING, BUT CASK AND ME SURE APPRECIATE YOU HELPING US TRAIN OUR BOYS HERE.
AFTER OUR... EXPERIMENTS...WE NEEDED TO TEST THEIR ABILITIES AGAINST A TRULY FORMIDABLE OPPONEN LIKE, SAY, THE BLACK WIDOW. THE VERSION NO ONE WOULD MISS.
THEY'RE PRETTY GOOD, RIGHT? FOR FORMER PRISONERS?
I MEAN, YOU SHOULD HAVE SEEN THE SHAPE THEY WERE IN WHEN CASK BOUGHT THIS PLACE.
NOT SEXY.
S.H.I.E.L.D. WAS AUCTIONING OFF THE CRAZIEST STUFF-- HELL, I DON'T THINK THERE'D BEEN GUARDS HERE FOR MONTHS BY THE TIME IT WENT UP FOR SALE, RIGHT GUYS?

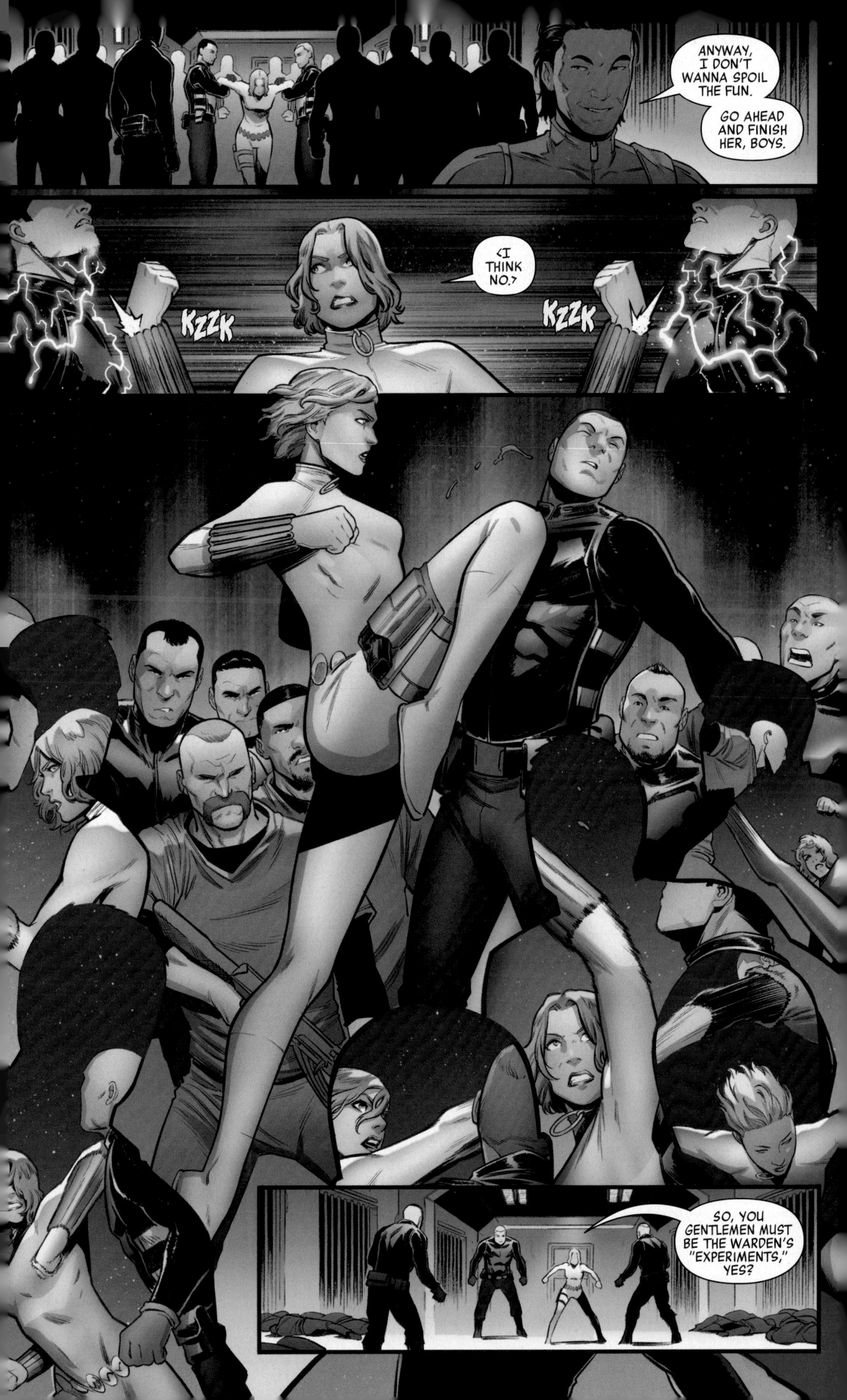

ANYWAY, I DON'T WANNA SPOIL THE FUN.
GO AHEAD AND FINISH HER, BOYS.
<I THINK NO.>
KZZK
KZZK
SO, YOU GENTLEMEN MUST BE THE WARDEN'S "EXPERIMENTS," YES?

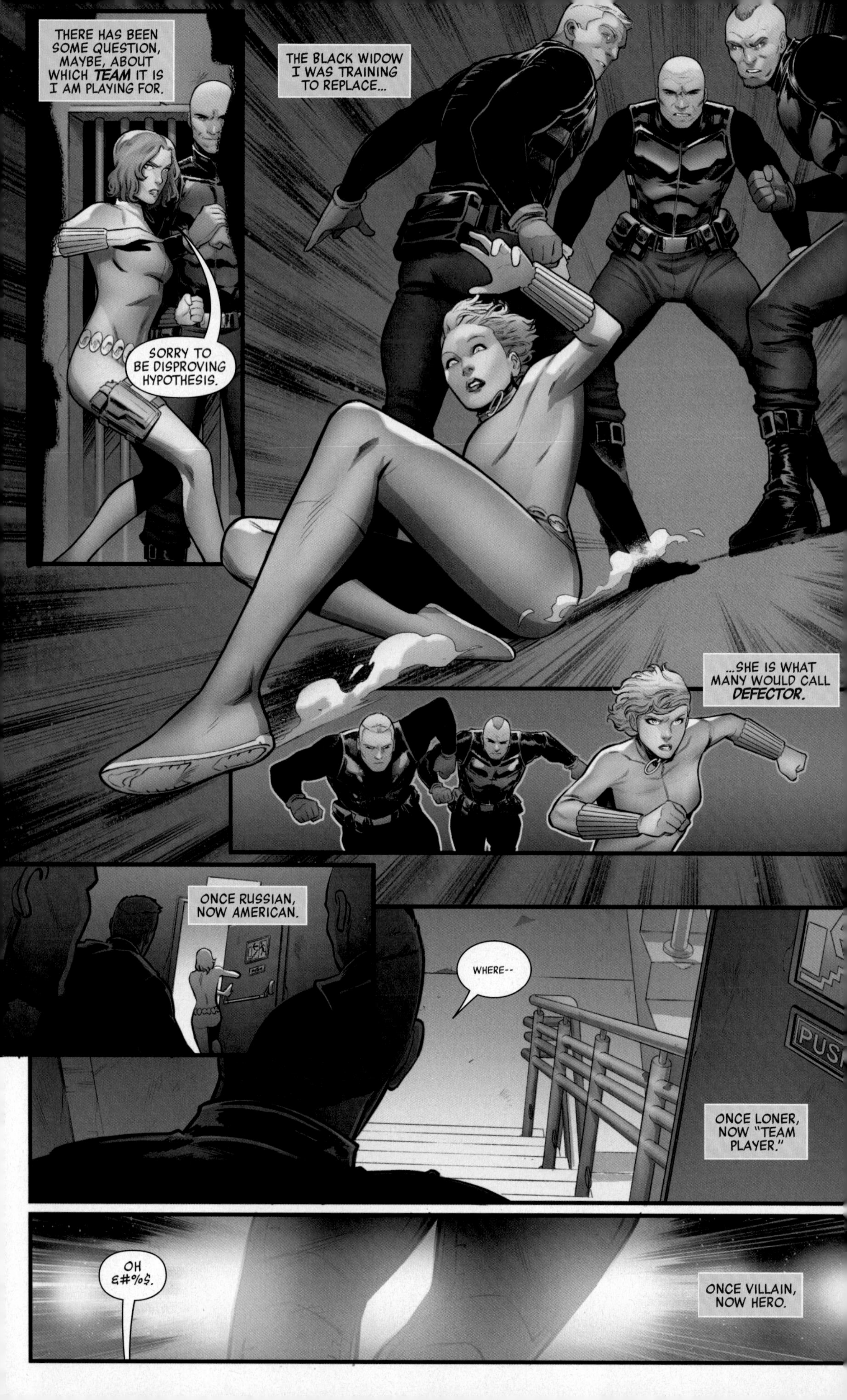
THERE HAS BEEN SOME QUESTION, MAYBE, ABOUT WHICH TEAM IT IS I AM PLAYING FOR.
SORRY TO BE DISPROVING HYPOTHESIS.
THE BLACK WIDOW I WAS TRAINING TO REPLACE...
...SHE IS WHAT MANY WOULD CALL DEFECTOR.
ONCE RUSSIAN, NOW AMERICAN.
WHERE--
PUSH
ONCE LONER, NOW "TEAM PLAYER."
OH &#%$.
ONCE VILLAIN, NOW HERO.

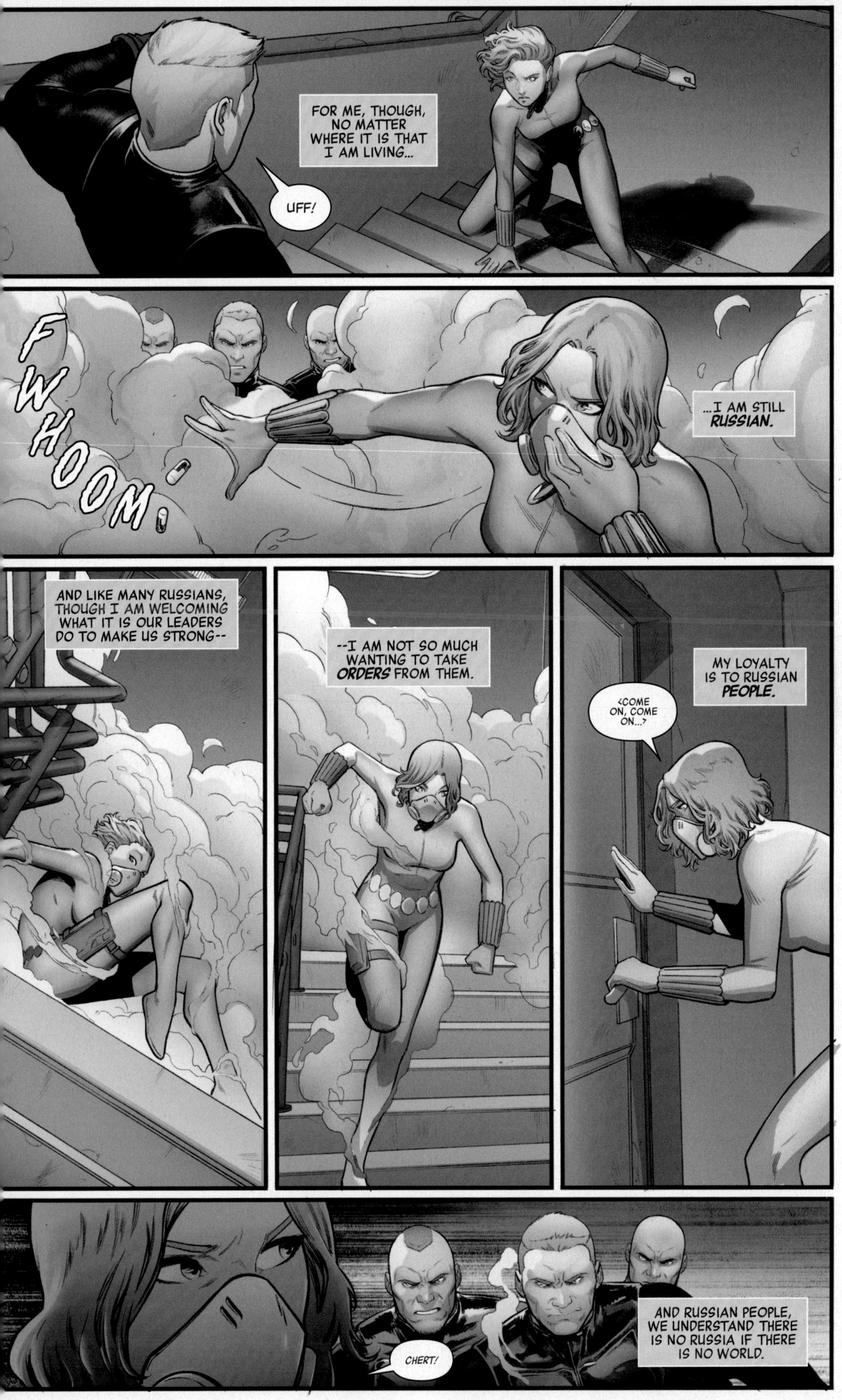
FOR ME, THOUGH, NO MATTER WHERE IT IS THAT I AM LIVING...
UFF!
FWHOOM
...I AM STILL RUSSIAN.
AND LIKE MANY RUSSIANS, THOUGH I AM WELCOMING WHAT IT IS OUR LEADERS DO TO MAKE US STRONG--
--I AM NOT SO MUCH WANTING TO TAKE ORDERS FROM THEM.
MY LOYALTY IS TO RUSSIAN PEOPLE.
<COME ON, COME ON...>
AND RUSSIAN PEOPLE, WE UNDERSTAND THERE IS NO RUSSIA IF THERE IS NO WORLD.
CHERT!

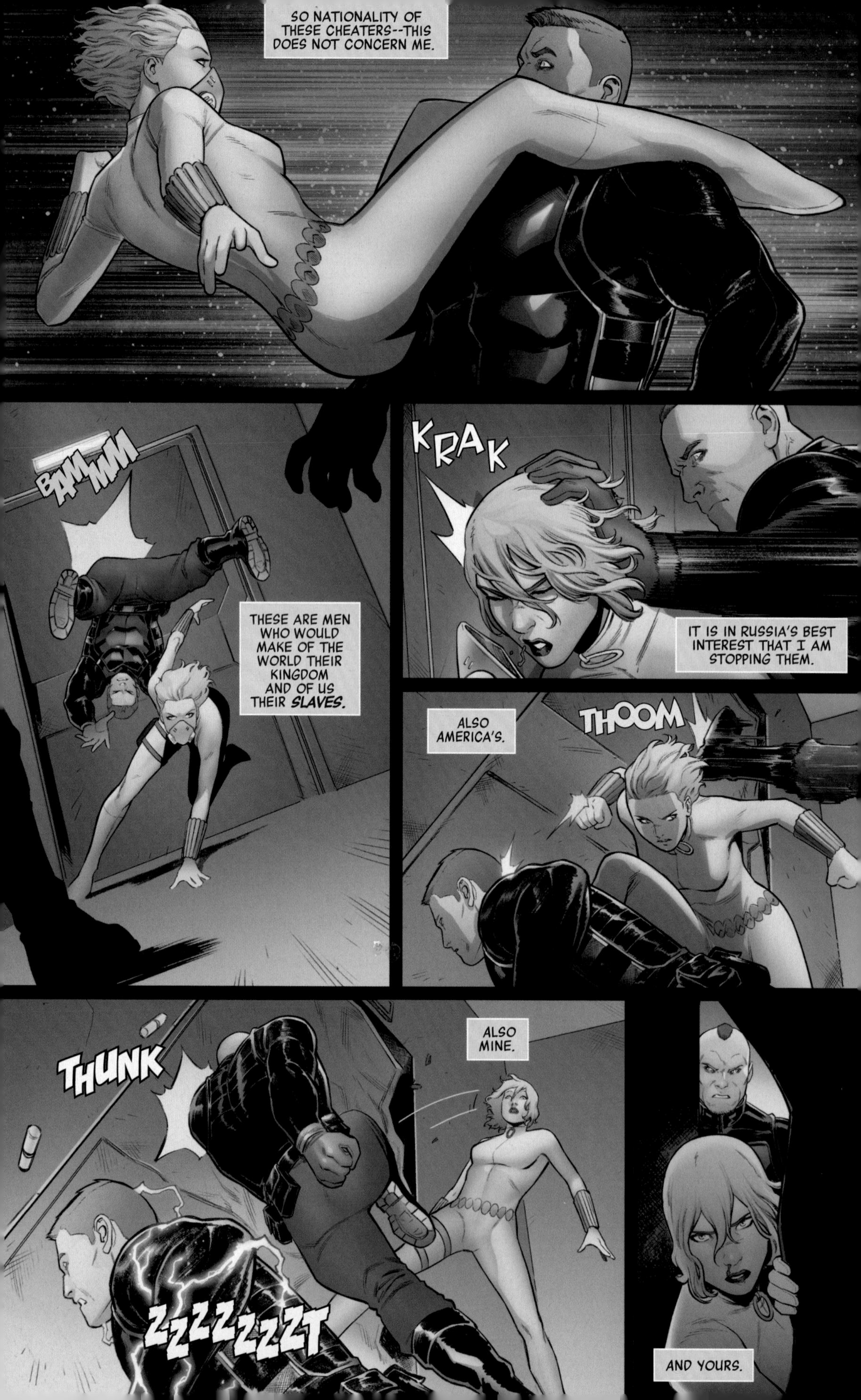
SO NATIONALITY OF THESE CHEATERS--THIS DOES NOT CONCERN ME.
BAMMM
THESE ARE MEN WHO WOULD MAKE OF THE WORLD THEIR KINGDOM AND OF US THEIR SLAVES.
KRAK
IT IS IN RUSSIA'S BEST INTEREST THAT I AM STOPPING THEM.
ALSO AMERICA'S.
THOOM
THUNK
ZZZZZZZT
ALSO MINE.
AND YOURS.

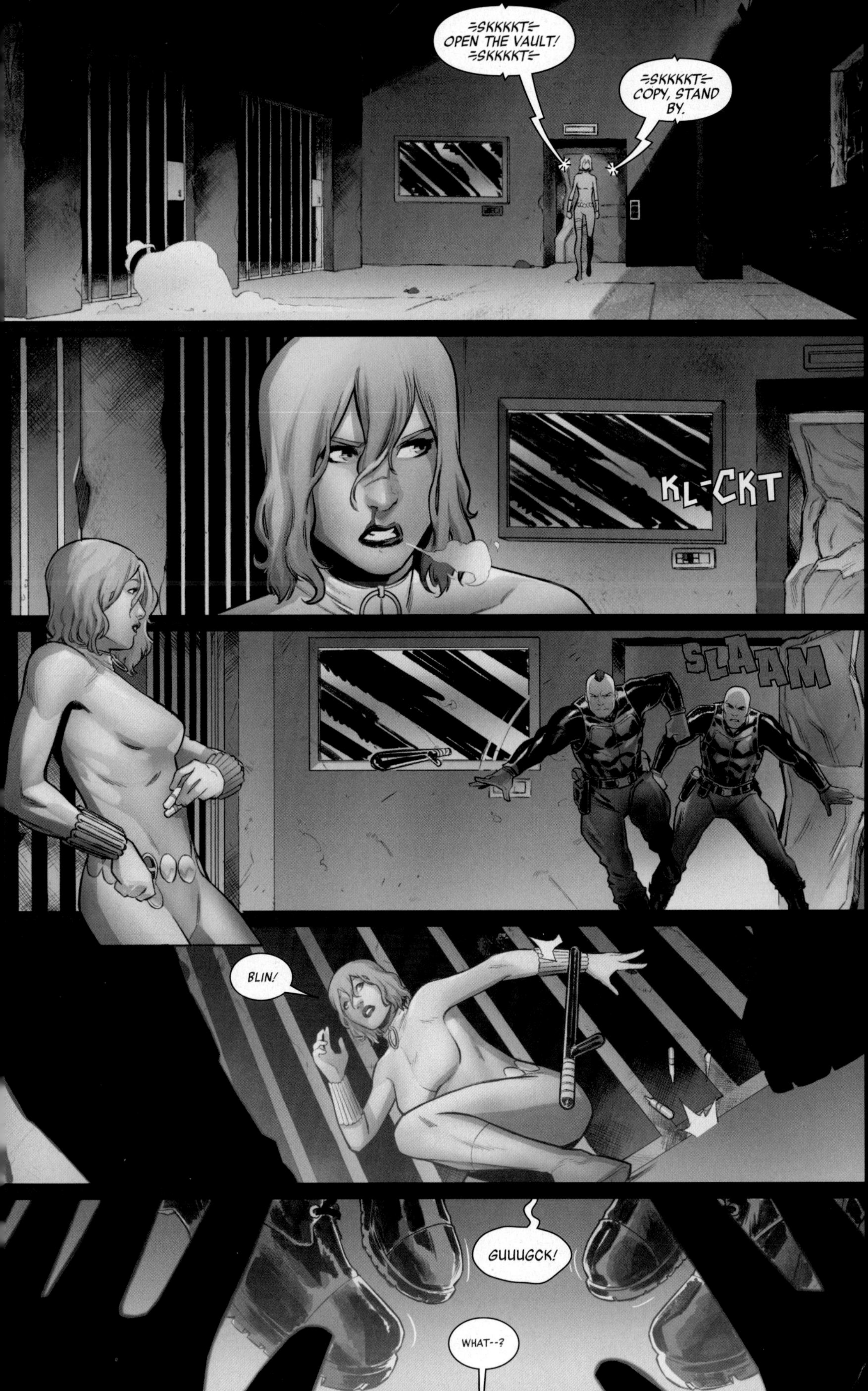

=SKKKKT= OPEN THE VAULT! =SKKKKT=
=SKKKKT= COPY, STAND BY.
KL-CKT
SLAAAM
BLIN!
GUUUGCK!
WHAT--?

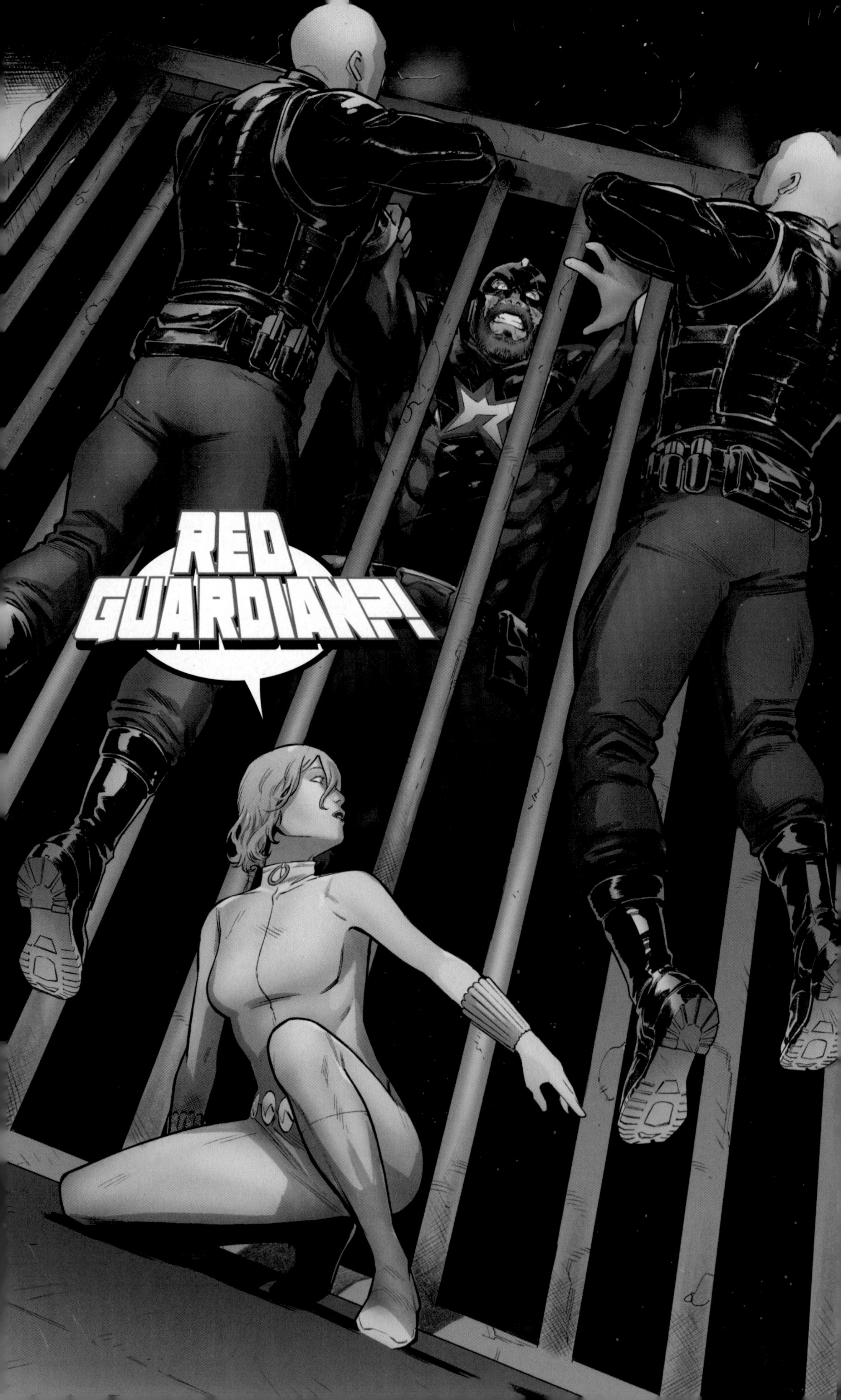
RED GUARDIAN?!

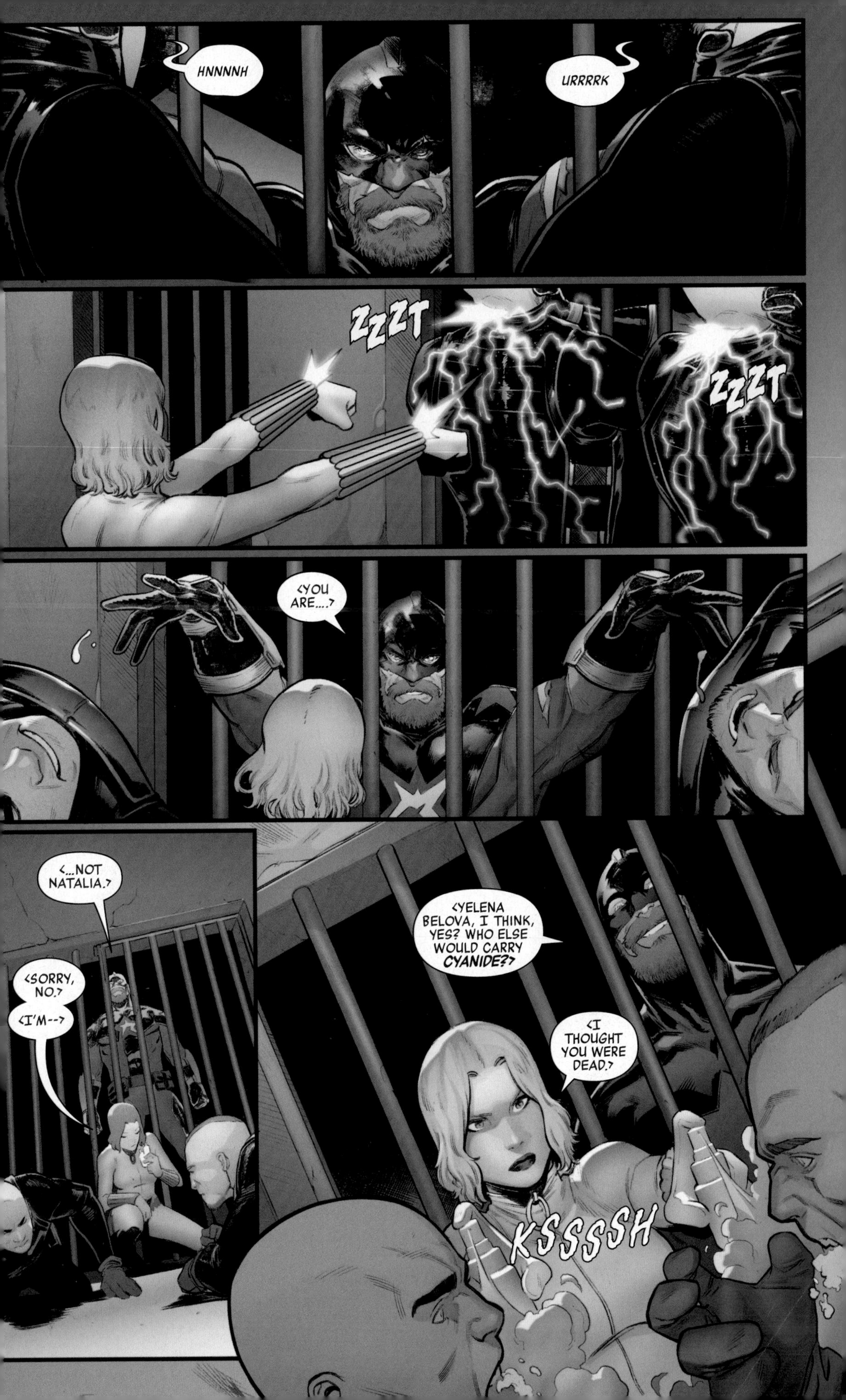
HNNNNH
URRRRK
ZZZT
ZZZT
<YOU ARE....>
<...NOT NATALIA.>
<SORRY, NO.>
<I'M-->
<YELENA BELOVA, I THINK, YES? WHO ELSE WOULD CARRY CYANIDE?>
<I THOUGHT YOU WERE DEAD.>
KSSSSH

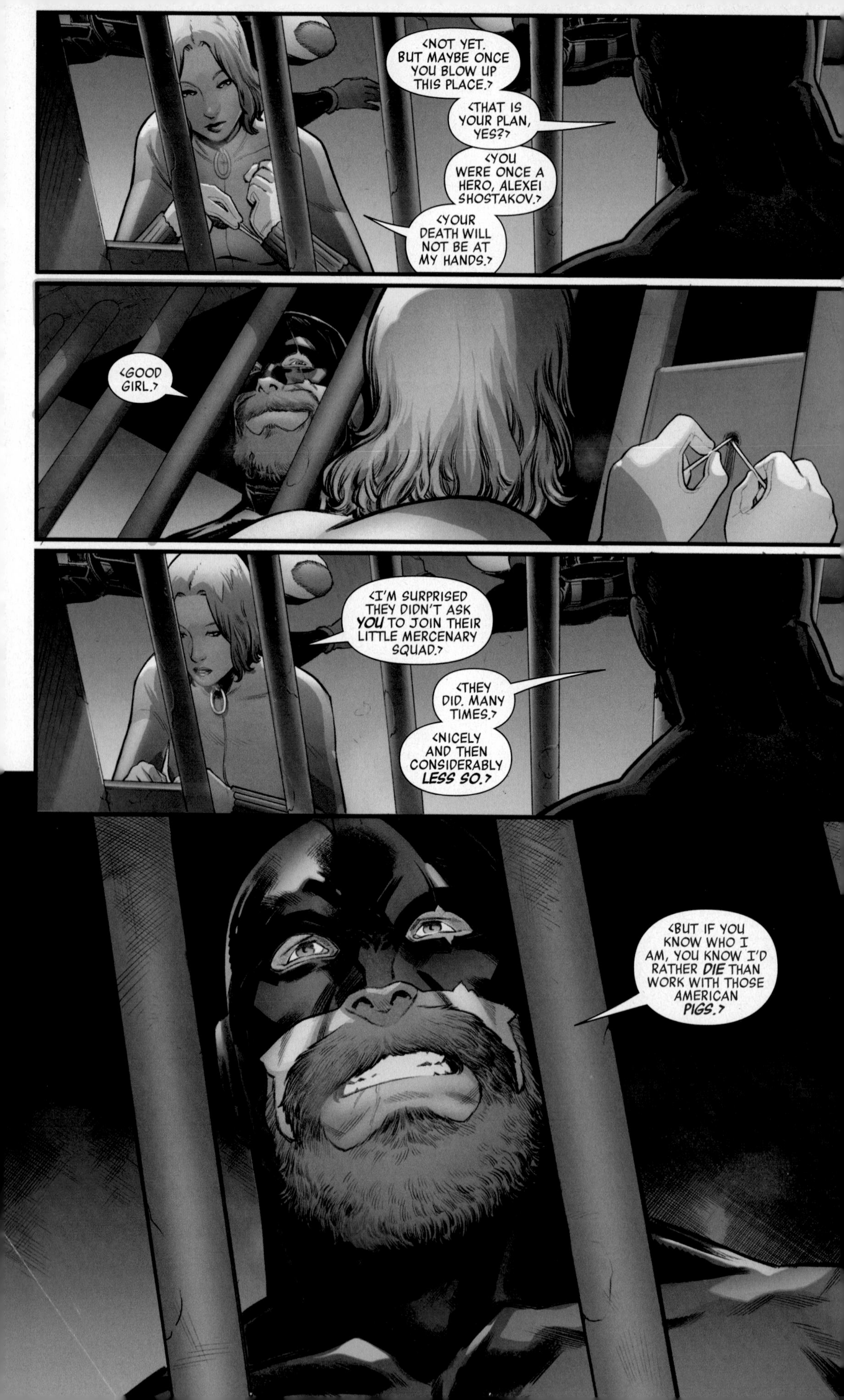
<NOT YET. BUT MAYBE ONCE YOU BLOW UP THIS PLACE.>
<THAT IS YOUR PLAN, YES?>
<YOU WERE ONCE A HERO, ALEXEI SHOSTAKOV.>
<YOUR DEATH WILL NOT BE AT MY HANDS.>
<GOOD GIRL.>
<I'M SURPRISED THEY DIDN'T ASK *YOU* TO JOIN THEIR LITTLE MERCENARY SQUAD.>
<THEY DID. MANY TIMES.>
<NICELY AND THEN CONSIDERABLY *LESS SO.*>
<BUT IF YOU KNOW WHO I AM, YOU KNOW I'D RATHER *DIE* THAN WORK WITH THOSE AMERICAN *PIGS.*>

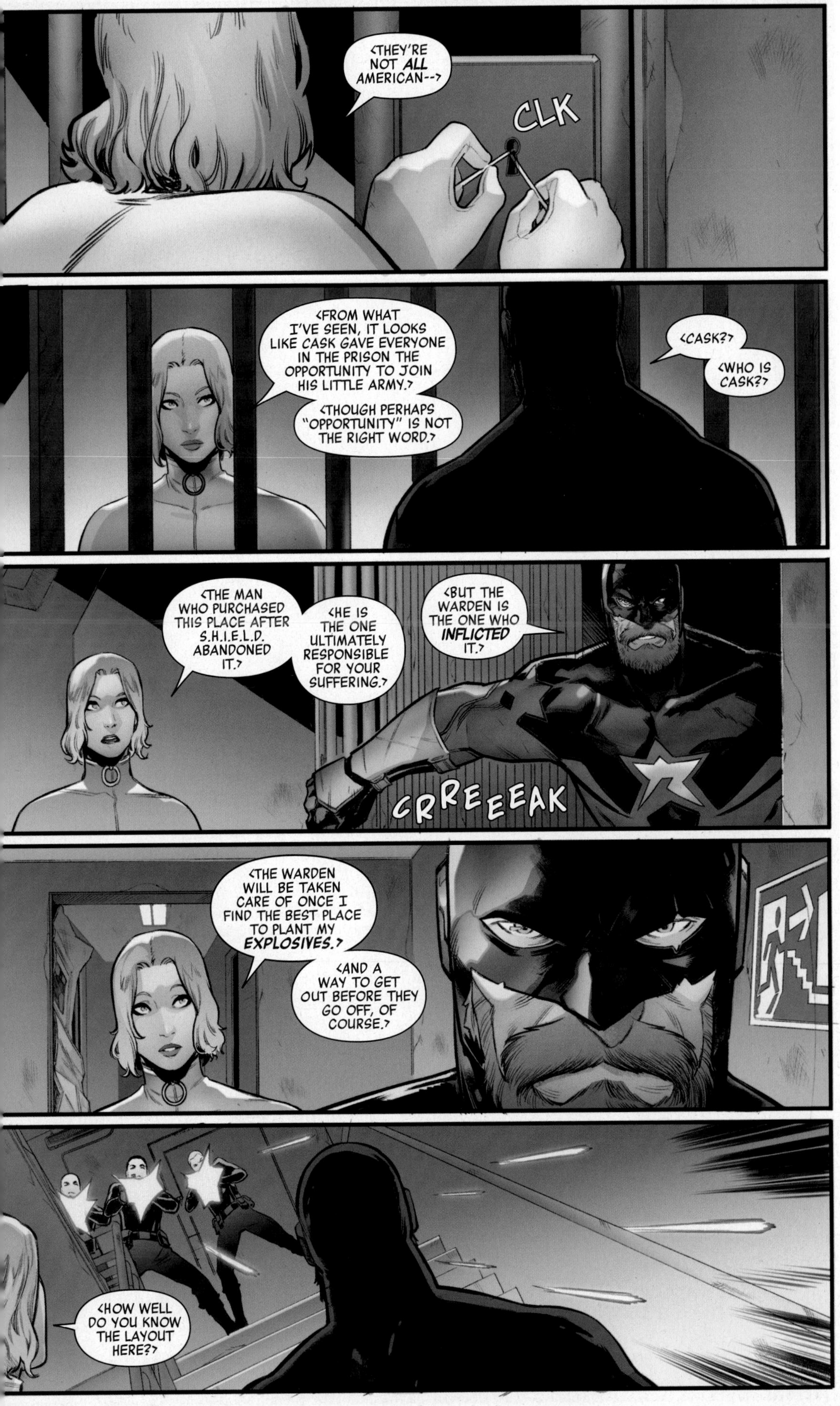

<THEY'RE NOT ALL AMERICAN-->
CLK
<FROM WHAT I'VE SEEN, IT LOOKS LIKE CASK GAVE EVERYONE IN THE PRISON THE OPPORTUNITY TO JOIN HIS LITTLE ARMY.>
<THOUGH PERHAPS "OPPORTUNITY" IS NOT THE RIGHT WORD.>
<CASK?>
<WHO IS CASK?>
<THE MAN WHO PURCHASED THIS PLACE AFTER S.H.I.E.L.D. ABANDONED IT.>
<HE IS THE ONE ULTIMATELY RESPONSIBLE FOR YOUR SUFFERING.>
<BUT THE WARDEN IS THE ONE WHO INFLICTED IT.>
CRREEEAK
<THE WARDEN WILL BE TAKEN CARE OF ONCE I FIND THE BEST PLACE TO PLANT MY EXPLOSIVES.>
<AND A WAY TO GET OUT BEFORE THEY GO OFF, OF COURSE.>
<HOW WELL DO YOU KNOW THE LAYOUT HERE?>

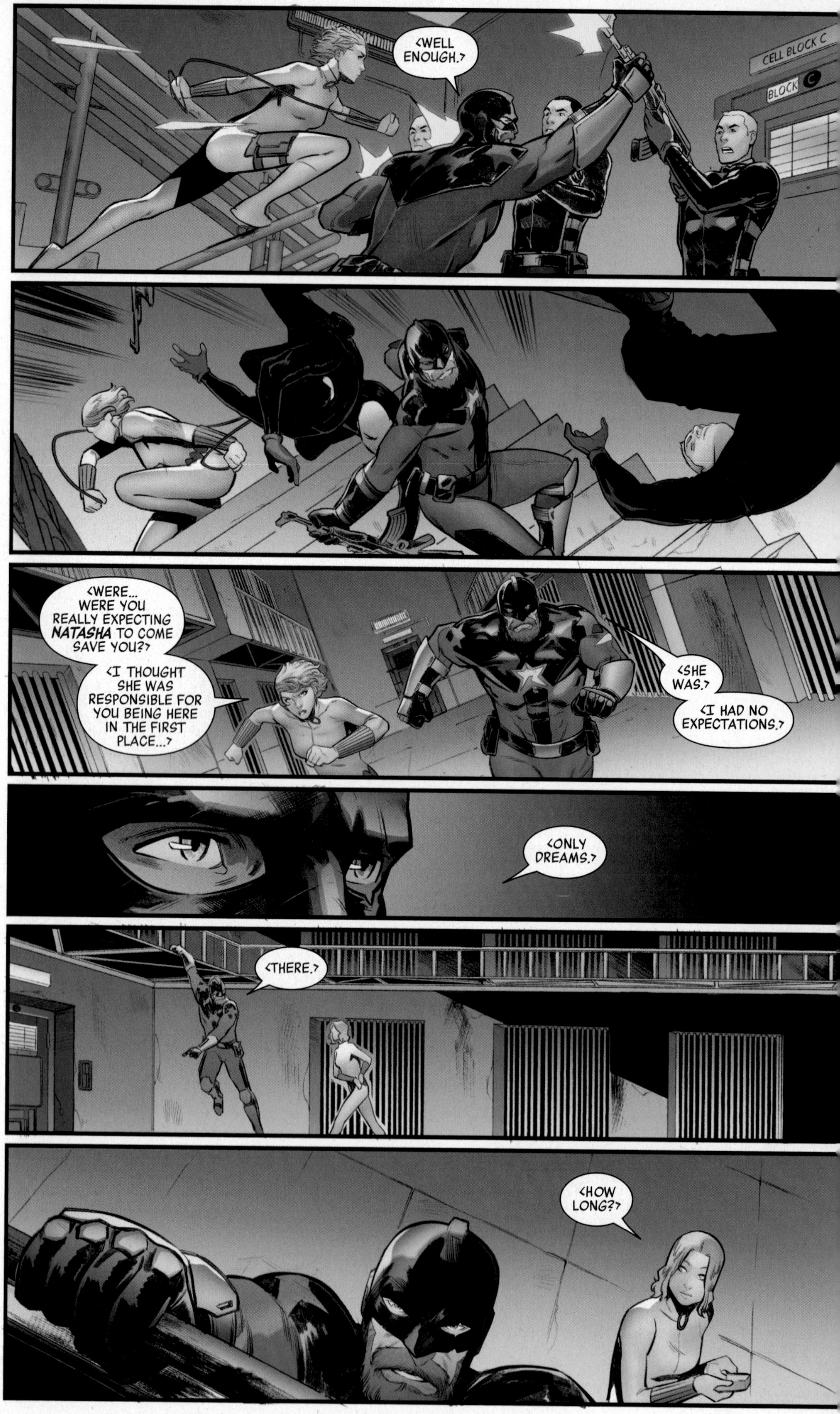

<WELL ENOUGH.>
CELL BLOCK C
BLOCK C
<WERE... WERE YOU REALLY EXPECTING NATASHA TO COME SAVE YOU?>
<I THOUGHT SHE WAS RESPONSIBLE FOR YOU BEING HERE IN THE FIRST PLACE...>
<SHE WAS.>
<I HAD NO EXPECTATIONS.>
<ONLY DREAMS.>
<THERE.>
<HOW LONG?>

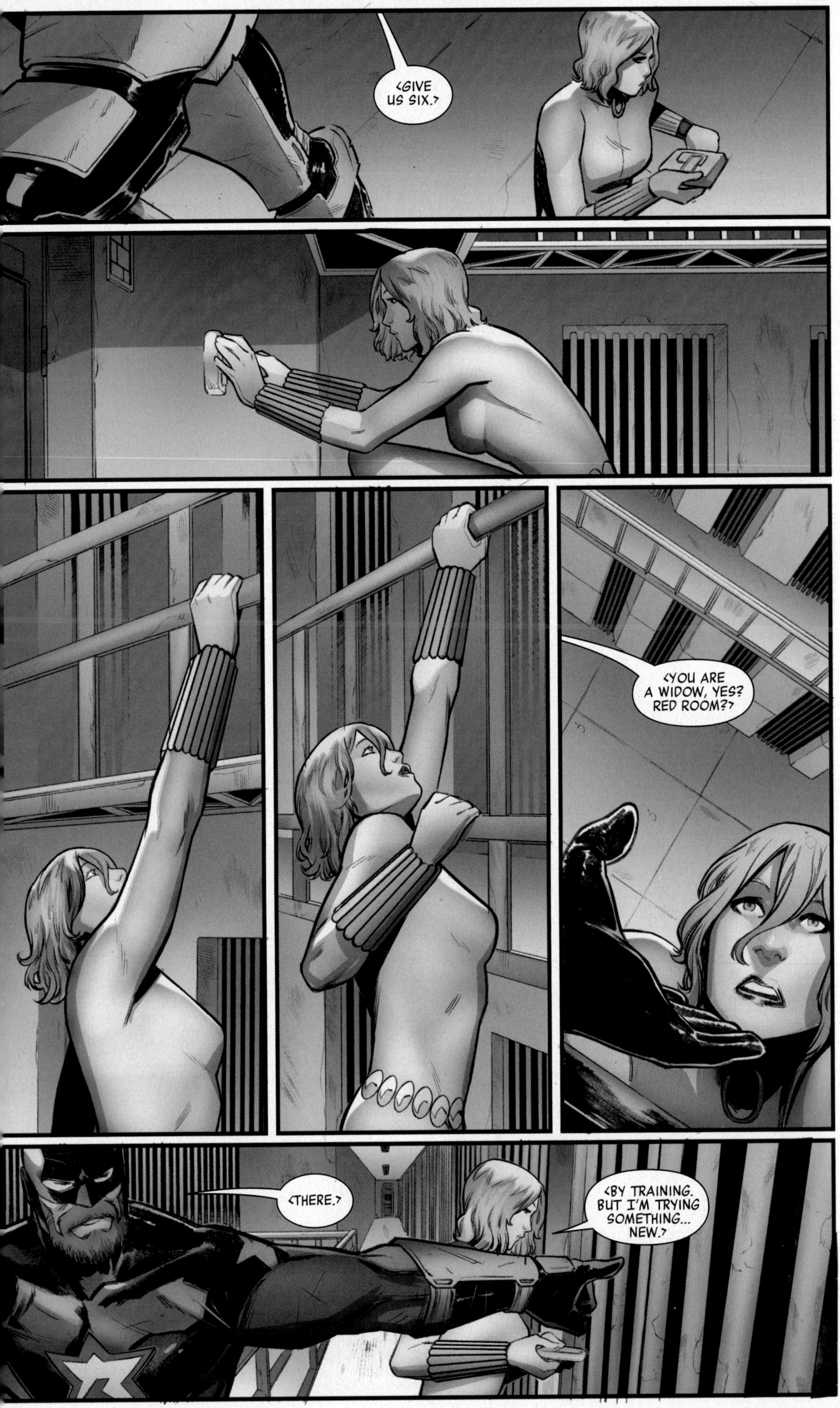

<GIVE US SIX.>
<YOU ARE A WIDOW, YES? RED ROOM?>
<THERE.>
<BY TRAINING. BUT I'M TRYING SOMETHING... NEW.>

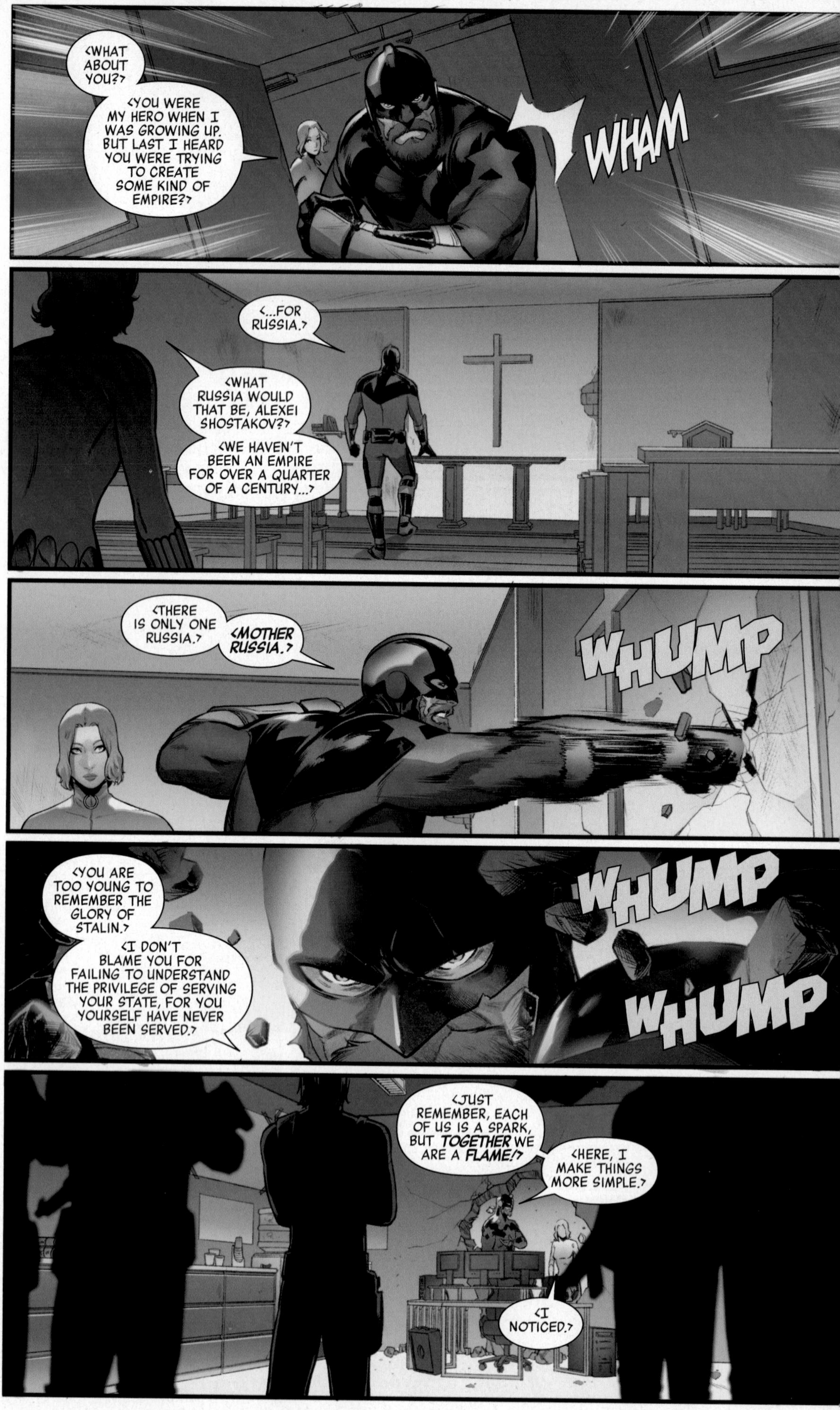

<WHAT ABOUT YOU?>
<YOU WERE MY HERO WHEN I WAS GROWING UP. BUT LAST I HEARD YOU WERE TRYING TO CREATE SOME KIND OF EMPIRE?>
WHAM
<...FOR RUSSIA.>
<WHAT RUSSIA WOULD THAT BE, ALEXEI SHOSTAKOV?>
<WE HAVEN'T BEEN AN EMPIRE FOR OVER A QUARTER OF A CENTURY...>
<THERE IS ONLY ONE RUSSIA.>
<MOTHER RUSSIA.>
WHUMP
<YOU ARE TOO YOUNG TO REMEMBER THE GLORY OF STALIN.>
<I DON'T BLAME YOU FOR FAILING TO UNDERSTAND THE PRIVILEGE OF SERVING YOUR STATE, FOR YOU YOURSELF HAVE NEVER BEEN SERVED.>
WHUMP
WHUMP
<JUST REMEMBER, EACH OF US IS A SPARK, BUT TOGETHER WE ARE A FLAME!>
<HERE, I MAKE THINGS MORE SIMPLE.>
<I NOTICED.>

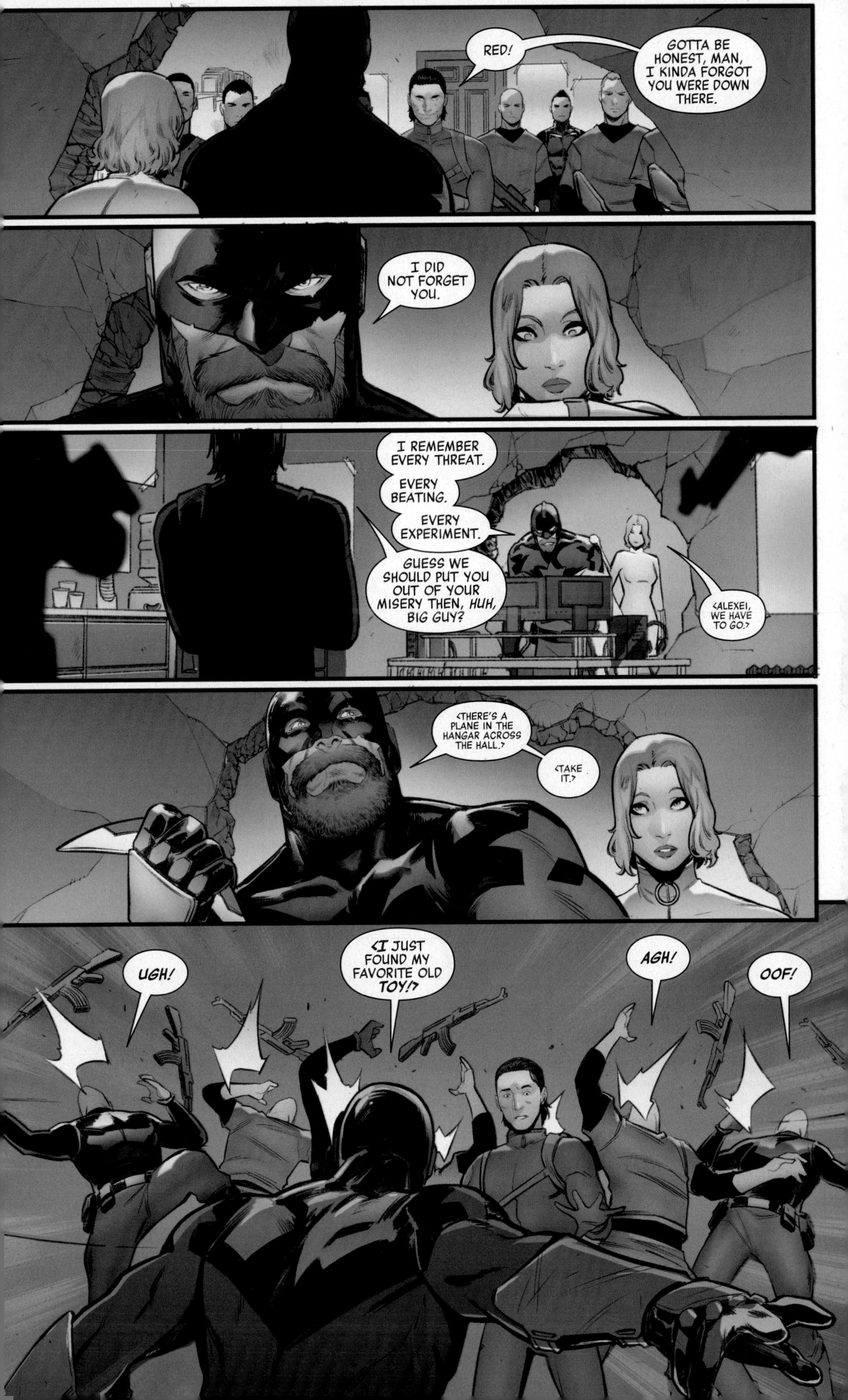
RED!
GOTTA BE HONEST, MAN, I KINDA FORGOT YOU WERE DOWN THERE.
I DID NOT FORGET YOU.
I REMEMBER EVERY THREAT.
EVERY BEATING.
EVERY EXPERIMENT.
GUESS WE SHOULD PUT YOU OUT OF YOUR MISERY THEN, *HUH*, BIG GUY?
<ALEXEI, WE HAVE TO GO.>
<THERE'S A PLANE IN THE HANGAR ACROSS THE HALL.>
<TAKE IT.>
UGH!
<I JUST FOUND MY FAVORITE OLD *TOY!*>
AGH!
OOF!

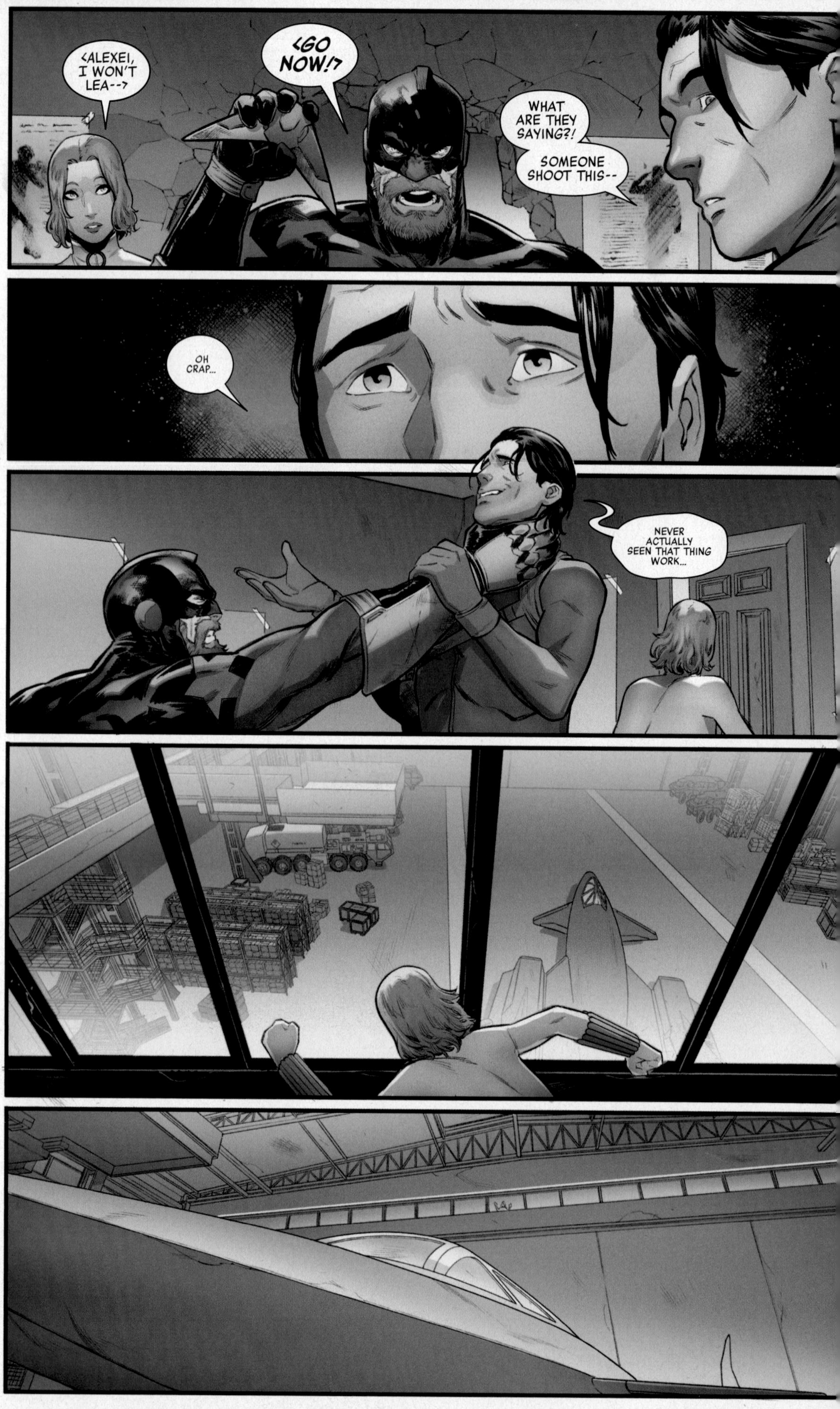

<ALEXEI, I WON'T LEA-->
<GO NOW!>
WHAT ARE THEY SAYING?!
SOMEONE SHOOT THIS--
OH CRAP...
NEVER ACTUALLY SEEN THAT THING WORK...

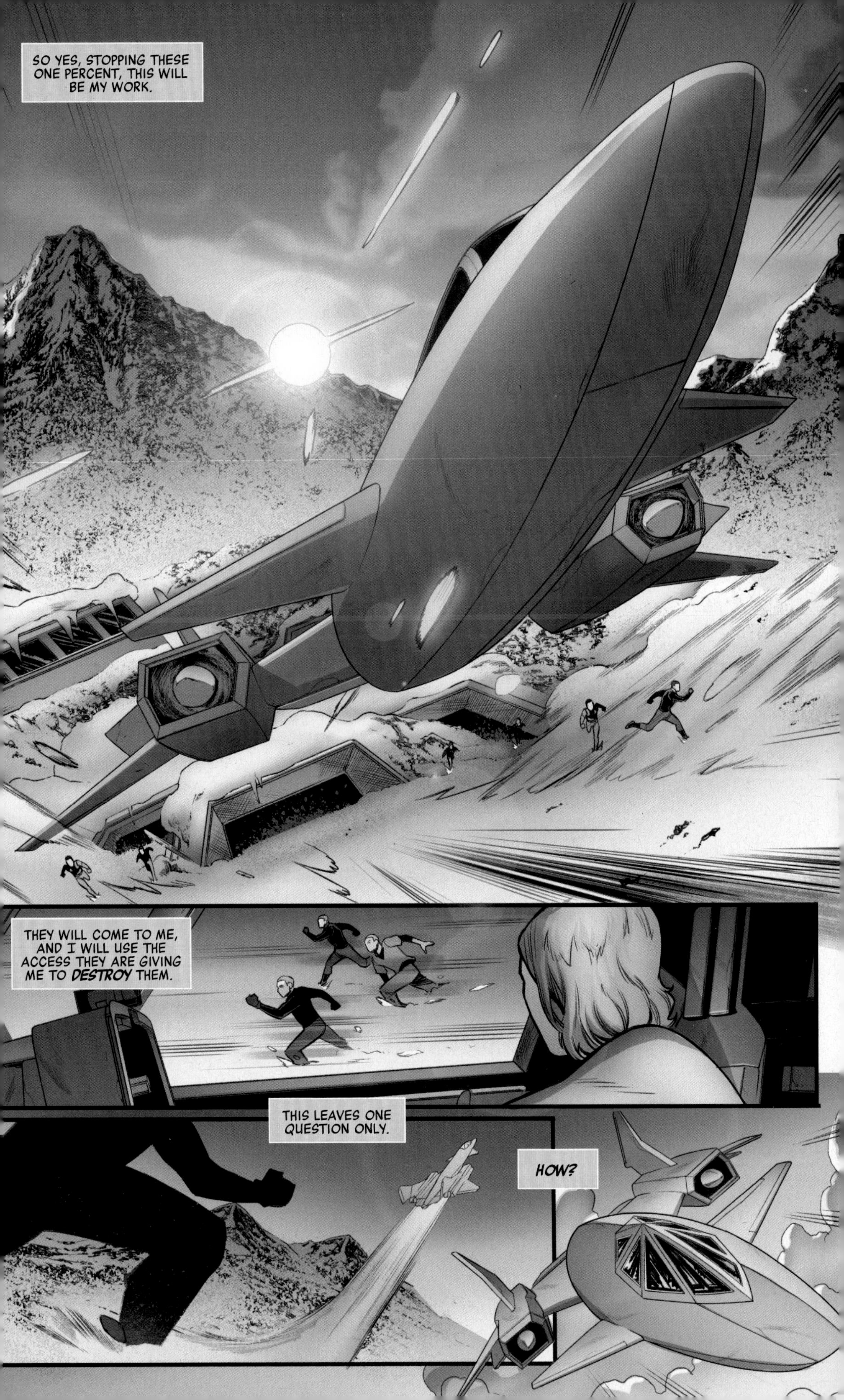
SO YES, STOPPING THESE ONE PERCENT, THIS WILL BE MY WORK.
THEY WILL COME TO ME, AND I WILL USE THE ACCESS THEY ARE GIVING ME TO *DESTROY* THEM.
THIS LEAVES ONE QUESTION ONLY.
HOW?

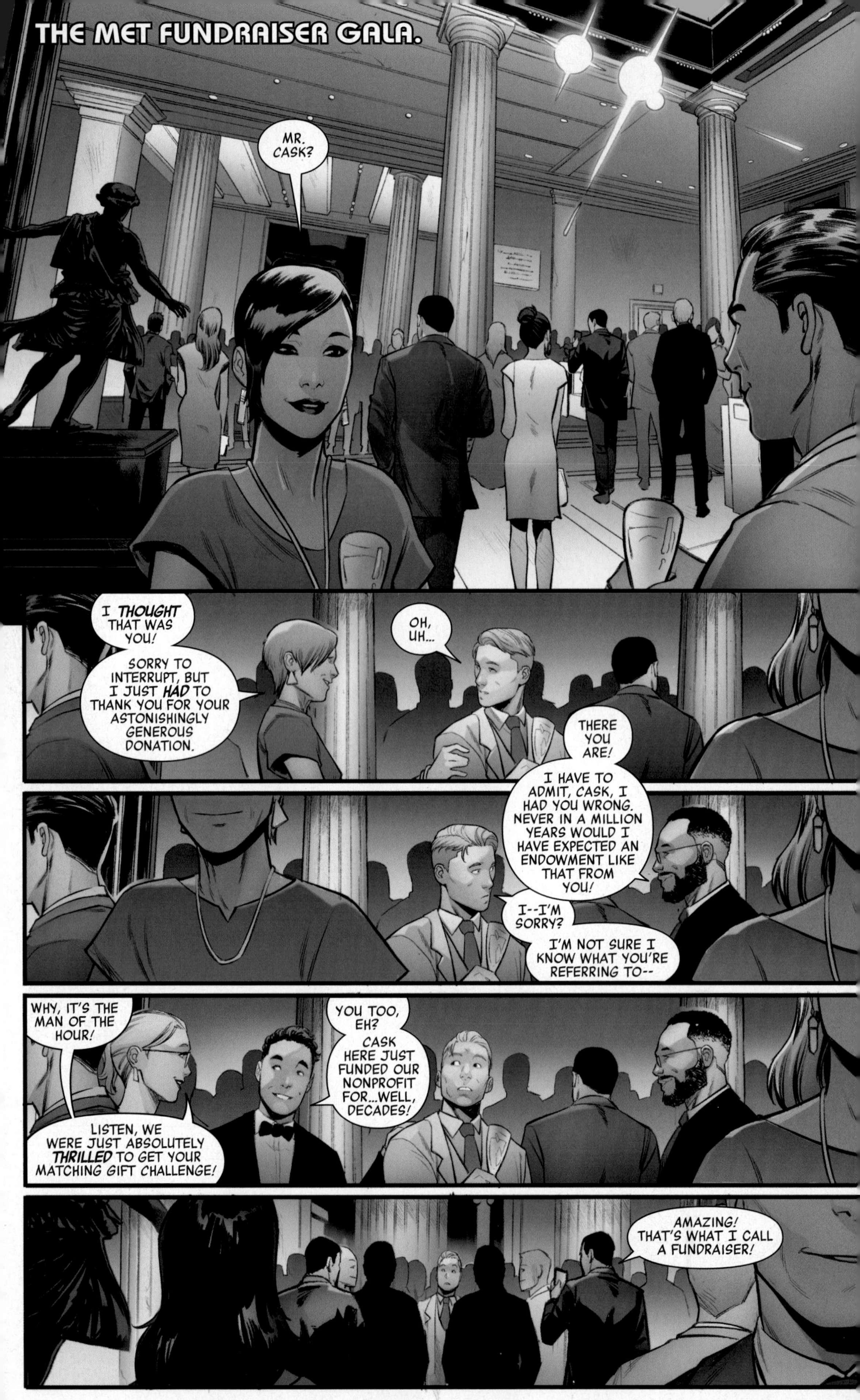
THE MET FUNDRAISER GALA.
MR. CASK?
I *THOUGHT* THAT WAS YOU!
SORRY TO INTERRUPT, BUT I JUST *HAD* TO THANK YOU FOR YOUR ASTONISHINGLY GENEROUS DONATION.
OH, UH...
THERE YOU ARE!
I HAVE TO ADMIT, CASK, I HAD YOU WRONG. NEVER IN A MILLION YEARS WOULD I HAVE EXPECTED AN ENDOWMENT LIKE THAT FROM YOU!
I--I'M SORRY?
I'M NOT SURE I KNOW WHAT YOU'RE REFERRING TO--
WHY, IT'S THE MAN OF THE HOUR!
LISTEN, WE WERE JUST ABSOLUTELY *THRILLED* TO GET YOUR MATCHING GIFT CHALLENGE!
YOU TOO, EH?
CASK HERE JUST FUNDED OUR NONPROFIT FOR...WELL, DECADES!
AMAZING! THAT'S WHAT I CALL A FUNDRAISER!

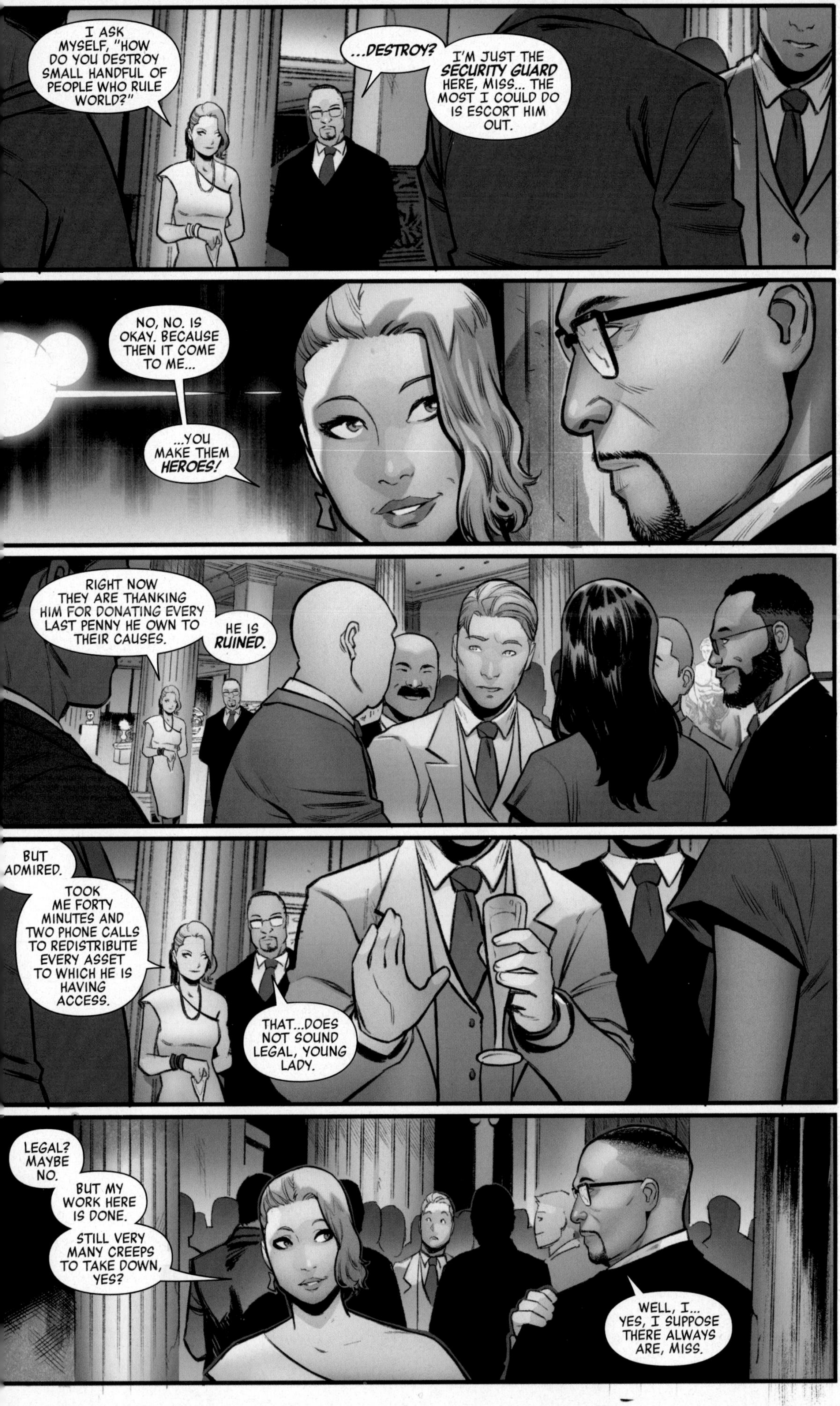

I ASK MYSELF, "HOW DO YOU DESTROY SMALL HANDFUL OF PEOPLE WHO RULE WORLD?"
...DESTROY?
I'M JUST THE SECURITY GUARD HERE, MISS... THE MOST I COULD DO IS ESCORT HIM OUT.
NO, NO. IS OKAY. BECAUSE THEN IT COME TO ME...
...YOU MAKE THEM HEROES!
RIGHT NOW THEY ARE THANKING HIM FOR DONATING EVERY LAST PENNY HE OWN TO THEIR CAUSES.
HE IS RUINED.
BUT ADMIRED.
TOOK ME FORTY MINUTES AND TWO PHONE CALLS TO REDISTRIBUTE EVERY ASSET TO WHICH HE IS HAVING ACCESS.
THAT...DOES NOT SOUND LEGAL, YOUNG LADY.
LEGAL? MAYBE NO.
BUT MY WORK HERE IS DONE.
STILL VERY MANY CREEPS TO TAKE DOWN, YES?
WELL, I... YES, I SUPPOSE THERE ALWAYS ARE, MISS.

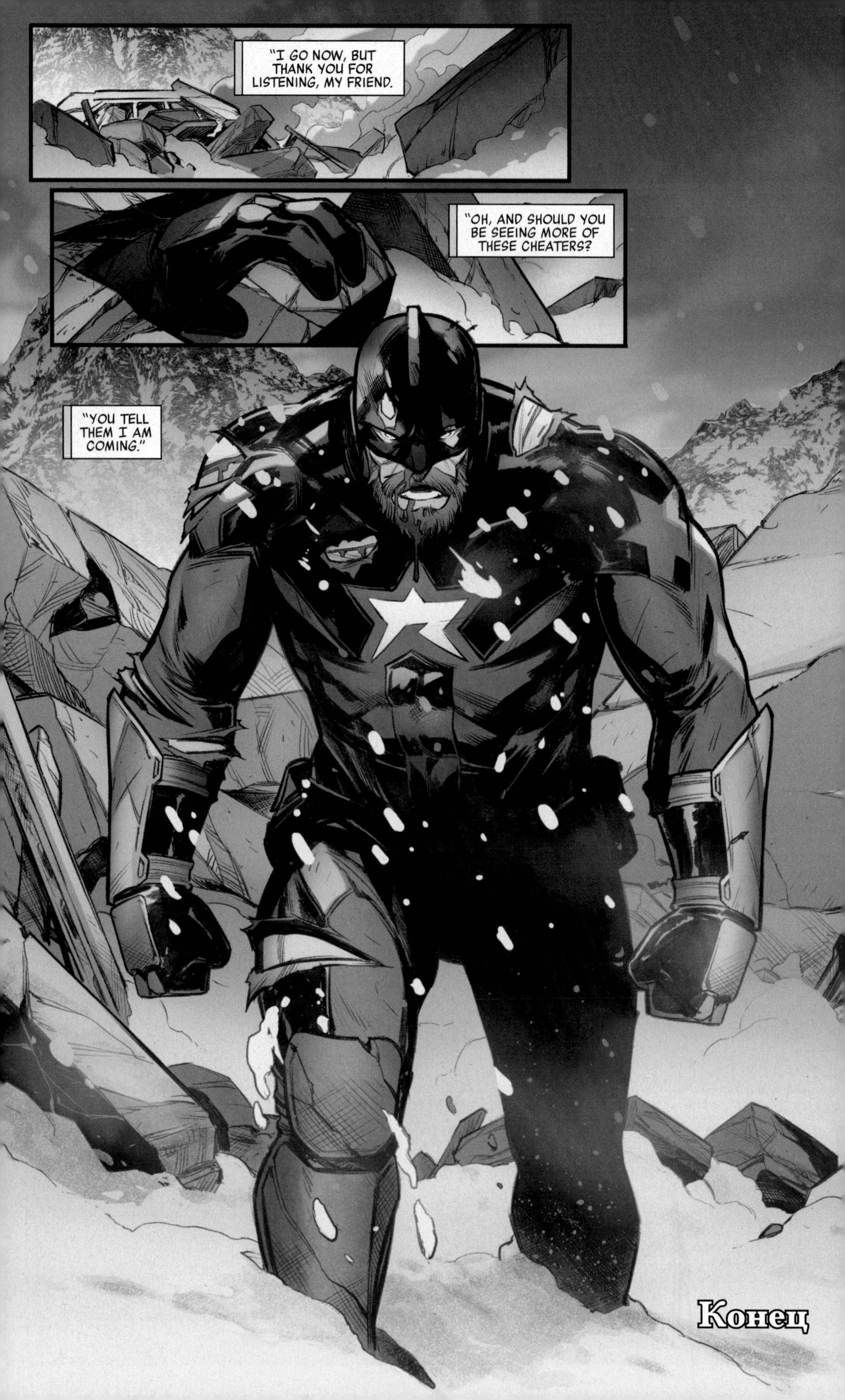
"I GO NOW, BUT THANK YOU FOR LISTENING, MY FRIEND.
"OH, AND SHOULD YOU BE SEEING MORE OF THESE CHEATERS?
"YOU TELL THEM I AM COMING."
Конец

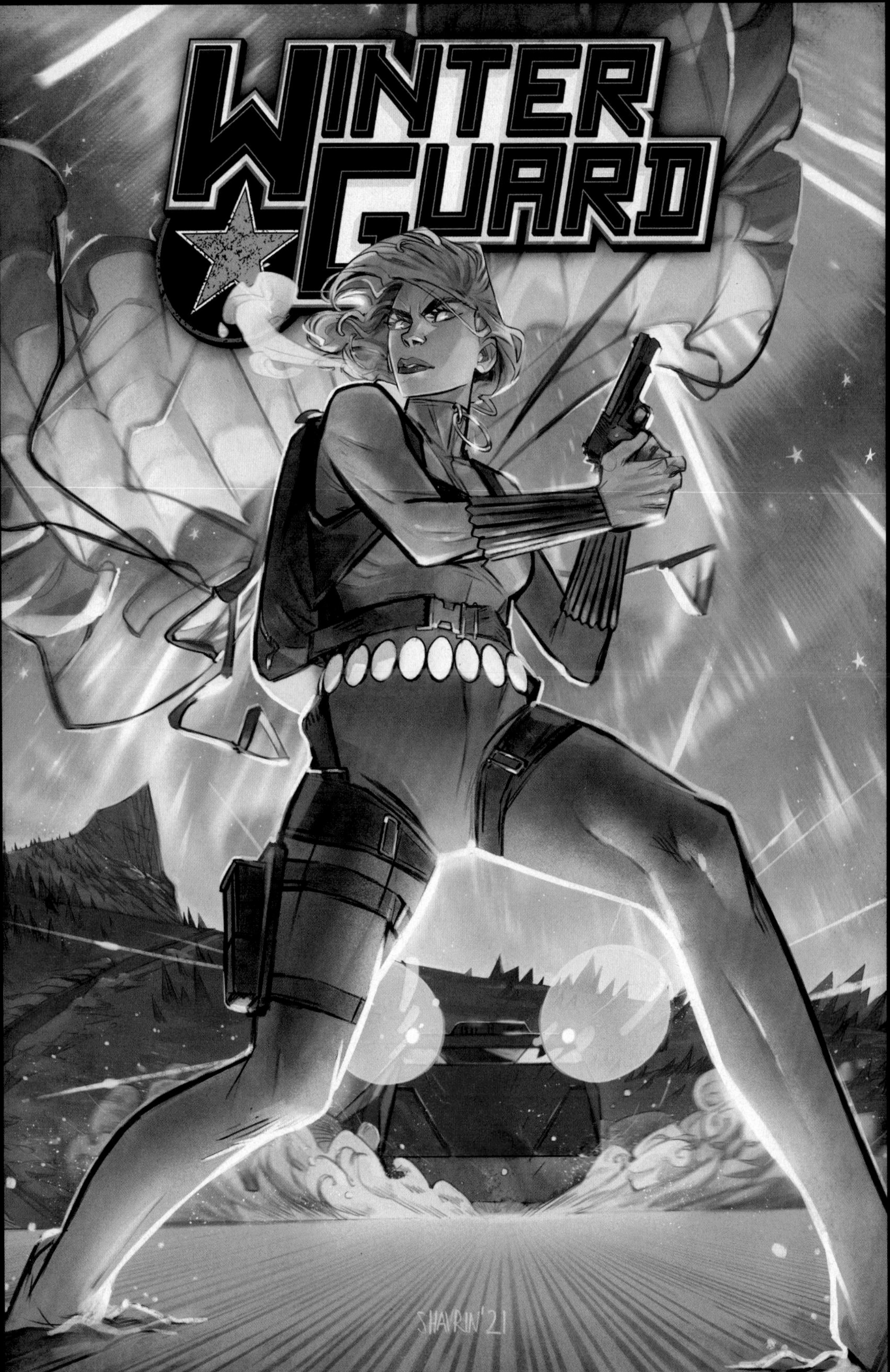
WINTER GUARD
SHAVRIN'21

Winter Guard #4 Variant
BY IVAN SHAVRIN

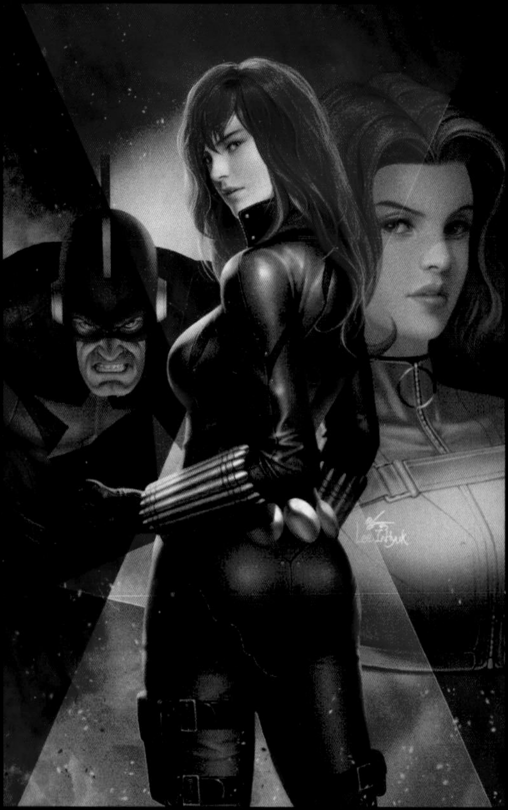

Widowmakers: Red Guardian and Yelena Belova Variant
BY INHYUK LEE

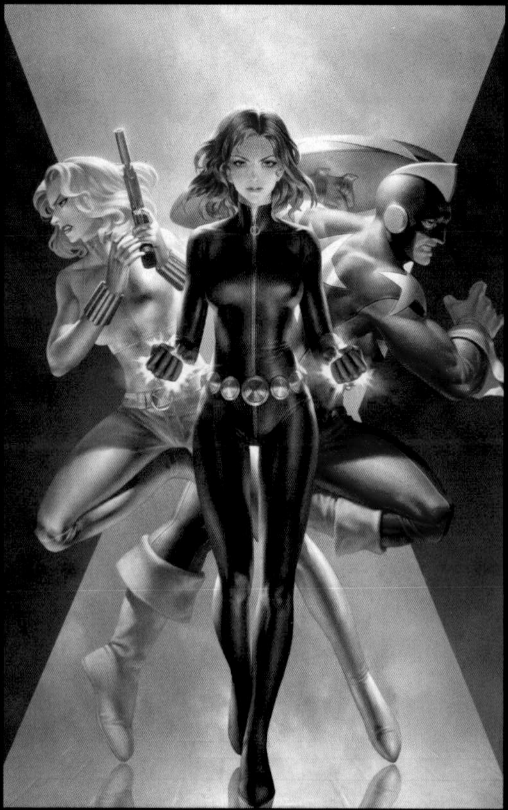

Widowmakers: Red Guardian and Yelena Belova Variant
BY JUNGGEUN YOON

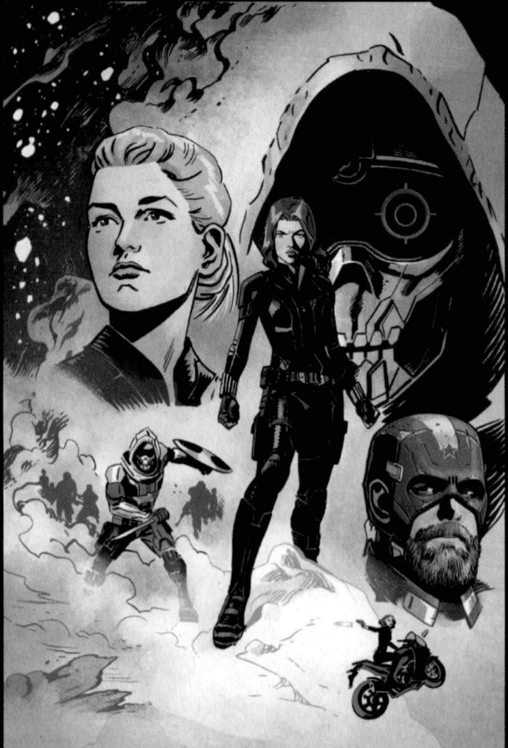

Widowmakers: Red Guardian and Yelena Belova MCU Variant
BY CHRIS SAMNEE & MATTHEW WILSON

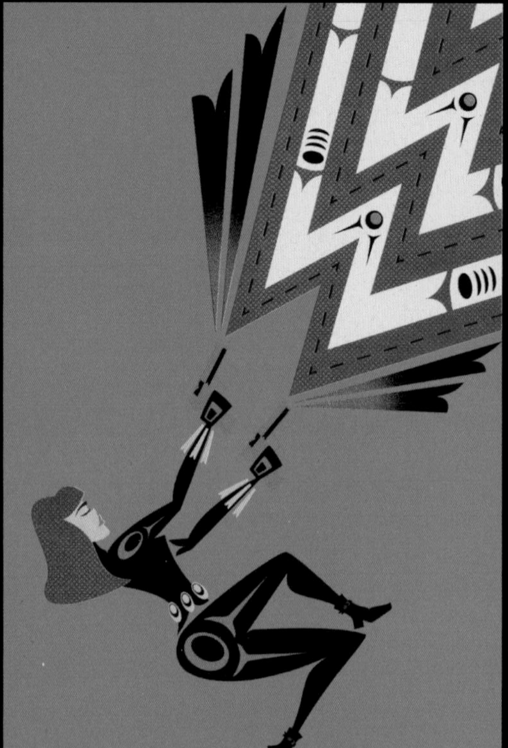

Widowmakers: Red Guardian and Yelena Belova Variant
BY JEFFREY VEREGGE